AMERICAN POPULAR CULTURE IN THE ERA OF TERROR

AMERICAN POPULAR CULTURE IN THE ERA OF TERROR

Falling Skies, Dark Knights Rising, and Collapsing Cultures

JESSE KAVADLO

PRAEGER™

An Imprint of ABC-CLIO, LLC

Santa Barbara, California • Denver, Colorado

Library of Congress Cataloging-in-Publication Data

Kavadlo, Jesse.
   American popular culture in the era of terror : falling skies, dark knights rising, and collapsing cultures / Jesse Kavadlo.
      pages cm
   Includes bibliographical references and index.
     ISBN 978–1–4408–3562–9 (cloth : alk. paper) — ISBN 978–1–4408–3563–6 (ebook) 1. Popular culture—United States—History—21st century. 2. Mass media—Social aspects—United States—History—21st century. 3. September 11 Terrorist Attacks, 2001—Influence. 4. September 11 Terrorist Attacks, 2001—Psychological aspects. 5. Fear—Social aspects—United States—History—21st century. 6. United States—Civilization—1970– 7. National characteristics, American. I. Title.
   E169.Z83K385   2015
   306.2′40973090511—dc23   2015017264

ISBN: 978–1–4408–3562–9
EISBN: 978–1–4408–3563–6

19 18 17 16 15   1 2 3 4 5

This book is also available on the World Wide Web as an eBook.
Visit www.abc-clio.com for details.

Praeger
An Imprint of ABC-CLIO, LLC

ABC-CLIO, LLC
130 Cremona Drive, P.O. Box 1911
Santa Barbara, California 93116-1911

This book is printed on acid-free paper ∞

Manufactured in the United States of America

Contents

Acknowledgments

Professors are asked about how their writing affects their teaching. For me, it's the other way around—the question is how my teaching affects my writing. I start with my classes, dreaming up topics I'd want to take as an undergraduate. This book's chapters grew out of those courses, including Aliens to Zombies: Monsters in Literature and Film, Superheroes in Literature and Culture, 9/11 and the Novel, Conspiracy and Paranoia in Contemporary American Literature and Film, New Voices and Forms in American Literature, Secret Worlds: Fantasy Stories and Their Fans, and Bedtime Stories After the End of the World. Thank you to my students in those classes over the years, for thinking about books, movies, and ideas with me. I especially want to single out May Ashour, Jaime Brown, Megan Burian, Amy Butz, Dustin Sifford, and Matt Wigley. Thank you for keeping me on my toes.

I am grateful to many people for helping me complete this project. Thanks to Bob Batchelor for encouraging me when I needed it most. Bob is crucial to this book's genesis. After founding the *Popular Culture Studies Journal*, Bob encouraged me to submit an essay for its inaugural issue. I did! Catherine Lafuente, acquisitions editor at Praeger, read that essay and wondered whether I was working on a book along the same theme. I was! Or at least I should have been. Catherine has been supportive, kind, and good spirited. Thank you, and thanks to Erin Ryan for helping me find and secure the rights to the book's images.

I am especially indebted to Abbie Nicoloff, Rebecca Rey, and Janessa Toro, who read and responded to chapter drafts. I'll read anything you send me, forever.

Many more thanks are in order: Mary Ellen Finch, Maryville University Vice President of Academic Affairs, for sustaining faculty members' freedom to pursue our passions, and President Mark Lombardi, who happens to share my enthusiasm for this book's subject. Although we are a teaching institution, both of you supported my scholarly ambition and helped award me the semester-long sabbatical I needed to complete the book. Thank you as well to Cherie Fister, Dean of Arts and Sciences, and the members of the Sabbatical Committee.

I am also thankful to my collogues in Maryville University's remarkable English Department: Bebe Nickolai, Germaine Murray, John Marino, who directed the writing center in my absence, and Johannes Wich-Schwarz, who coordinated University Seminar for me and, more importantly, chided me on a regular basis to get back to work. Thank you as well to my Maryville colleagues in the Center for First Year Experience and Academic Success, Jen McCluskey, Kelly Mock, Anna Kisting, and Kathy Mann, fellow zombie enthusiasts in the College of Arts and Sciences Kyra Krakos and Chris O'Connor, and perpetual sources of encouragement Marilyn Cohn, Linda Pitelka, and Nadine Ball.

I am fortunate to have had plenty of online support: Kathy Knapp, Rick Magee, Rebecca Hussey, Janice Cable, Elson Bond, Anna Mae Duane, and Jennifer Gilchrist, my Fordham University alums, as well as Sam Cohen, Marjorie Worthington, Matt Kavanagh, Norma Jones, and David Abbott.

I also thank the officers of the Don DeLillo Society: Anne Longmuir, Andrew Strombeck, Aaron DeRosa, Paul Petrovic, Karim Daanoune, and Matt King, and past officers I've known, Philip Nel, Mark Osteen, and Marni Gauthier.

Special thanks to my wife, Aura, and my children, Jonah, Dorian, and Daphne, who sat through hours and hours of movie monsters, superheroes, and dystopias with me, and maybe even liked some of them. Thanks to our friends, who made me try to explain what exactly I was working on. And thank you to my parents, Rosalie and Carl, and brothers, Dan and Alan, who were there in New York when I was not.

I am happy to have developed a few ideas that made their way into the book on my blog, *Hourman: Cultural Analysis in 60 Minutes or Less*. In addition to a version of Chapter 5 published in the *Popular Culture Studies Journal*, parts of Chapter 1 were published, in a different form and context, in *Reading Chuck Palahniuk: American Monsters and Literary Mayhem*, edited by Cynthia Kuhn and Lance Rubin (Routledge, 2009) and *You Do Not Talk About Fight Club*, edited by Read Schuchardt (BenBella, 2008). A section of Chapter 3 was published in different form in *Humanities Review*, vol. 6, no. 2 (Spring 2008). A version of Chapter 4 was published in *Looking for Lost: Critical Essays on the Enigmatic*

Series, edited by Randy Laist, 2011, included by permission of McFarland & Company, Inc., Jefferson, North Carolina (www.mcfarlandpub.com). Finally, a short section of Chapter 7 is a revised version of a chapter published in *X-Men and Philosophy*, edited by Rebecca Housel and J. Jeremy Wisnewski (Wiley, 2009). Thank you to each of the editors and publishers for their permissions.

Introduction

One World Trade Center under a blue sky. (Pivariz/Dreamstime.com)

Pile the bodies high at Austerlitz and Waterloo.
Shovel them under and let me work—
I am the grass; I cover all.

                    —From "Grass" (1918), Carl Sandburg

I am a native New Yorker, Brooklyn born and Brooklyn bred, and when I die I'll be Brooklyn dead. It's a song I learned from my mother, herself a native Brooklynite, decades before the borough's endemic gentrification. I left New York in 2000 for Winona, Minnesota, about as far culturally, if only halfway geographically, as I could have traveled in America. When the Twin Towers fell 13 months later, I, like the vast majority of Americans, could only look on numbly at my television screen, even as I knew that my parents were a few miles away and that one of my brothers was in Lower Manhattan that morning. He would soon be among the thousands walking across the Brooklyn Bridge that day, a scene of mass exodus that would become a recurring image in subsequent literature and film. People who know I'm from New York have asked me if I chose to write about terror based on my own experience on 9/11, but I am not writing because I was there. I'm writing because I wasn't.

But this is not a book about terror—not exactly. It is about examining relationships between the phenomenon of terrorism, the pervasive millennial feelings of terror in America, and their myriad manifestations in popular culture. The topic and scope go back further than 2001, and then extend further, into the mid-2010s. The 1990s, more than September 11, 2001, serves as the foundation. Perhaps it was not the fall of the towers alone that precipitated contemporary representations of terror, but rather, another fall: that of the Berlin Wall, and with it the Soviet Union, in 1989. What if America's millennial preoccupations—its depictions of collapsing cultures, absent fathers and threatened children, monstrous impulses in humans and humane impulses in monsters, fragmented or half-forgotten narratives, as well as heroes who would tell the story and rise again—is a post–Cold War, not post-9/11, phenomenon? What if, artistically and culturally, September 11 is not the day that changed the world, but instead the most powerful symbol of a world whose stories and perceptions were already transforming?

What, then, do the stories of a culture gripped with terror look like? They come in different forms—fiction, film, and television—through different viewing technologies. They span multiple genres—including disaster, adventure, science fiction, and horror—and implied audiences: mass market, literary fiction, independent, and young adult (YA). Some of them address terrorist plots explicitly, or incorporate the events of 9/11 directly into their story lines. More often, however, they merge terror with wishes of safety—and sometimes, fears of excessive safety and wishes for terror's power—integrating recognizable fragments of reality from real-life terrorist attacks or the post-9/11 war on terror into styles and story lines more frequently associated with fantasy. And as we will see, these seemingly disparate cultural, literary, and even epistemological categories turn out to have traits in common. But what, how, and why? How do narratives that revolve around terror create meaning, what do they mean, and why do they matter? In the end, I hope to show ways in which terror helps us to understand popular culture, and how popular culture may also help us to understand terror.

The Sky Is Falling

I am writing these words on September 11. Not *the* September 11, of course, what has now become known simply as "9/11." Unlike other dates strongly associated with their historical importance like the Fourth of July, our shorthand for Independence Day, or December 7, better known as Pearl Harbor Remembrance Day, 9/11 has no other name. Its date alone will suffice. It feels symbolic enough, evoking 911, our phone number for emergencies, and its two ones visually evoke the fallen towers themselves. Many people who are old enough to remember 9/11 think about where they were and what they were doing when the planes crashed into the World Trade Center, the Pentagon, and the ground in Pennsylvania. We remember the "perfect blueness of the sky that Tuesday morning," as President George W. Bush put it, the postcard fall day, juxtaposed against the moment when the sky was falling.[1] By midday, American well-being and the blue were together blotted out; chaos and white dust enshrouded downtown Manhattan. Or perhaps, if the weather in your part of the world didn't look like New York City or Washington that morning, you instead remember the images from television, played again and again, futilely, as though reenactment might, just this once, yield a different outcome. There is a good chance, in fact, that even if you were in New York City, the images from memory are, by now, inextricably entwined with those that have been rebroadcast, edited, developed, and shaped, both visually and narratively, ever since.

On September 11, 2014, 13 years later, a New York baker's dozen, Americans seemed unsure exactly how to commemorate this undistinguished anniversary. Despite the decade, perhaps not much had changed since the satirical newspaper *The Onion* published its story "Area Man Not Exactly Sure When To Take Down American Flags": "After more than four months of proudly displaying American flags on his car, home, and body, 47-year-old computer consultant Jerry Wenger is uncertain when the appropriate time will be to take them down."[2] The Freedom Tower at 1 World Trade Center opened on November 3, 2014, to little national fanfare. Yet even if—or, if we take the bombing of Pearl Harbor as one of the few possible historical comparisons, even *when*—9/11's national injury begins to recede into the rearview mirror of history, it may still be closer than it appears. As the commemorations ebb, popular culture continues to reflect it.

We have entered what I am calling the era of terror. Americans began to shift their anxieties from the Soviet Union to Middle Eastern and domestic terrorism, from World War III to the World Trade Center in 1993. But since 9/11—the day the planes, the buildings, and the people fell—the sky has been falling ever since. Movie after movie, book after book, and image after image have replaced the initial news coverage of the falling towers and fleeing Manhattanites with new, fictionalized versions of an imperiled, damaged, or dystopian nation. Taken together, they remind Americans what we lost and that we have not narratively moved on—but, perhaps, they also intimate what we may still yet accomplish.

The forms of these stories vary. While a body of what might be called 9/11 novels (and 9/11 movies) began to emerge in the 2000s, as I discuss in Chapter 2, many of the most popular and significant genres to dominate the 2000s and 2010s at first bear little resemblance to any literal reenactment of 9/11 itself. Yet they have much to do with terror—and with 9/11, symbolically. Throughout distinct genres and over different chapters, I'm interested in mining the subtexts, or implicit themes beneath the surfaces, of these pop-cultural texts. How are stories that seem to be about the trauma of 9/11 also expressions of other, related wishes, fears, and phenomena—and how do stories that seem unrelated to 9/11 metaphorically appropriate it? But with subtext, context matters as well. How may ostensible fantasy stories—about monsters, desert islands, dystopias, superheroes, and more—be interpreted through the lens of life after 9/11, our era of terror?

People strive to avoid terror in life, of course. Yet many of us crave those feelings from the safety of our armchairs, enjoying stories that provoke fear and incorporate real-life images, events, and ideas from the terrors of the everyday. Terror, of course, is personal, subjective, and difficult to define. In his book *Terror, Terrorism, and the Human Condition*, Charles P. Webel offers this possibility: "The term 'terror' denotes both a phenomenological experience of paralyzing, overwhelming, and ineffable metal anguish, as well as a behavioral response to a real *or perceived* life-threatening danger" (my emphasis).[3] Even as most people disdain real danger, they crave its "perception"—its representations, its narrative or visual simulations. Targets of terrorism—the World Trade Center and the Pentagon, but also the Alfred P. Murrah Federal Building in Oklahoma City or the Centennial Olympic Park in Atlanta—were symbolic, so that the death and damage inflicted would be perceived as even more threatening, even greater, than it was. Creating fear through symbolism, ostensibly the work of the terrorist, is also the goal of many authors and filmmakers, their craft devoted entirely to producing alarm through imagery. Artists and audiences abhor terrorism. But we have complex feelings about terror.

Critics have been less ambivalent, at least about popular culture's reaction to terror. In her book *The Terror Dream*, Susan Faludi laments that "virtually no film, television, drama, play, or novel on 9/11 has begun to plumb what the trauma meant for our national psyche."[4] Similarly, in *After the Fall: American Literature since 9/11*, Richard Gray decries the wave of post-9/11 novels that seek to "assimilate"—rather than challenge—"the unfamiliar into familiar structures. The crisis is, in every sense of the word, domesticated."[5] Perhaps Faludi, whose excellent analysis focuses politics and journalism, looks too narrowly, too literally, at what fiction "on 9/11" might mean. Many of the novels, films, and television shows analyzed in this book fall outside what one might initially consider "on 9/11." And Gray underestimates what literature does, and can do: after the shock of 9/11, followed by the global war on terror, imaginatively assimilating the unfamiliar into the familiar may be more difficult, and necessary, than Gray acknowledges. Or perhaps we can look at it another way: what if much of popular culture after 9/11 has instead been attempting to assimilate the now-familiar—the concomitant events and emotions associated with terrorism—into *un*familiar structures: of horror, dystopia, and superhero stories?

As we will see, many of these novels and films may be less familiar than they appear to be. Their artistic and linguistic explorations contrast their supposed domestication. Chapter 1 analyzes 1990s domestic terror in two novels by Chuck Palahniuk, *Fight Club* and *Survivor*, to understand the ways in which they prefigure 9/11 but also suggest that Americans were already conflicted about terror before 9/11. Chapter 2 addresses the novels and films of 9/11 directly, including *World Trade Center*, *United 93*, *Extremely Loud and Incredibly Close* by Jonathan Safran Foer, and *Falling Man* by Don DeLillo, and the ways in which incorporating 9/11 in some ways does "domesticate" it, transmuting it into a search—if often, futile—for literally or metaphorically missing family. More than assimilating the familiar, however, through their forms and experimentation, these novels potentially discomfort and confront their readers, daring us to make sense of the story's events, knowing that we cannot. Chapter 3 analyzes the power of the phrase "war on terror," looking at the ways in which monster stories—about zombies, in *World War Z*; vampires, in *Twilight* and *Cosmopolis*; and aliens, in *Avatar*—have changed in the aftermath of a real terror attack, and how the attacks change how we read earlier novels like *Frankenstein* and *Dracula* in retrospect. Chapter 4 shifts angles and media to the way in which television's *Lost* has not only incorporated the themes and subtexts of 9/11 and the aftereffects of two wars abroad but has also adjusted them over time, with each additional season complicating its multi-layered story line as well as its emblematic connections with the culture. Chapter 5 analyzes a different trend after 9/11: the epidemic of amnesia—metaphorically in American culture, literally in American film—and its rela-tionship to stories of dystopia, which temporarily ceased immediately after 9/11, to be revised appropriately by Cormac McCarthy in his postapocalyp-tic novel *The Road*. Chapter 6 broadens the discussion of dystopian fiction and film: while *The Road* and other novels written for adults matter, the more important shift in the 2000s came from the success of young adult end-of-the-world novels and their film adaptations, particularly of Suzanne Collins's series, *The Hunger Games*. If dystopias became suited for kids, superheroes were aimed toward adults. Chapter 7 examines the preponderance of mature superhero movies in the era of terror, looking closely at Christopher Nolan's *Dark Knight* trilogy and the ways in which themes and imagery of the terrorism shape his revision of Batman and the challenge of saving the world. Finally, the book concludes with a complica-tion: while much of popular culture has emphasized an endangered America, Americans in the 2010s are arguably safer than ever before. What does it mean, then, that our pop-cultural perceptions do not match our political reality? Is the sky really falling?

While chapter by chapter this book takes on a wide array of works, at the same time I also want to trace the ways in which seemingly dissimilar responses to terror nevertheless create discernible thematic and narrative parallels. From *Fight Club* to *Twilight*, *World Trade Center* to *World War Z*, literary master Don DeLillo's *Falling Man* to mainstream movies' Batman, *Lost*'s desert island to YA's dystopia, popular culture in the era of terror reconfigures existing genres, and mixes and matches themes and narrative approaches, to create an identifiable set of conventions. Throughout these works, we encounter protagonists who are sympathetic antiheroes or outsiders. In different ways, the stories depict the loss of the nuclear family, erosion of heteronormative marriage, the disappearance of a father, or the precarious bonds between fathers and sons. In keeping with contested patriarchy and family, the stories present challenges to larger institutions, including the possibility of social breakdown and fear of governments and corporations. Throughout and despite genre, readers feel a pervasive atmosphere of terror that even a happy ending—the restoration of family's or society's status quo, or the conquest of fear—cannot allay. Finally, frequently (although not always) these stories complicate or defy conventional points of view and linear narrative; with the challenge to gender and societal order comes a self-reflexive reexamination of storytelling itself. As a response to terror, these features, taken together, question every kind of authority: morality, family, law and order, safety, and story.

As Carl Sandburg writes in his World War I–era poem "Grass," quoted in the epigraph, while time goes on and grass grows over battlefields after warfare has ended, the aftermath of violence lingers for survivors, a word lamentably applicable to many of the protagonists discussed in this book. The prevailing feeling of imminent breakdown pervades millennial American pop culture, with no sign of abatement. Americans feel just as unsafe in 2015 as they did in the aftermath of 9/11; despite that, statistically, we have never been safer.[6] As the feeling of terror in America far surpasses actual instances of terrorism, terror seems less like the specific, unlawful acts of the terrorist and more of a state of being, a cultural phenomenon. After trauma, Sandburg's poem asks, what then? How has living in the era of terror, and the afterglow of the televised 9/11 attacks, affected the way we tell and interpret stories? We are looking up at the sky, waiting for it to fall again, but should we be looking down, beneath our feet, to let the grass do its work? How much time must pass for the grass to grow over the graves—and can it really ever cover all?

CHAPTER 1

With Us and Against Us:
Chuck Palahniuk's Homegrown
Terror of the 1990s

From *Fight Club* (1999): the composed symmetry and duality of Brad Pitt's and Edward Norton's characters. (20th Century Fox/Photofest)

In this chapter: *Fight Club* (1996) and *Survivor* (1999), Chuck Palahniuk; film adaptation of *Fight Club* (1999), directed by David Fincher.

9/11, the day that changed everything, ushered in a new era in American history and America's pop cultural representations of terror and terrorism. Or did it? This chapter closely examines Chuck Palahniuk's novels Fight Club *and* Survivor *in order to demonstrate that their political themes prefigure 9/11. At the same time, a reading of these novels after 9/11 can provide ways of understanding the problems of prescience in popular culture, sympathetic characters who do terrible things, and narrative plots that, like terrorist plots, lead toward death and explosive conclusions. In many ways, Palahniuk's stories of violence, self-destruction, and the possibility of redemption, of angry young men bent on destroying financial centers and crashing airplanes, may reveal more to us today than readers in the 1990s may have imagined.*

"**A**mericans were not accustomed to what so much of the world had already grown weary of," *Time*'s cover story ominously intoned, "the sudden, deafening explosion . . . , a hail of glass and debris, the screams of innocent victims followed by the wailing sirens of ambulances. Terrorism seemed like something that happened somewhere else—and somewhere else a safe distance over the horizon. And then last week, in an instant, the World Trade Center in New York City became ground zero."[1] *Time*, of course, was reporting the attack on the World Trade Center—in 1993.

Americans did not discover terrorism after September 11, 2001. Contrary to how we may have come to think of it, terrorism came to the forefront of American consciousness, and pop culture, in the 1990s, when suddenly, it seemed, real-life terrorism demanded attention just as the threat of a nuclear war with Soviet Union had ebbed. Using homemade explosives placed in a rented van, a group of Middle Eastern terrorists attempted to destroy the World Trade Center in 1993. They failed to bring down the buildings but killed six people and injured more than 1,000.

More often, however, Americans in the 1990s had reason to fear domestic terrorism, threats from Americans themselves. Mentally ill former Berkeley mathematician Theodore Kaczynski, known as the Unabomber, eluded the FBI for two decades while killing three people and injuring 29 others using homemade explosives. He pressed the *Washington Post* into publishing his manifesto against technology and environmental destruction, which ultimately led his brother to recognize the delusions and unusual turns of phrase.[2] In 1997, Timothy McVeigh, an army veteran and antigovernment extremist, like the World Trade Center bombers, used a rental truck filled with explosives made from readily available, inexpensive materials to destroy the Alfred P. Murrah Federal Building in Oklahoma City, killing 74 people.[3] The Animal Liberation Front and Earth Liberation Front, nearly forgotten by many Americans after 9/11, were, according to the FBI in 1999, responsible for "the third major wave of domestic terrorism evident since the 1960s."[4] Motivated by religion and politics and using homemade explosives, Eric Robert Rudolph killed two people and injured 111 others, bombing two abortion clinics and a lesbian bar, and most famously deploying a backpack bomb in Atlanta during the 1996 Summer Olympics.[5] Confrontations between federal agents and an accused militia group were fatal in Ruby Ridge, in Idaho, in 1992; the following year, a government standoff between agents and David Koresh, leader of the religious sect Branch Davidians, in Waco, Texas, similarly ended in death. Influenced by the Oklahoma City bombing and seeing themselves as self-styled terrorists, Eric Harris and Dylan Klebold killed 13 people and injured at least 21 more before committing suicide in what became known as the Columbine High School massacre, the first such shooting to be aired on live television.[6] The raw ingredients for narratives about domestic terror, like components for the homemade bombs, were all present in the culture before 9/11, an explosive mixture of psychopathy, delusions of grandiosity, cult mentality, the need for spectacle and exposure, and anger over personal mistreatment, government excess, or corporate overreach, whether imagined or not.

Filmmakers and authors noticed. While crime and detective stories go back to Edgar Allan Poe and Arthur Conan Doyle in the nineteenth century and pulp fiction and film noir in the first half of the twentieth century, these earlier forms differ sharply from the real-life incursion of terror into the American popular consciousness of the 1990s. Stories about what now looks like terrorism certainly existed: James Bond foiled what could be called terrorists in his very first film, *Dr. No*, in 1962. Yet while occasional terrorists appear in Cold War–era films, for the most part they seem the exceptions. International villains were far more often shadowy Soviets or their surrogates. From *Red Dawn* to *Rambo*, the original *Manchurian Candidate* to *War Games*, the Soviets, their agents, or their pernicious influence provided decades of cinematic villains and storylines. Even the vanquished Third Reich managed to live on for decades, through John Wayne's celluloid warfare, subsequent nostalgia films, and individual Nazi villains like *Marathon Man*'s depraved dentist. After the Cold War ended in 1989, however, and World War II receded further from the popular imagination, the uncomplicated villains of the World War II–era and the nuclear threats that accompanied Communist fears seemed moot. Even the 1980s anxiety of an ascending Asia—emblemized in Ridley Scott's *Black Rain* and science-fictionalized in *Blade Runner*, also directed by Scott—seemed unlikely after Japan's Great Recession began in the early 1990s.

While films of the 1970s like *Badlands*, *Taxi Driver*, *Dog Day Afternoon*, and *The Godfather* began to introduce complex, ambiguous criminals, many pop culture killers tended to be masked horror movie ghouls. A coherent narrative or perspective about terror or terrorists in mainstream popular culture did not emerge until the 1990s. What seems striking, however, is that the portraits of terrorists in popular culture of the 1990s, in keeping with the spirit of the 1970s, often treated them as heroes rather than protagonists, villains, or even antiheroes. While not terrorists, *Pulp Fiction*'s hitmen were humanized and funny. HBO's Tony Soprano was smart and sympathetic. And interestingly, one actor in the 1990s appeared again and again in a spectrum of films about likable psychopaths and good men turned wrathful: Brad Pitt, the apotheosis of white Hollywood handsome masculinity. In *Kalifornia*, *Se7en*, and *Twelve Monkeys*, plus other genre-busting killing-spree movies like *True Romance*, *Interview with the Vampire*, and *Snatch*, Pitt showed off his perfect teeth and his blazing guns. One role in particular, however, stands out and helps us to understand the pop culture's emerging terror narrative: Tyler Durden, founder of terrorist organization Project Mayhem, in director David Fincher's adaptation of Chuck Palahniuk's novel *Fight Club*. *Fight Club*, together with Palahniuk's *Survivor*, serves as the centerpiece of this chapter, allowing a particular lens into terror's nascent pop cultural ascent.

Chuck Palahniuk's 9/11

A homegrown terrorist cell, led by a fanatic, uses everyday items to destroy a center of financial skyscrapers. A religious fundamentalist hijacks an airplane, not to make demands or take hostages, but in order to crash it for the sake of story, statement, and spectacle. These sentences summarize two novels by Chuck Palahniuk, *Fight Club* and *Survivor*, as well as, of course, the events of September 11, 2001, when 19 Islamists took control of four airplanes, destroying the World Trade Center and damaging the Pentagon, killing 2,977 people. Like author Don DeLillo before him, whose fictionalized portrait of the Kennedy assassin, *Libra*, noted "the tendency of plots to move toward death,"[7] Palahniuk's work demonstrates the disturbing intersections between the multiple meanings of the word "plot"—narrative, conspiratorial, and funereal—reminding us of the linguistic connections between our stories, our secrets, and our entombment.

With the possible exception of DeLillo himself—who published *White Noise* (1985), about a massive chemical spill, only a month after the Union Carbide chemical disaster in India, and *Underworld* (1997), with its cover image juxtaposing a cross with World Trade Center like a tombstone or crosshairs—readers are not used to such cultural foresight from their novelists, especially those, like Palahniuk, who seem to traffic specifically in the outrageous, the supposedly unimaginable. Writing in 1960, novelist Philip Roth already lamented that

> the American writer in the middle of the twentieth century now has his hands full in trying to understand, describe, and make *credible* much of American reality. It stupefies, it sickens, it infuriates, and finally it is even a kind of embarrassment to one's meager imagination. The actuality is continuously outdoing our talents, and the culture tosses up figures almost daily that are the envy of any novelist.[8]

For the most part, 50 years have rendered Roth's pronouncements prophetic. In the case of Chuck Palahniuk, however, it was the culture that needed to catch up with the novelist. After the events of September 11, 2001, pundits, politicians, and even the president declared the attacks "unthinkable." Yet five years earlier, Philip Roth and George W. Bush to the contrary, Chuck Palahniuk had thought it. Palahniuk claims to have written *Fight Club* after publishers rejected his first work, *Invisible Monsters*, in order to " 'offend, to shock and to punish' people who wouldn't publish 'my "good" work.' "[9] How can it be, then, that *Fight Club*, Palahniuk's work of imagination—a novel worse, he felt, than *Invisible Monsters*' tale of a fashion-model whose face was shot off and her transgender secretly-long-lost brother taking a violent road trip— could turn so quickly from dark fantasy to tragic prediction?

On the one hand, analyzing Palahniuk's novels through the retroactive lens of 9/11 can help us understand how the novels work and why the movie adaption of *Fight Club* became a far bigger pop culture phenomenon in the ensuing decade than it was when it was released in 1999. The novels can even provide a way into understanding of America's reaction to 9/11, helping to usher in a pop culture obsessed with terror and what I see as its concomitant characteristics of complicated heroism, fathers separated from families, mistrust of authority, and nonlinear and unreliable narration.

Even as they prefigure the pop culture decade to come, though, *Fight Club* and *Survivor* are works of fiction that capture the frustrations inherent to the stultifying corporate and materialistic homogeneity associated with 1980s Wall Street culture through the 1990s commerce-driven dot-com bubble. They are novels very much of their time. As literary critic Alex Tuss puts it, "[T]he anxious narrator who morphs into Tyler Durden, spokesman for White Rage and the disenfranchised male, becomes the persona through which Palahniuk probes and then explodes the seemingly serene surface of masculine success in the boom era of the 1990s."[10] In addition to forecasting coming trends in popular culture, they drew upon their context. Susan Faludi's book *Stiffed: The Betrayal of the American Man*, published the same year as *Survivor*, makes no mention of *Fight Club*, yet maintains many of the same themes. The Promise Keepers, an organization of Christian men that held events in football stadiums; the advent of the Million Man March, a gathering of African American men to Washington, D.C., in 1995; to say nothing of the first bombing of the World Trade Center, the Unabomber, and the Oklahoma City bombing together suggest that the novels were a part of, not just ahead of, their time, like other art of the era.

Yet the novels also stand out. With over 300,000 copies of *Fight Club* in print and a prolific publication pace, Palahniuk's following remains strong, particularly among young men, a demographic widely known to the publishing world for its reluctance to read. This appeal is unsurprising: combining violent surrealism, suspenseful noir, and psychological and narrative twists, the novels depict middling men who find themselves raging against political, economic, and social systems. Palahniuk's popularity is more complex, however, than chronological or cultural proximity to the emerging men's movement suggests. His books' manic charm transcends a core readership of disaffected young men galvanized by the books' stylish nihilism, violent chic, or tongue-in-cheek contravention. On the surface, the books celebrate testosterone-drenched, wanton destruction—*Fight Club*'s nameless narrator finds relief from stultifying consumerism by forming an underground boxing network, but the violence escalates to attempted bombings; *Survivor* revolves around twin conceits of cult suicides and narrator Tender Branson's reverse-paginated countdown to a hijacked plane crash. On the other hand, despite this outward sadism, the pain inflicted on others, the violence in the novels also embodies a peculiarly masculine brand of masochism: "Maybe self-improvement isn't the answer," *Fight Club*'s narrator imagines. "Maybe self destruction is the answer."[11] In the context of *Fight Club*'s 12-step programs, self-destruction does not sound nearly as dangerous as it does later in the novel, when Project Mayhem's volunteers—"Space Monkeys"—like suicide terrorists, are willing to kill and die for their cause.

Yet the novels are less acts of fantasized revenge than elaborate rituals of self-ruin. In *Fight Club*, the narrator's injuries, we discover in the ending's twist, have all been self-inflicted, because he and his nemesis, Tyler Durden, are in fact the same person, two sides to a split personality. The narrator and Tyler turn their acts of sadomasochism into masochism alone. Palahniuk's narrators rebel against what the books position as the emasculating conformity of contemporary America (IKEA takes a bigger beating than the fight club's members), but what the narrator has really been fighting, literally and figuratively, is himself.

Writing in 1996, *New York Times* book critic Michiko Kakutani lamented the prevalence of what she termed "designer nihilism," citing as examples conceptual artist Damien Hirst, famous in the 1990s for his exhibits "The Physical Impossibility of Death in the Mind of Someone Living" (a formaldehyde shark) and "Mother and Child Divided" (a cow and calf sliced and shown in a series); the film *Leaving Las Vegas*, about a screenwriter who plans to drink himself to death; and industrial rock band Nine Inch Nails, among others. While she does not discuss Palahniuk, who had not yet risen to prominence, her language pinpoints the critical sentiments expressed toward Palahniuk by critics such as Laura Miller and Janet Maslin, who have been disparaging of Palahniuk's work: "contemporary artists ... are just interested in sensationalism for sensation's sake. Their peek into the abyss isn't philosophically interesting; it's just an excuse for a self-congratulatory smirk."[12]

Yet in retrospect, Kakutani may have been overly dismissive. Palahniuk's novels signal, and ushered in, a movement from the fringes of popular culture into the mainstream. Chuck Palahniuk did not just understand 1990s male rage, or even its upcoming global equivalent, the attacks on September 11, 2001. He understands the distinctly human needs of both isolation and connection, and the ways in which our paradoxical ambivalence toward other human beings frequently goes awry, often horribly so. And he understands that the solution is neither fight-club brutality nor scorched-earth fundamentalism, neither bombing buildings nor crashing planes; those alternatives merely mirror the problems that they purport to solve. Instead, Palahniuk suggests the possibility of storytelling, even as his most prophetic stories, *Fight Club* and *Survivor*, proved disturbingly familiar.

In *Fight Club*, the narrator meets Tyler Durden, who seems to be everything that the narrator is not: aggressive, individualistic, charismatic, powerful. At the same time, however, Tyler's nihilistic Generation X critiques of an exhausted earth—" 'Recycling and speed limits are bullshit ... They're like someone who quits smoking on his deathbed' " (124)—and post-Nietzschean philosophies—" 'It's only after you've lost everything ... that you're free to do anything' " (70)—have been taken too literally by both fans and critics alike. Durden is not a generational spokesperson; even within the fiction of *Fight Club*, he is a fictional character, a hallucination, another kind of copy of a copy of a copy, his own simulacrum. While throughout much of the book the narrator is convinced by Tyler, and thus wants to "destroy everything beautiful I'd never have" (70), by the end, through Marla Singer, his antagonist turned love interest, he can find solace only in his attempt to save, not destroy, the world. After almost 200 pages of pummeling irony, he allows himself the sincerity to tell Marla, " 'I think I like you' " (197), and in the end, just as the building they occupy is poised to explode, Marla says, " 'It's not love or anything ... but I think I like you, too' " (205). Fight club never saves the narrator, as he says it does early in the novel; instead, Marla does. But first the narrator, like the reader, has to look past Tyler Durden's allure to find her. When he can, the desire to destroy himself is rendered as another kind of fiction, replaced by his desire for Marla. Though wounded and institutionalized in the book's final pages, he— and Marla—survive. Tyler does not.[13]

Yet rather than using fiction or popular culture to understand what had happened, America reacted to 9/11 by moving away from anything that seemed too close.[14] Plans for a *Survivor* movie—which would revolve around a hijacked airplane—to follow on the DVD success of *Fight Club* were put on hold.[15] Even Palahniuk seemed rattled by the ways in which his two major pre-9/11 novels so precisely anticipated what was to come. As interviewer Peter Murphy says, "[P]ost-9/11, Palahniuk reckoned it was all over for transgressive tales of angry young saboteurs, so ... he devoted his attentions to rehabilitating and subverting the horror genre with yarns like *Lullaby* and *Diary*."[16] After 9/11, even *Lullaby*'s plot, featuring recurring infant death, or *Diary*'s trope of human sacrifice, seemed less provocative than those of their predecessors; at least their plots pivot on the supernatural, as opposed to the intersections between the psychological, political, and philosophical.

In retrospect, however, we need to understand the impulses represented by *Fight Club* and *Survivor*. The works provide a voice to increasingly frustrated and alienated young men. Yet even as these men flock to Palahniuk's readership, his narrators function more as cautionary tales than moral exemplars: *Fight Club*'s nameless narrator is a split personality capable of punching himself bloody (116), among other things, and

Survivor's Tender Branson is a semi-suicidal ex-cult member who "can't bear the thought of being free."[17] Each struggles to create some kind of meaning, yet the only way he can, through most of the books, is through particularly physical and peculiarly masculine forms of self-destruction, perfectly embodied by *Fight Club*'s Tyler Durden.

Indeed, throughout most of the book, it is Tyler—and not Marla—who attracts and preoccupies the narrator. And what makes Durden attractive to the narrator—his potency, wit, and sly subversion—are the same qualities that appeal to a readership of solitary young men. Critics of the film find it ridiculous that buff idol Brad Pitt, playing Durden, can sincerely recite lines like " 'We are the middle children of history, raised by television to believe that someday we'll be millionaires and movie stars and rock stars, but we won't' " (166). Critic Henry Giroux calls it "a contradiction that cannot be overstated," and *Salon*'s Andrew O'Hehir says, "[T]here's something more than a little ludicrous about sitting in a theater while Brad Pitt preaches at you about the emptiness of materialism."[18] What these critics see as contradictory or ludicrous, however, I see as comic irony to underscore the narrative drama. As attractive as Tyler seems, and that is the power of Pitt's casting, his philosophies are a fantasy and a delusion, as Tyler himself turns out to be.

Even after discovering that he and Tyler are one, the narrator denies their connection in the novel: "I love everything about Tyler Durden, his courage and his smarts. His nerve. Tyler is funny and charming and forceful and independent, and men look up to him and expect him to change their world. Tyler is capable and free, and I'm not" (174). Or as the film's Tyler/Pitt bluntly puts it, "All the ways you wish you could be, that's me. I look like you want to look, fuck like you want to fuck. I am smart, I am capable, and most importantly, I'm free in all the ways that you are not." An epitome of the American masculine ideal, Pitt is a perfect Tyler, exactly the star most men would wish to play them (to borrow a conceit from *Survivor*) in the movie version of their lives. As a result, however, we must never take Tyler literally: to do so would be madness, as it is for the narrator, or fascism, as it is for the members of Project Mayhem. Palahniuk's fiction conveys the appeal but ultimately warns against both.

Critics, however, take Tyler, like Pitt, at face value. In a scathing analysis, Giroux calls *Fight Club* "[a] morally bankrupt and politically reactionary film. Representations of violence, masculinity, and gender in *Fight Club* seem all too willing to mirror the pathology of individual and institutional violence that informs the American landscape, extending from all manner of hate crimes to the far right's celebration of paramilitary and protofascist subcultures."[19] Yet Giroux, I think, substitutes what the film and novel *depict* for what they ultimately *prescribe*. *Fight Club* rails against consumerist conformity, but its alternative, Project Mayhem, which evolves out of fight club—the "protofascist subculture," to use Giroux's term—takes far more of its members' individuality— names, clothes, hair, identities—than consumer culture can. That is, until Big Bob—the narrator's friend Robert Paulson—is inadvertently killed by a police officer during a prank gone wrong. The narrator, now aware that his followers believe him to be Tyler Durden, attempts to put an end to Project Mayhem, but instead, echoing the language of fanatic religious martyrdom (in anticipation of *Survivor*) more than fascism, they say, "[O]nly in death will we have our own names since only in death are we no longer art of the effort. In death we become heroes" (178). The narrator, however, no longer believes this, and Palahniuk's irony thus subverts Giroux's reading—the book's endorsement of violence, rather than the narrator, self-destructs.

The Fiction of Self-Destruction

Unlike their narrators, who always experience a change of heart, Palahniuk's novels ultimately enact their own self-destruction, through their self-deconstruction—the ironic sense that the reader's cultural views by the end of the novel should be precisely the opposite of the views expressed by the narrator at the beginning, a kind of moral chiasmus. And unlike the terrorist's self-destruction, this narrative self-destruction ironically becomes an act of creation. Again and again, the supposedly espoused machismo, masochism, and nihilism must be traded hastily for something else, and that "something else" seems consistently to be love. Once Palahniuk's narrators learn the truths about themselves, they turn to their love interests for redemption. In *Fight Club*, we must go back to beginning and relearn the novel from the new perspective that the narrator and Tyler Durden are one, or in *Survivor* that the barren Fertility Hollis is pregnant with Branson's child. The stories, like the characters, self-destruct—but never completely. There is just enough left of them, and the narrative, to begin rebuilding.

Yet the return of the Husband/Father Figure seems potentially satirical as well—it's hard to imagine an unironic happily-ever-after in these books—even as they anticipate the rescue and reunion narratives that have become associated with 9/11 in popular culture, as the next chapter will examine. At the same time, though, books, unlike real life so far, may offer another way out of masculine martyrdom, aside from the obvious point that Palahniuk's main characters survive: the possibility of redemption. Michiko Kakutani seems not to see that prospect; instead, she concludes her 1996 essay by lamenting that

> [t]he New Nihilism is the absurd end product of years of 12-step thinking, recovery-movement mea culpas and daytime-television cries of victimization. After a decade defined by the spin cycle of sin and redemption, sin and redemption, it's not surprising that people would finally give up on redemption altogether and just wallow in sin and pain and guilt, the way Ben does in "Leaving Las Vegas."[20]

Here, Palahniuk's fiction sharply differs from Kakutani's analysis, and her complaint provides precisely the model against which Palahniuk rebels. For his work, in its own contemporary context, in the sudden context 9/11 imposed on it, and for the future, is, in the end, concerned with little other than a narrative of masculine redemption, first by satirizing what he sees as contemporary America's trivialization of it and then by pondering what salvation may look like in a world numbed by the very satire and hyperbole he so deftly employs.

Fight Club's nameless narrator, rather than the book itself, is "the absurd end product of . . . 12-step thinking."[21] He begins his story without questioning his life, that of a cubicle-dwelling, catalogue-reading, condominium-dwelling consumer—"You don't understand any of it, and then you die" (12)—with the language of materialism that extravagantly dwells on minutiae: "my Haparanda sofa group with the orange slip covers . . . [the] Johanneshov armchair in the Strinne green stript pattern . . . [the] Rislampa/Har paper lamps" (43) and more.[22] By about halfway through the novel, his apathy turns into the amorphous nihilism that critics accuse Palahniuk himself of espousing: "I wanted to destroy everything beautiful I'd never have. . . . Open the dump valves on supertankers and uncap offshore oil wells. I wanted to kill all the fish I couldn't afford to eat, and smother the French beaches I'd never see" (123). The impulse is apolitical destruction of an apathetic world, a way for the powerless to fantasize about spiting nature. Yet the language is still that of consumption—seeing fish as an edible commodity, for example. He still employs the same consumerist thinking, only with the sentiments reversed: the obsession with acquisition has turned into a desire for its removal.

By the end, however, we see the impulse evolve. The narrator, presumably in a sanitarium, hears the whispers of former followers, who tell him "we're going to break up civilization so we can make something better out of the world" (208). The message is meant to be ominous, the ending that is not an ending, a reminder that while Tyler seems gone and the narrator incapacitated, the same anger that began fight club remains seething beneath the surface, another bomb waiting to detonate, a terrorist cell waiting to be called up. Yet to me the language suggests more than menace: the narrator is no longer acquiring or destroying, but, rather, recycling. When an item—or even, perhaps, a culture—has outlived its purpose, we hope to return it in order to make something new out of it. Both physical consumption and ethereal spirituality even use the same verb: redeem.

In this sense, the novels' conclusions seem less traditional, and less a repudiation of the notion that "I'm a thirty year old boy, and I'm wondering if another woman is what I need" (51) than the possibility of genuine connection. For *Fight Club*'s narrator and Tender Branson do not use their potential new status as survivors as a means to control Marla and Fertility, respectively; indeed, neither woman seems in any position to be controlled. Rather, each narrator is finally in a position to claim his own story. As *Fight Club*'s narrator begins, "I remember everything" (15), the line's meaning clear only by the end, when the reader realizes that he, the narrator, has not been aware of his experiences as Tyler. In *Survivor*, Branson similarly realizes that

[i]t's all done. It's all just a story now.
     Here's the life and death of Tender Branson, and I can just walk away from it. (1)

Their discovery of narrative authority seems crucial, emblematic of Palahniuk's own sense of the connective, redemptive powers of story. Both books pivot upon the point in which the characters take control of their lives by taking control of their story. The narrators' ironic first-person unreliability—*Fight Club*'s narrator does not know the most basic truth about himself, that he shares a body with Tyler Durden; Tender Branson, again among many other examples, does not realize that his attempt to prevent the plane's hijacking *is* the very hijacking he is trying to prevent—posits narrative uncertainty as moral uncertainly. In doing so, the novels ask readers to go along with their wounding and wounded protagonists, even as we laugh at and recoil from their confusion. Unlike the world after 9/11 that he anticipates, Palahniuk asks readers to be with *and* against his narrators, just as they are with and against themselves.

Yet at the same time, I do not want to suggest that Palahniuk's stories of redemption should lose the subversive edge for which they are best known. More than threats of bombing buildings, which had already recently taken place during the first attempt to destroy the World Trade

Center in 1993 and the 1995 Oklahoma City bombing; suicide cults, enumerated at length in *Survivor* itself (144–143); recursive narratives (both *Fight Club* and *Survivor* begin at the ending, then work their way back) or twist endings (the split personality of *Fight Club*; Tender's twin's survival or Fertility's pregnancy, rendering her name appropriate rather than ironic), Palahniuk has presented something even more disturbing than sympathetic sociopaths: the thesis that our culture creates the means for its own people to turn against it. Palahniuk's men feel as though they have so little power and so little choice that they would rather perform mindless menial and potentially harmful tasks working *against* the system than, like the narrator at the beginning, perform mindless menial and potentially harmful tasks *for* it. Indeed, Project Mayhem arguably performs nothing as lethal on a large scale as the narrator's corporate task as a car recall analyst: "Everywhere I go, there's the burned-up wadded-up shell of a car waiting for me. I know where the skeletons are. Consider this my job security" (31). The passage is ambiguous: is his knowledge of corporate malfeasance—figurative skeletons in the closet—his security, as it later proves to be? Or, just as likely, is he referring to the actual corpses in the cars, and his security comes from further death because of corporate greed?

In that sense, the moral Manichaeism that the post-9/11 age has ushered in—as President George W. Bush memorably put it, "You are either with the terrorists or against them"—was already a faulty either/or distinction in *Fight Club*. The terrorists are neither with us nor against us but are a part of us. This is literally true of the narrator and Tyler; they are obviously inextricably linked, two minds in one body. But it is also figuratively true of the other characters: like the members of *Fight Club*, like the Creedish in *Survivor*, the men hiding in terrorist cells are functioning members of the culture, not obvious aliens or outsiders, even as they occupy the lowest social and economic rungs of the global economy and culture. As the *9/11 Commission Report* states, all the so-called muscle hijackers—the ones who would "storm the cockpits and control the passengers"—"were between 20 and 28 years old; most were unemployed with no more than a high school education and were unmarried."[23]

Clearly, in their preoccupation with bombings, plane crashes, plotting, and frustration, *Fight Club* and *Survivor* are uncomfortably close to the actual traumatic events of 9/11. Yet other aspects of the novels display a more nuanced—a word seldom associated with Palahniuk's often-explicit work—and perhaps more disturbing vision of 9/11-era America. *Fight Club*'s Tyler Durden epitomizes Generation X's frustration at the hyped and failed promises and excesses of the Baby Boomer, MTV, and IKEA culture, delivering speech after speech of portentous yet visceral pronouncements: " 'We are the middle children of history,' " Tyler declares more than halfway through the novel, in the line singled out by critics, " 'raised by television to believe that someday we'll be millionaires and movie stars and rock stars, but we won't. And we're just learning this fact . . . So don't fuck with us' " (166). The sentiment captures the genuine frustrations of a generation of men left feeling powerless, and radicalized, by a culture that is, like the narrator, a split personality: its men must conform to a rigid code of masculine self-sufficiency, but at the same time they must allow for crying and buying, grooming and consuming. Fight club simplifies everything; as Alex Tuss says, "The brutal immediacy of destruction, like the brutal immediacy of the individual combat in Fight Club, liberates the narrator and makes him an icon for all the other alienated and angry white men who flock to be members of Fight Club and Project Mayhem."[24]

Yet the less-quoted build-up to the "middle children of history" speech, ignored by critics who find Brad Pitt's delivery absurd, may be more revealing, despite its toned-down rhetoric:

> "Remember this," Tyler said. "The people you're trying to step on, we're everyone you depend on. We're the people who do your laundry and cook you food and serve you dinner. We make your bed. We guard you while you're asleep. . . . We are cooks and taxi drivers and we know everything about you. . . . We control every part of your life." (166)

This section, more than the reminder of thwarted riches and rock stardom, reveals the painful intersection between gender and class at the heart of the Space Monkeys' anger that even fight club cannot eradicate. The list of who "we" are comprises caretakers and domestics, jobs thought of as traditionally feminine and subservient: cooking (mentioned in three different ways in the same passage), doing laundry, directing calls. These are, not surprisingly, the same jobs relegated to the "tenders" in *Survivor* (239).

Unlike *Fight Club*'s narrator, Tender Branson's name is suffused with significance. As the novel explains, Tender is "not really a name. It's more of a rank. . . . It's the lowest rank. . . . Tenders are workers who tend" (240). In the rigid hierarchy of Palahniuk's Creedish religion, the role of each son after the first (who is always named Adam) is to tend to others' needs. In addition, though, "tender," as an adjective, means "easily cut or chewed, not tough; susceptible to pain or grief; sensitive, delicate, fragile; loving and affectionate." As Tender actively encourages desperate people to kill themselves ("try barbiturates and alcohol with your head inside a dry-cleaning bag" [282]), he does not immediately seem to qualify as "tender." But the word also means "requiring tact or careful handing," and Tender is indeed carefully handled throughout the novel, first by his church elders, then by his depraved employers, then by his manager, and finally by Fertility Hollis. And despite his outward hardness and meanness, Tender is indeed tender—loving and affectionate, as well as susceptible to pain and grief.

But these positions—Tender of *Survivor* and the figurative tenders of *Fight Club*—seemingly at the bottom of the capitalist system, are, in the novels, reversed: there is tremendous power, total control, and complete trust, Durden suggests, in working—in groups together and in secret—from the bottom. Similarly, Tender's seeming docility and invisibility are the very qualities that render him dangerous to others but safe from capture when he sets up his phony suicide hotlines, and the same qualities that allow others, including Fertility, to manipulate him later. The working man's weakness, his subservient feminizing, becomes his potential masculinist strength.

The emerging fight clubs become a way for disenfranchised young men to attempt control of the world through ostensible control of their bodies, even if that means self-destruction. As the narrator explains, "Fight club gets to be your reason for going to the gym. . . . The gyms you go to are crowded with guys trying to look like me, as if being a man means looking the way a sculptor or an art director says" (50). Exercise—indeed, the body—exists not for vanity, which would be coded feminine, but utility, which is coded masculine. Not surprisingly, the 9/11 hijackers felt the same way: according to the *9/11 Commission Report*, "several [of the muscle hijackers] also joined local gyms, presumably to stay fit for the operation."[25] Yet Durden's "We're the people . . ." speech, like much of the novel, is about more than anger, even more than about struggle and power. It is also, implicitly, about loss. Part of the novel's appeal—even more so in *Survivor*—becomes the reader's implicit sympathy for these characters. No wonder so many readers did not see Tyler Durden as the delusion he turns out to be, but rather as the savior he professed to be.

Tyler Durden's indifference to suffering should not transfer onto the reader, who may identify with his position but also recoil, by the end, at his acts of violence. Even the narrator cannot remain morally neutral. If *Fight Club* embodies Giroux's protofascism, it is in order to condemn it. In their brutality and futility, Tyler's followers, the nameless and faceless Space Monkeys, blur the lines between rebellion and conformity with the zeal of conversion, discarding tie wearing, Starbucks sipping, and

IKEA shopping to become mantra-repeating black shirts. The book's cryptofascism is not unambiguously 1960s-style anticonsumerism per se, Tyler's charisma (and Brad Pitt) notwithstanding. It is, rather, a call to recognize that fascism is the endgame of a capitalist system that would reduce workers to drones and all personal identification to brand names and commercial transactions.

Even family is implicated in the depersonalized strictures: the narrator notes with his usual detachment that his father serially divorced and started a new family every six years: "This isn't so much like a family as it's like he sets up a franchise" (50). Anticipating the novels, television shows, and films under consideration over the rest of this book, including *Extremely Loud and Incredibly Close*, *Lost*, *Hunger Games*, and the *Dark Knight* trilogy, *Fight Club* becomes an abandoned child's quest to find or replace his absent father. Throughout the novel, the narrator intones, "Tyler never knew his father" (49); "I asked Tyler what he'd been fighting. Tyler said, his father" (53); "his father was never home" (55); "I am Joe's Broken Heart because Tyler dumped me. Because my father dumped me" (134). The book's political subtext insinuates that our cherished bastions of American liberty—the free market, liberal autonomy, fatherhood, and family values—come loaded with nascent totalitarianism.

Terror of the Everyday

In the end, Tyler and the narrator are the same person, yet their literal split personality comes to emblemize the symbolic schizophrenia of American culture, the way in which we have two sides—a with and an against—that seem in conflict without our knowledge. The terrorists—of the novel, but also, metaphorically, of 9/11—come from inside of us, very different from the Cold War image of takeovers, body snatchers, and nuclear strikes. Tyler may seem to brainwash his Space Monkeys, but they show up on his doorstep—and stay for three days—on their own accord (129). We now fear a revolt not from the outside, but from within, that we may be infiltrated, as the members of fight club hide but tacitly acknowledge each other. Or worse, that our own progress, our own possessions, will be redirected against us. As political columnist Thomas Friedman puts it, the 9/11 terrorists used "the networked world, the Internet and the very high technology they hate, to attack us ... They turned our most advanced civilian planes into human-directed, precision-guided cruise missiles—a diabolical melding of fanaticism and our technology."[26]

This reversal, the sense that the means of our own destruction are also of our own making, lies at the heart of *Fight Club*. The book establishes this potential for violence beneath each of its bland, bourgeois exteriors: because of the narrator's extortion, his morally bankrupt corporate workplace—which weighs the value of human lives against the cost of recalling a faulty automobile—finances the equivalently morally bankrupt Project Mayhem. As if anticipating Timothy McVeigh and the Oklahoma City bombing, the narrator explains that there are "three ways to make napalm: One, you can mix equal parts of gasoline and frozen orange juice concentrate. Two, you can mix equal parts gasoline and diet cola. Three, you can dissolve crumbled cat litter into gasoline until the mixture is thick" (13), and again near the end: "Gasoline or gasoline mixed with frozen orange juice concentrate or cat litter" (186). The recipes are humorous and disturbing, for the same reason: the characters combine familiar consumer objects to make them lethal, just as box cutters and airplanes turn from symbols of a consumer culture to the very weapons against it. Tyler Durden, like the architects of 9/11, understood that there is no way to defy a culture as powerful as America without using the same machinations of that culture against itself.

Similarly, Tyler steals "liposuctioned fat sucked out of the richest thighs in America" to make soap, which he then sells "back to the very people who have paid to have it sucked out" (150), transmuting the substance itself but also its symbolism, from cleanliness to quasi-cannibalism (especially as he stores the fat from Marla's mother in the freezer). Soap is no longer a product of consumer capitalism but a way to subvert it while ironically profiting. Like gasoline, bedrock of the American way of life, and orange juice, symbol of California's manifest destiny and breakfast, most important meal of the day, soap, symbol of American hygiene, now undermines rather than strengthens the culture. *Survivor* maintains the metaphor, but reversed: the ways to "get bloodstains out of a fur coat" or "get blood off piano keys" (269), to "hide bullet holes in a living-room wall" (268) or "repair stab holes in night gowns, tuxedoes, and hats" (265), exposes the violent, secret lives beneath the bourgeoisie exteriors of both people and their products.

In *Fight Club*, beneath the facades of regular, everyday products lie the means for terror and violence, much like the men who inhabit the world of *Fight Club* itself. Here, behind the world of stain removal or hole repair is the inescapable fact of bloodshed, a bullet fired, a knife used, skin slapped. *Fight Club* uses seemingly harmless merchandise to expose the potential for violence; *Survivor* uses everyday products to conceal the violence that has already been inflicted. Somehow, soap and cleanliness are never next to godliness, and "the copy of a copy of a copy," at least suggestive of an original, gives way to sanitized suppression in the name of perfection. Tender's cleaning tips in the novel's opening lead directly to the conclusion's pornography landfill, the *reductio ad absurdum* of American hypocrisy, secrecy, obsessive compulsion, and misophobia. The potential for danger and destruction lurks beneath seemingly harmless merchandise and benign consumer culture. Similarly, Tyler Durden is the split personality that "just happen[s] to have the same fingerprints" as the narrator; he is the angry, murderous reverse of the innocuous pencil pusher. In the era of terror, people and products alike have an unseen, dangerous flipside to their identity and existence. Tyler's solution to corporate conformity and immorality, however, is anticorporate conformity and immorality.

Palahniuk's moral imperative directs his social criticism toward greater targets than fringe religions. As the book progresses, it becomes clear that whatever obvious criticism Palahniuk proffers toward the Creedish, those same criticisms apply to mainstream American culture. When Tender Branson remembers the thousands of cooking and cleaning instructions that he leaned in order to be of service to his future employers, he understands that the teaching "made us stupid. . . . With all the little facts we learned, we never had time to think. None of us ever considered what life would be like cleaning up after a stranger day after day. Washing dishes all day. Feeding a stranger's children. Mowing a lawn. Painting houses. Year after year. Ironing bedsheets" (193). Add the possibility of also going to a *Fight Club*–style corporate job, substitute "husband," "wife," or "children" for "stranger," and the complaint is typically middle-class American. With all of its other meanings, "tender" is also a verb, meaning "to offer or present," with its accompanying nouns, "bid, proposal," as in legal tender (this very phrase is used in the novel itself). And that, in Palahniuk's social criticism, is what Tender Branson, like too many Americans, has let himself become: a kind of legal tender, a means to an end, living capital ready for exchange, whether cleaning a house, urging suicide, or, later, telling people the proper spiritual way to live. Tender, like too many Americans, is indistinguishable from his tasks.

Tender begins to understand that everything he had been taught was fabricated, as artificial as the fake flowers that inspire him and that he tends with compassion usually associated with the care of the living. Of course, since they are not alive, "the best place to find bulbs for forcing is in the Dumpster behind the mausoleum" (257) and while there, Tender wishes to be "chased by flesh-eating zombies," out of the romantic, wistful yearning that "it would prove some sort of life after death" (255).

The notion is tender—immature (another meaning of "tender")—but suggestive of his emotional fragility and susceptibility to existential pain. The book then becomes a black-comic update of Keats's "Ode on a Grecian Urn": Palahniuk examines the ironic tension between the immortal perfection and perfectibility art—or, for Palahniuk, the fake, the artificial, the simulation—versus life's flaws and finiteness. As the novel continues, Tender becomes a false prophet but makes real profits, in the process buffing his body with a StairMaster (a kind of artificial exercise) and chemical supplements, wearing a wig when the supplements make his hair fall out, capping his teeth, bronzing his skin, reading the words of a teleprompter, learning about cures that exist in name only (but "of course they're real" [146]), and attending his own televised, fake wedding (no love, no ring, no spoken words, and even the ostensibly fake bride is replaced at the last minute by an understudy), so that, as Tender says of the flowers, "from a distance, everything looks perfect" (71, paraphrased 257). "Perfect," while fine for fakes, by the end demoralizes Tender.

Palahniuk's signature plot twists extend the trope of artificiality further: Tender's long-lost brother, Adam, is revealed as a murderer; Tender is a wanted man; and Adam, Tender, and Fertility Hollis invent a fictional terminally ill child and live in prefabricated houses before winding up in the Tender Branson Sensitive Materials Sanitary Landfill (a pornography junk yard), where Tender kills Adam at his request. Finally, Fertility pulls from her bag real flowers: "These flowers will be rotten in a couple hours. Birds will crap on them. The smoke here will make them stink, and tomorrow a bulldozer will probably run them over, but for now they are so beautiful" (24). The life of the real flowers, however temporary and imperfect, is preferable to the artificial ones that haunt Tender, the mausoleum, and the novel's pages.

Tender continues to survive his mistreatment at the hands of his family, his cult, his employers, his caseworker, and his manager. He continues to tell the tale, even as the reader, more than in a conventional novel, is constantly reminded of the story's ending and finiteness by Palahniuk's reverse pagination (the story opens on 289 and ends on page 1). The countdown appears to be to the plane crash, explosion, and death, even as the novel concludes contentedly: "The sun is total and burning and just right here, and today is a beautiful day" (1). Tender both celebrates and laments the power of narrative, finishing in circular fashion, with the same "Testing, testing, one, two—" of the opening, a dash substituting for the completion that "three" provided on the first page. The reader has no way to know whether Tender has miraculously survived or whether the last dash is the final crash.

Palahniuk revealed his "real"—a complicated word choice—ending on the Cult's website:

> The end of *Survivor* isn't nearly so complicated. It's noted on page 7(8?) [*sic*] that a pile of valuable offerings has been left in the front of the passenger cabin. This pile includes a cassette recorder. Even before our hero starts to dictate his story—during the few minutes he's supposed to be taking a piss—he's actually in the bathroom dictating the last chapter into the cassette recorder. It's just ranting, nothing important plot-wise, and it can be interrupted at any point by the destruction of the plane. The minute the fourth engine flames out, he starts the cassette talking, then bails out, into Fertility's waiting arms (she's omniscient, you know). The rest of the book is just one machine whining and bitching to another machine. The crash will destroy the smaller recorder, but the surviving black box will make it appear that Tender is dead.[27]

The reader, without this information, could fairly assume that Tender dies, although the book presents no way to show his death, since he himself is narrating. (The ending's dash, however, reminiscent of Emily Dickinson's many poems about death, does not bode well.) The reverse pagination suggests a countdown to the crash, as opposed to the takeoff. But this optimistic ending is revealed on his website, specifically and deliberately hidden to all but Palahniuk's online confidants, bonding, like members of fight club, through the secret.

While 9/11 discussions tend to emphasize the hijackers' foreignness, Palahniuk—again, with Don DeLillo—understood those aspects of contemporary American life that would lead to the kind of fanaticism, martyrdom, and destructiveness that the hijackers would go on to exhibit. Palahniuk sees the terrorist as a sympathetic figure, for, rather than emphasizing his difference from his victims, Palahniuk sees the terrorist's disturbing everyman quality, an ambiguous line between killer and victim, one that allows readers to root for Tender's survival even after he has hijacked a plane. *Fight Club*'s narrator has no specific name and little physical description, not just because he could be anyone, but because he is, in a sense, everyone. The book's revelation of male bonding through secrecy implicitly positions male readers as members, again strengthening potential sympathy, if at the potential expense of a female readership. As Alexander Boon suggests, "To write about *Fight Club* is to violate the first rule of Fight Club, to engage in a discourse rendered illicit by Tyler Durden's directive in the novel and unspeakable by a post-war cultural politic that posits violence as the exclusive domain of men and brands male violence as *the* monolithic evil overshadowing American culture."[28] Thus, any man reading *Fight Club* becomes a symbolic member.

Here, however, Palahniuk departs from DeLillo, who in his 1991 novel *Mao II* also used terrorists as foils for his everyman figure, Bill Gray. DeLillo's terrorists remain oppositional, marginal, and distinctly anti-Western. Palahniuk's terrorists, by contrast, are the logical and direct outgrowths of the culture they wish to supplant, not foreign reactions against it. And this distinction enforces one of the most striking discoveries of 9/11: that the suicide attackers, as the *New York Times* reported just days after the attacks, simply did not fit the established hijacker profile; they were "not hopeless young zealots. ... They mingled in secular society, even drinking forbidden alcohol, hardly typical of Islamic militants ... [and] had, in some cases, spent years studying and training in the United States ... facing many opportunities to change their minds."[29]

The *New York Times* reporter, however, also misses a point that Palahniuk understood: just as American culture provides material opportunity, to do so it must at the same time accentuate material inequality. Writing in the age of the Unabomber and Timothy McVeigh, Palahniuk understood that an enemy after the Cold War could come from within, a homegrown right-wing movement insistent on resisting what it perceives as the feminizing of American culture through the government's intrusion onto the privacy of (male) Americans, versions of which appear as both Project Mayhem as well the Creedish cult. Or it could come from an anticorporate left-wing movement like the groups that led Seattle to declare a state of emergency during the protests against the convention of the World Trade Organization in 1999. Yet what the novels, coupled with the advent of 9/11, also reveal is the similarity between groups that seem to be on opposite sides of the political spectrum—that militant, fundamentalist Islam shares the same ideas about attacking an overreaching, materialist, decadent, feminizing culture and government with native reactionaries. Palahniuk thought that he was exaggerating the worst aspects of a culture that, in the terrorists' view, seeks to emasculate its male citizens, but what 9/11 shows is that the effects were even more far reaching than Palahniuk understood. It was not just American men who felt as though their manhood and individuality were being taken away from them, but men around the world, who would then come here and use the freedoms and technologies of the culture to destroy it from within.

While the charges that Project Mayhem set up for the Parker Morris Building themselves are supposed to explode, they do not technically blow up the buildings. As demolitions experts understand, once the charges detonate, the building, rather, implodes, its own weight used against its now-weakened infrastructure.[30] The troubling legacy of 9/11 that Palahniuk preemptively understood is not that we would be attacked, Cold War–style, by expensive, explosive technologies from across the globe, as much as the possibility of implosion, of being attacked by people hiding in plain sight, waiting for their activation. The terrorist threat in *Fight Club* is not the bombs, which fail to detonate in the book but succeed in the film. The true explosive threats are the people themselves. The post–Cold War era, as Palahniuk anticipated, shows the greatest danger as coming from people, human bombs awaiting activation.

After 9/11, Don DeLillo, who, like Palahniuk, has built a literary career on both his prescience and his understanding of marginal figures, published his essay "In the Ruins of the Future," in which he again displayed his understanding of plots:

> Terror's response is a narrative that has been developing over years, only now becoming inescapable. It is our lives and minds that are occupied now. This catastrophic event changes the way we think and act, moment to moment, week to week, for unknown weeks and months to come, and steely years. Our world, parts of our world, have crumbled into theirs, which means we are living in a place of danger and rage.[31]

Yet again, in the 1990s Palahniuk saw the ways in which we were already living "in a place of danger and rage" and that terror is less a tactic than a way of thinking, living, and, disconcertingly, creating a narrative. In *Fight Club*, Palahniuk's distinctly American perpetrators want "to blast the world free of history" (124); for DeLillo, "[t]he terrorists of September 11 want to bring back the past."[32] Yet ideologies advocating erasing history, as opposed to merely bringing back a past that may never have been, are, in practice, the same. *Survivor*'s Creedish, whose fundamentalism resembles Islamist groups more than, say, the Amish, after which they seem visually modeled, deny modernity in the name of a spirituality that paradoxically mirrors the mainstream's own violence and self-absorption; similarly, *Survivor*'s America sneers at the Creedish religion even as it yearns for its own unironic religious icons. Palahniuk's narratives powerfully undermine the Us and Them dichotomies even before they had fully formed in the national consciousness. In the end, novels such as *Fight Club* and *Survivor* demonstrate the futility of a With Us or Against Us mindset, while finally, in perhaps the novels' most subversive touch, revealing that any war on terror must be a spiritual one, within our culture and our selves, one that must end in redemption, not, like the Twin Towers, in collapse.

Philip Roth seems to prefigure this concern with collapse and implosion, concluding "Writing American Fiction" even less happily than he begins. Assessing the works of William Styron, Saul Bellow, and Ralph Ellison, Roth sees a turn inward. The characters of the novels under review, he says, "come through a serious personal struggle, [and] simply to have survived . . . is nothing to be made light of." But too often, he continues, as in the end of *Invisible Man*, "the hero is left with the simple stark fact of himself. He is as alone as a man can be. Not that he hasn't gone out into the world; he has gone out into it, and out into it, and out into it—but at the end he chooses to go underground, to live there and to wait. And it does not seem a cause for celebration for him, either."[33] Again, the solipsistic despair Roth sees exhibited here, like his fear of the novelist outstripped by the news, has mostly come to pass. But he did not anticipate Palahniuk's work, for, as Palahniuk describes in the introduction to *Stranger Than Fiction*, "all my books are about a lonely person looking for some way to connect with other people."[34] Yet it is the reader, not just the characters, who is drawn out of solitude by the books' themes. As Palahniuk explains,

> My pet theory about *Fight Club*'s success is that the story presented a structure for people to be together . . . Look at books like *How to Make an American Quilt* and *The Devine Secrets of the Ya-Ya Sisterhood* and *The Joy Luck Club*. These are all books that create a structure . . . that allows people to be together and share their stories. . . . Of course, they're all women's stories. We don't see a lot of new models for male social interaction. There's sports. Barn raisings. That's about it.
>
> And now there's fight clubs. For better or worse.[35]

More than terrorist cells, suicide cults, and fight clubs, there is *Fight Club*. Together with *Survivor*, *Fight Club* presents "terror's response," in DeLillo's words, but also, even more subversively, the implicit counternarrative: that redemption may be in the palm of the reader's hands, in the form of storytelling itself. After the carnage of 9/11 and its ongoing aftermath abroad, perhaps Roth underestimated the value of survival. After all the falling buildings, falling planes, and falling men, Palahniuk's plots, despite DeLillo's pronunciation in *Libra*, move toward life. However bleak Palahniuk's worlds may seem, even after planes crash, even after buildings fall, the story—and storyteller—survive.

The books render the concept of self-destruction as unreliable and unsustainable as the bombs that fail to detonate at the end of *Fight Club*. In the film, of course, the bombs do explode, and the buildings indeed crumble, in pre-9/11 imagery that would surely never have been produced just a few years later. At the same time, however, the film ironically uses the metaphor to fortify, rather than demolish, the final romance between Marla and the narrator, by using the bursting bombs and imploding buildings as the literal backdrop to their replete romance, their explosive embrace. Their world, rather than ending, is just beginning. The film concludes with the humorous shot of the "subliminally" spliced-in image of the penis, reminding viewers of the film's much-touted masculinity, but more importantly of the main characters' emerging sexuality and, self-reflexively, that what we're seeing is really just a movie capable of being spliced at all. The eerie guitar refrain (and apt lyrics) of "Where Is My Mind" by the Pixies plays, the credits roll, and astute viewers experience the shock of recognition that *Fight Club* turned out to be, of all things, an uplifting movie.

In the trappings of postmodern apocalypses and existential absurdities, Palahniuk's novels are old-fashioned romances. But they're not decked out in Brad Pitt-as-Tyler Durden's neo-hipster get-up. Tyler's vintage denim, red leather, wraparound shades, and mussed pomade hairdo exist only in the film; when the narrator meets him in the book, Tyler is naked. Palahniuk may nod to designer nihilism, but he knows that the emperor has no clothes.

CHAPTER 2

Falling Towers, Falling Planes, and Falling Men: Trauma as Domestic Drama

The 9/11 Memorial in New York City, the names etched and enshrined. (Tootsie2/Dreamstime.com)

In this chapter: *World Trade Center* (2006), directed by Oliver Stone; *United 93* (2006), directed by Paul Greengrass; *Extremely Loud and Incredibly Close* (2005), Jonathan Safran Foer, and its film adaptation (2011) directed by Stephen Daldry; *Falling Man* (2007), Don DeLillo. Additional discussion: *The Writing on the Wall* (2005), Lynne Sharon Schwartz; *A Disorder Peculiar to the Country* (2006), Ken Kalfus; *The Reluctant Fundamentalist* (2007), Mohsin Hamid; *Netherland* (2008), Joseph O'Neill.

Falling and redemption, humor and horror, fragmented consciousness and narrative—the premises and characteristics of Fight Club *and* Survivor *would be the unlikely templates for popular culture of the next millennium. But on September 11, 2001, terror would move from the American subtext and symbol and into the American story. After the attacks, many filmmakers and writers incorporated the events of 9/11 into their explicit subject matter. Discussing these films and novels requires a different way of thinking. While these stories may use the back-drop of the 9/11 attacks, images of the Twin Towers, and recurring images of searching and falling, they are ultimately less about global or extraordinary events than about the intersections between national trauma and everyday American family life. While Oliver Stone's film* World Trade Center *relies on familiar pre-9/11 genre conventions, Paul Greengrass's movie* United 93, *and the novels* Extremely Loud and Incredibly Close, *by Jonathan Safran Foer, and* Falling Man, *by Don DeLillo, each provides different narrative and emotional challenges in the ways in which they absorb terror into their plots and characters' lives.*

On the evening of the September 11, 2001, attacks, President George W. Bush appeared on television to address a fearful and tearful nation, and his first response initiated what would become the prevailing American narrative of 9/11:

> Today our fellow citizens, our way of life, our very freedom came under attack in a series of deliberate and deadly terrorist acts. The victims were in airplanes or in their offices: secretaries, business men and women, military and Federal workers, moms and dads, friends and neighbors. Thousands of lives were suddenly ended by evil, despicable acts of terror.[1]

That "our way of life, our very freedom came under attack" and the concluding image of "evil, despicable acts of terror"—what would soon be called "the war on terror" on September 20, 2001—would in the next few years certainly shape the United States' actions abroad and perceptions at home. But in between, the litany of casualties, the "secretaries, business men and women, military and Federal workers, . . . friends and neighbors," but especially "moms and dads," established the characters in the stories we would begin to tell. Early reports suggested that upwards of 6,000 people had died that day. Even as the casualties have been adjusted to 2,977, the number was, and is, far too high to comprehend: a statistic, an abstraction. The death of an individual, however, paradoxically can feel like more, by allowing us to connect with specific, personal histories and stories.

And so we looked for individuals. Three days later, President Bush's next speech, for the National Day of Prayer and Remembrance Service, would establish the importance of identities further:

> Now come the names, the list of casualties we are only beginning to read. They are the names of men and women who began their day at a desk or in an airport, busy with life. They are the names of people who faced death, and in their last moments called home to say, be brave, and I love you. They are the names of passengers who defied their murderers, and prevented the murder of others on the ground. They are the names of men and women who wore the uniform of the United States, and died at their posts. They are the names of rescuers, the ones whom death found running up the stairs and into the fires to help others. We will read all these names. We will linger over them, and learn their stories, and many Americans will weep.[2]

Bush's impulse to repeat the word "names," name the names, "learn their stories," and mourn the losses of people, not a collective, would soon become articulated in the New York Times's Portraits of Grief, vignettes and images of the people who died. Loss could be understood only one life at a time, through the lens of each individual. And yet, by the end of the series, the Times had collected over 2,500 portraits—an encyclopedia more than a portrayal, too many names, histories, details, and stories to read and process.[3] Even if one were to read them all, he or she would have difficulty imposing a shape or shared language. If anything, the diversity of entries, rather than any cohesion, was precisely the point. Later, along the two pools that now symbolize the absent towers, the 9/11 Memorial would inscribe all of the names of the dead as a solemn, unified register. Yet a stone memorial alone cannot voice their stories. For the combination of voice and vision, the shape and scope that comes from the interplay of character and plot, symbol and theme, we usually turn to a longer, more personal form: fiction. Yet this shift from numbers to names, and then names to narratives, creates new problems as well.

Towers and Planes: *World Trade Center* and *United 93*

Appropriately, but in some ways disconcertingly, the emerging narrative, like Bush's speech and Portraits in Grief, focused on the particular lives and loves of specific focal characters rather than a larger cultural sweep or representation. The impulse is understandable, a way to emphasize human feeling and family. Yet beneath the sincerity remained anxiety: the attack on America was domestic, in the sense of our own soil and our own families, continuously experienced through the cold light of constantly present screens. One of the first national, posttraumatic attempts to process the attack into a single, linear, nondocumentary narrative was *World Trade Center*, directed by Oliver Stone, in 2006. Rather than seeing 9/11 as a day that changed everything, *World Trade Center* instead fits it into a familiar film framework. As Susan Faludi puts it, *World Trade Center* does "precisely what it meant to do, and what other American cultural presentations of 9/11 have done before and since: replicate, not delve."[4] Yet its replication is more complex than Faludi suggests, and other cultural presentations have done more than merely repeat what we thought we knew.

"A true story of courage and survival," according to the description on the DVD, the plot revolves around two Port Authority police officers, John McLoughlin (Nicolas Cage) and Will Jimeno (Michael Peña), who, in their attempt to rescue trapped victims after the attacks on the Twin Towers, become trapped themselves. The inescapable feeling throughout the first 15 minutes of the film, before the planes hit the towers, before the rescues begin, before the officers lie trapped beneath the wreckage, is dramatic irony: the idea that the viewer knows something important that the characters do not. Stone presumes that any likely viewer of the film had also been watching, and re-watching, the footage of the attacks for the past five years. The film's opening scene seems to depict a day just like any other, George Bush's blue sky, for Cage's character, with a lingering shot where he kisses his wife, Donna (Maria Bello), goodbye. We, unlike them, know the separation that the day will bring, and we are powerless to stop it.

Once the planes inevitably hit, however, the laid-back air and the famous blue sky withdraw. The film becomes emotionally severe, even claustrophobic, as Stone blacks out the screen and silences what had just been the roar of the collapsing first tower. A half-hour into the film, with the fall of the South Tower, Stone incorporates real-life footage, heightening the film's sense of realism and familiarity. For most of the rest of the film, viewers stare helplessly as the fallen officers lie buried beneath the fallen building, rescuers in need of rescue. Deep beneath the rubble, when the prospect of salvation seems lost, McLoughlin breathlessly tells Jimeno, "Tell my family that I love them." Suddenly, the darkness dissolves into a halo of light, and a backlit penumbra of Jesus Christ himself appears, offering a water bottle, in another image that has come to be associated with the post-9/11 rescue. A symbolic montage ensues, featuring a soft-focus Donna making the bed and holding the sheets—white and supple, all maternal warmth and comfort—as McLoughlin repairs the roof—synecdoche for the house and fatherly protection—in perfect, gender-specific domestic harmony.

The officers are saved by Marine Sgt. Dave Karnes (Michael Shannon), who tells the grateful, incredulous Jimeno, "You are our mission," and after a lengthy effort, they are rescued. The film concludes when Karnes reports that "[w]e're gonna need some good men out there to avenge this," the referent for the pronoun "this" too broad to specify. As CGI smoke obscures the damage done to Manhattan, the film concludes with an optimistic expression of hope: the reunification of family and the reiteration of domesticity. As we discover in the final titles, "only 20 people were pulled out alive," which makes McLoughlin's and Jimeno's survival even more miraculous, even as it also has the troubling effect of potentially implying that the mostly unseen deaths were somehow necessary to elevate McLoughlin's and Jimeno's exceptionalism. Despite the day's catastrophe, where we understand that thousands have died, the film wants us to root for these particular men to live, as though their endurance were an extension, a symbol, of America's own.

On the surface, *World Trade Center* eschews politics entirely, let alone political intrigue, to focus on its story and character. Its seeming political agnosticism, though, becomes another form of politics: it does not challenge the solidifying mythos of 9/11, but instead reinforces, even reifies, President Bush's first speeches, what by 2005 were the accepted symbols and signifiers of 9/11. The film makes sure to dramatize the reams of paper that poured from broken towers, blanketing lower Manhattan, just as the novels *The Writing on the Wall*, by Lynne Sharon Schwartz; *Extremely Loud and Incredibly Close*; by Jonathan Safran Foer; and *Falling Man*, by Don DeLillo describe as well. The camera captures the businessmen who jumped to their deaths, just like the man serendipitously caught on camera by Richard Drew, christened the Falling Man by writer Tom Junod in *Esquire*, appropriated as the title of DeLillo's novel, and another recurring image in *Extremely Loud and Incredibly Close*. The audience hears and feels the sub-bass rumble and sees the enshrouding dust storm of the falling towers, familiar from so many fantasy movies featuring massive destruction but made strange and discomforting by the viewers' knowledge that it really happened. The film's symbolism renders 9/11 an attack not just on America, but on America's masculinity, taking down our phallic towers and entrapping and emasculating our best men, so that only "good men" can "avenge" what has happened.

Perhaps most crucially of all, television dominates and saturates *World Trade Center*, becoming the way in which its characters—indeed, all Americans—were united in the very moments when fear loomed largest. If Vietnam was America's first televised war, 9/11 was its first televised domestic disaster.[5] Unlike the film footage of President Kennedy's assassination—inadvertently captured by home video enthusiast Robert Zapruder, incorporated at length into Oliver Stone's *JFK*, and almost impossible to view for decades after Kennedy's death—the image of the second plane hitting the South Tower, the subsequent footage of the towers falling, and the turmoil in the streets became available for all to see, in real time. Rather than conspiring, lying, or dividing, as detractors have suggested, the media in *World Trade Center* are part of the very experience of 9/11, the coverage of the events inextricably linked to the events themselves.

The confusion as it unfolded on the real September 11, 2001, the on-air reporters struggling to make sense of what happened, the tentative hand-cams and home videos, is replaced by the confident cameras in—and of— Stone's 9/11, to transmute reality's uncertainty into cinematic cohesion. The day on which many Americans felt the least safe in their lifetime could now unfold as a familiar Hollywood three-act structure. First, the exposition, establishing the officers' characters and family ties, followed by rising action, brought on by the catastrophe and, in typical movie convention, worsened through the attempt to resolve it. And finally, resolution, through the climactic moment of when the officers are found, with our protagonists' reunion with their wives and children as the dénouement.

Stone seems not to have made a movie about the fall of the real World Trade Center, exactly. Rather, he created a comprehensible, and familiar, narrative of disappearance and recovery. In that sense, using September 11 and the World Trade Center as the sites for the disaster and rescue story seems arbitrary. *World Trade Center* follows the conventions of catastrophic movies from any era, including *The Poseidon Adventure* (1972), or its remake, *Poseidon*, appearing in 2006 along with *World Trade*

Center. Much more presciently, *Poseidon Adventure* producer Allen Irwin followed with *The Towering Inferno* (1974), a film that, as Stephen Prince writes, "prefigures the events of 9/11 in numerous ways."[6] Yet perhaps that film did not quite prefigure 9/11; rather, Stone's pop-cultural representation of 9/11 harks back to past forms.

Despite *World Trade Center*'s use of darkness and confinement, it serves to comfort, not confront, by transmuting the supposedly unimaginable events of 9/11 into a film that had been imagined, many times. In that sense, *World Trade Center* is less an enactment than a simulacrum of 9/11: Stone based his film on the day that, to so many onlookers, felt like a movie, in part because it had been. While it goes without saying that 9/11 was not like a movie because real people died and real geopolitics were altered, in another crucial way the events of 9/11 were not like a movie at all: it had no sustained focal characters, no clear story line, no sense of narrative development, no conventional time limit, and no ending. Stone then makes a movie about the day that felt like one by retroactively imposing these narrative constraints after enough time had passed for them to be recognizable.

With *World Trade Center*, these narrative conventions are more than recognized: they become ingrained. McLoughlin and Jimeno are rescued by the Marines, but they are also rescued by Oliver Stone. Their rescue is meant to be ours as well, with nearly all of the deaths, and all of the aftermath, left off camera so that we can rejoice in the miraculous survival of the only characters viewers were primed to care about. Some of that conditioning comes from seeing McLoughlin and Jimeno trapped and suffering, but much of it is created by the repeated shots of anguish from Donna and visibly pregnant Allison Jimeno (Maggie Gyllenhaal). The cameras, and the resultant film, are there to comfort them, and us.

In contrast with Stone's reassuring gaze, Paul Greengrass's *United 93* is confusing and frenzied. While three of the four planes hijacked on September 11, 2001, crashed into the terrorists' targets, the fourth, supposedly directed toward the White House, crashed in rural Pennsylvania, after passengers thwarted the hijackers. Stone casts Nicolas Cage, provides lengthy exposition and backstory for his two fallen officers, and employs steady cameras, creating a sense of literal and symbolic stability and a unified field of vision around 9/11. On the contrary, Greengrass casts unknowns and actual flight attendants,[7] eschews flashback, and uses increasingly wild handheld cameras, disjointed cuts, diegetic sound (surrounding sounds, rather than added effects or music), and subjective shots (angles that seem to be from someone's perspective rather than the more typical Hollywood approach where viewers are not supposed to think about the camera at all). While Tom Pollard refers to the camera techniques as "cinema vérité"[8]—a naturalistic, documentary style of filmmaking—the effect of *United 93* is much more than a heightened sense of realism or cinematic equivalent of the promotional materials "based on a true story" tag. Taken together, these choices foster feelings of chaos that are central to Greengrass's 9/11. While Stone's 9/11 soothes viewers into believing someone is in charge and rescue is just on the way, Greengrass's 9/11 is like the ill-fated flight itself: out of control and doomed. Stone's fallen men rise again, but Greengrass's falling planes do not.

Like *World Trade Center*, *United 93* pivots upon dramatic irony—the film also opens with what seems to be a day like any other. One of the recurring, powerful refrains about 9/11 is that the attacks were "out of the blue," an inadvertent pun that combines the surprise and the perfect skies. The first 30 minutes, in fact, seem so familiar that they could be depicting almost any plane, any flight. But the audience knows what characters do not, so that the opening scenes, juxtaposing the would-be hijackers' preparations with their prayers, take on ominous tones. As passengers head to the airport for what they assume will be a routine flight, we see a highway sign saying "God Bless America." We hear air traffic controllers bantering about "clear skies, ought to be a good day in the East coast." Waiting passengers chat on their cellphones about trivia, as only viewers can recognize the hijackers sitting among them. One passenger makes it onto the flight just in time and believes himself lucky, a detail seemingly lifted straight from *Speed* (1994), about a terrorist bomb placed on a bus. The flight attendants' safety procedures, ignored by the passengers and that would not have kept them safe at any rate, become powerfully, painfully ironic. Without the slightly shaky camera, through which only we can see, and portentous sounds, which only we can hear, the film's early sequences would play like a benign documentary about a typical day for an airline.

As the film progresses, however, the camera grows more precarious, the sounds ever more ominous. Even then, Greengrass relies on some of Stone's 9/11 tropes: he incorporates real-life footage as well and makes sure that, even without elaborate biographies, we see that the passengers aboard United 93 have families waiting for them and who will grieve for them. The terror in these scenes is quiet and latent. Unlike the camera work and narrative of *World Trade Center*, *United 93* cannot reenact a rescue mission. Instead, its dramatic ironies begin to resemble those of a different genre: the horror movie. We want to warn passengers not to get on the plane, warn the pilots not to take off. When the terrorists say that no one will be hurt, we want to scream to the passengers not to believe them. Once the first planes crashes into the World Trade Center, the film's cinematography mirrors the day's massive sense of confusion. While time has revealed the answers to the viewer, the characters cannot know how many planes were hijacked, which planes, by whom, or why, the certainties provided in the ensuing months and years as yet unknown. By the end, as the passengers realize that there can be no rescue for them, they make their final phone calls, in symmetry with those made in the waiting area earlier. And while the "I love yous" are the same familiar, even banal words that we heard before and are used to overhearing from other people's grating conversations, the film reminds the viewer how crucial they are. With the final fall, *United 93* ends with the descent from light to darkness, the visual, literal, and symbolic opposite of *World Trade Center*'s ascent.

Unlike *World Trade Center*'s recognizable narrative and ultimately uplifting rescue (the officers are even literally uplifted), viewers can only watch in dismay, rather than suspense, as the story of the fated flight over Pennsylvania plays out. Just as we know that McLoughlin and Jimeno must live, *United 93* works as a film because we know that the plane must—will, did—crash. Yet somehow, in the retelling, some part of us believes that, this time, perhaps it will not. As one of my students wrote in response to the film, I "hate when you watch a movie and you know how it ends and yet you find yourself hoping for the best anyway."

While *World Trade Center* fits the genre of disaster and rescue movies with or without the context of 9/11, *United 93* never falls into the pre-9/11 film subgenre of terrorists taking over an airplane (or, alternately, a bus, boat, or building). Perilous flights have been a staple of disaster film since the 1950s, with James Stewart in *No Highway in the Sky* (1951) and John Wayne in *The High and the Mighty* (1954). Films like *Airport* (1970) seem in keeping with contemporaries *The Poseidon Adventure* and *The Towering Inferno*, in that their threats come from errors or accidents, not directly from hijackers. It was not until the 1990s that the trend of terrorists and criminals hijacking a plane becomes a commonplace film trope. *Passenger 57* (1992), about airplane terrorists that only Wesley Snipes can stop, was quickly followed by *Executive Decision* (1996), *Air Force One* (1997), and *Con Air* (1997). As a result, however, audiences have become conditioned to believing that hijacked planes in films do not crash, whereas Greengrass begins with the premise that the planes of *United 93* must.

United 93, however, departs further from *World Trade Center* in its portrayal of the terrorists themselves. *World Trade Center* portrays no visible villain—indeed, no clear group, country, or even ostensible motive behind the attacks other than to set its plot in motion. Yet Greengrass's hijackers are not portrayed as typical villains, masterminds, or, until the concluding, horrific violence on the plane, monsters. With their light beards, they seem innocuous, young, and nervous, lacking backstories, specific nationalities, and even names, nothing like the terrorists we have come to expect from pre-9/11 movie terrorists like Alan Rickman's sophisticated Hans Gruber in *Die Hard* or Dennis Hopper's bitter, maniacal Howard Payne in *Speed*. Those terrorists were intense and personal, power hungry, ingenious, laden with stories and agendas. In contrast, the terrorists of *United 93* are, until much of the way thought the film, very much like the passengers: everyday people who suddenly become part of an extraordinary moment in history they know they will not survive.

Greengrass conducted extensive research to insure that the movie was as accurate as possible.[9] What, though, becomes the point of such a film? Frank Rich argues that "rather than deepening our knowledge of them or their heroism, the movie caps an hour of air-controller nail-biting with a tasteful re-enactment of the grisly end."[10] Susan Faludi says that the film "seemed to have no other purpose than to repeat what we already know."[11] I think it achieves more than "re-enactment" or repetition—but that it is also more complex than the many websites listing it as one of the most "patriotic" films of all time would have viewers believe. It depicts the hijackers' premeditated violence, yet at the same time, it defiantly manages to humanize them; they often seem as though they might not go through with the plan, even as we know they will. The film is a perfect marriage of form and content: the camera's perspective grows more frenetic and less stable just as the passengers' lives, day's events, and the airplane itself simultaneously spin out of control. In style and substance, *United 93* provides a crucial counterpoint to *World Trade Center*. In some ways, of course, the films are similar: Greengrass again emphasizes the bravery of the passengers aboard the ill-fated flight. Yet for all of its seeming fidelity, that it is based on a true story, *World Trade Center*'s attempt to provide narrative logic and comfort creates as many problems for critical viewers as it solves. While Oliver Stone easily folds the events in New York on 9/11 into the familiar filmic conventions of the search and rescue genre, Greengrass's story, cinematography, and sound specifically resist many of the expectations established by pre-9/11 hijacking films.

Taken together, *World Trade Center* and *United 93* embody what became many of the features of popular culture in the era of terror. While the officers and marines of *World Trade Center* represent traditional film heroes, *United 93*'s passengers—in contrast with Wesley Snipes's former officer and terrorism expert John Cutter—remain average people, men and women, in a way that emphasizes their courage but also challenges what it means to be a film hero. Both movies create drama by stressing the separation of husbands and wives and parents and children, a theme that remains central to many of the stories under analysis. And while Stone suggests that even on 9/11, the pillars of society still stand, Greengrass viscerally depicts the breakdown of power, feelings of terror, and ways in which the technique of storytelling itself can be used to re-present these collapses. In breaking with the conventional approaches to genre, character, and more comforting modes of storytelling, like *Fight Club* before it, *United 93* challenges the viewer to rethink how living under the specter of terror affects the ways in which we conceptualize and comprehend our stories. As we will see, its challenges are consistent with fiction's approach to 9/11, and they presage the conventions that will dominate popular culture for the next decade.

Falling Men: The Novels of 9/11

Although different in approach, *World Trade Center* and *United 93* provide a sense of filmmakers' main response to trauma and terror: to make it about American families. The approach of otherwise dissimilar novelists is—strangely, or perhaps soothingly—the same. A list of what might be called "9/11 novels" could just as easily be a compendium of contemporary fiction of husbands and wives, or fathers and sons, separating, with attempts to reunite the fallen families. One of the first was *A Disorder Peculiar to the Country* (2006), by emerging writer Ken Kalfus, which revolves around both 9/11's falling towers and the failing marriage of Joyce and Marshall Harriman. Unlike any of the other subsequent 9/11 novels, however, Kalfus opts for the black comedy: both husband and wife believe the other has died and are dismayed and disappointed to find the other still alive. *Netherland* (2008), Joseph O'Neill's second novel, is ostensibly about 9/11 but depicts no falling towers or terrorists, instead creating the elaborate interior monologue of Hans van den Broeck, whose wife has left him in New York City in the aftermath of 9/11 and returned to England with their son; the novel's title punningly suggests Hans's in-between state, his lack of place, more than his country of origin. Claire Massud's *Emperor's Children* (2006) similarly dramatizes the effects of the tragedy on upper-middle-class New Yorkers who previously thought their privilege protected them from harm; their relationships, and in one case, marriage, unravel.

Another of the first novels to incorporate 9/11, *The Writing on the Wall* (2005) by Lynne Sharon Schwartz, captures the emotional tenor of life in New York. Renata, having survived the death of her twin sister and loss of her surrogate daughter, who disappeared years earlier, struggles to maintain her relationship with Jack. The novel brings together nearly all of the tropes and themes of the 9/11 novel: walks over the Brooklyn Bridge, posters for the missing, the idea that paper fueled the flames that ultimately brought down the towers, and of course, the images of twins—as in Twin Towers—and a heterosexual romantic relationship. Other, more famous authors, including Jay McInerney in *The Good Life* (2006, which, like *The Writing on the Wall*, features twins); Neil LaBute, with his play *The Mercy Seat* (2003); and Don DeLillo, with *Falling Man* (discussed in greater detail later in this chapter), each dwell on struggles between men and women and the ways in which the events of 9/11 bring these conflicts to the dramatic forefront.

Despite what seems inescapably political subject matter, nearly all of the novels, like *World Trade Center* and *United 93*, seem to avoid politics directly. *The Reluctant Fundamentalist* (2007), by Mohsin Hamid, is one of the only overtly political 9/11 novels. Its disarming monologue, by narrator Changez, chronicles his lateral move, rather than fall, as he converts from fundamentalist capitalism to fundamentalist Islamism. Yet in many ways, the turning point is not 9/11 itself, despite that, "despicable as it may sound," the narrator's "initial reaction was to be remarkably pleased ... I was caught up in the *symbolism* of it all, the fact that someone had so visibly brought America to her knees."[12] Instead, it is Changez's relationship with Erica, the woman with whom he is smitten but who cannot recover from the death of her first love, Chris, that drives him toward what seems to be jihad. The novel's conclusion, and its particular political stance, remains open ended: we never know whether Changez plans to kill his silent, unnamed conversation partner, or vice versa. But the novel itself shares Changez's preoccupation with symbolism, in that it is overtly allegorical: Erica is America, less a person than an emblem, while America is coded female ("brought America to her knees); Changez's name ("changes") could not be more overtly symbolic; and "Chris" seems a stand-in for Christopher Columbus, a ghost of America's colonial past. The political conflict between jihadists and America is rendered through the analogy of yet another struggling heterosexual couple. Jonathan Safran Foer's *Extremely Loud and Incredibly Close* (also discussed in greater detail later in this chapter), while focused on nine-year-old narrator Oskar Schell's grief over his father, who "died in 9/11," is also highly symbolic, even as it is clear to depict the way in which the death of the father represents, for Oskar, the death of the family.[13]

What about 9/11 has led so many writers to have the same literary reaction—that is, to treat it as a domestic incursion more than a political or international one? Again and again, a diverse group of writers looked at 9/11 and saw in it the novelistic opportunity to reevaluate marriage. For critic Richard Gray, "The crisis is, in every sense of the word, domesticated."[14] Agreeing with Gray, Michael Rothberg writes, "The fiction of 9/11 demonstrates ... a failure of the imagination."[15] Novelists, apparently, did not write the books that Gray and Rothberg wanted to see. But what if the domestic impulse does not represent a shortsightedness on the part of contemporary writers at all? Gray laments that these novels merely "assimilate the unfamiliar into familiar structures."[16] I want to suggest that, after 9/11, assimilating the unfamiliar into the familiar may be much more ambitious, and desirable, than Gray assumes. And perhaps the seemingly coincidental consistency raises important questions about the metaphorical links between 9/11 and marriage, to families, and to fallen fathers.

In order to understand how these novels reconfigure the global and national scale of the attacks into small, personal, and domestic stories of grief and strife within the American family, particularly involving lost husbands and fathers, I want to look closely at what for me are the two exemplary novels of 9/11, even as analyzing them suggests that they may not be as much about 9/11 as they first appear to be—and perhaps not conventional novels at all.

Jonathan Safran Foer's Search for the Father

New York Times critic Frank Rich and others objected to *United 93*, saying that "of course" it "exploits 9/11. It's a Hollywood entertainment marketed to make a profit."[17] Similarly, critics like Anis Shivani accused Jonathan Safran Foer of riding "the 9/11-novel gravy train,"[18] and *New York Press* reviewer Harry Seigel condemned him for "snatch[ing] 9/11 to invest his conceit with gravitas, thus crossing the line that separates the risible from the villainous."[19] I want to suggest, though, that with *Extremely Loud and Incredibly Close*, Foer makes use of 9/11 not cynically, but symbolically. The novel provides the necessary strangeness mixed with sentiment that the list of names on a memorial, a brief newspaper biography, or films about rescues or crashes cannot.

Shortly after *Extremely Loud and Incredibly Close* was published, the online satirical magazine *Yankee Pot Roast* featured a special issue devoted entirely to lampooning the novel's style, with one piece, for example, titled "Extremely Long and Incredibly Bad Writer's Block."[20] More seriously, Harry Siegel, in his review "Extremely Cloying & Incredibly False" refers to the novel as a "cut-and-paste assemblage of words, pictures, blank pages and pages where the text runs together and becomes illegible," concluding that "Foer isn't just a bad author, he's a vile one."[21] On first glance, the book can seem all literary pyrotechnics, bells and whistles, with the possibility that including 9/11 is merely another, more manipulative gimmick. Unlike most fiction for adults, it *is* filled with photographs, particularly of hands, birds, doorknobs, and most shockingly, a recurring image of man falling from one of the Twin Towers, like the famous photo and image from *World Trade Center*. But these pictures seldom accompany the narrative, like pictures in a children's story. Instead, they are diegetic—a part of the very story itself. Rather than illustrating actions, they represent images that Oskar Schell, the nine-year-old primary narrator, himself sees or takes. When readers look at those pictures, they are seeing what Oskar sees, as Oskar sees them.

The photos, the first of which appears even before the title page, are only the beginning. The book shifts perspective in ways that seem as though Foer, like Paul Greengrass, wants to jar the reader. Oskar's grandmother and grandfather each suddenly narrate chapters in their own voices and even typographies. The narrative is interrupted by an image of a newspaper column with a phrase, "not stop looking," circled in red pen (10), just as Oskar sees it; later, a whole article features these red-pen circles (208–216), again through Oskar's perspective. Sections feature a single fragment of writing taking up a whole page in order to reproduce the book of phrases that Oskar's grandfather—"the renter"—uses to navigate his life after he becomes mute: "I want two rolls" (19); "And I wouldn't say not to something sweet" (20); "I'm sorry, this is the smallest I've got" (21). Later, when the context changes, the meaning of the lines changes even as the words themselves cannot. For one section, the pages are completely blank (121–123); another section deliberately uses more spaces between words than is typographically acceptable (174–186), while yet another reduces the spacing between words until the page is illegibly black (284), an image that find its counterpoint in a similarly black photograph of space (318) near the conclusion.

These supposedly cloying techniques are never meant to stand alone. Instead, they illustrate, sometimes literally, the search for meaning and its representation in the wake of trauma, just as the plot of the novel becomes about a search as well. The novel uses its language, but also its typography and very space on the page, as metaphor. The book becomes a visual guide to the problems and possibilities of being close, a word used 21 times throughout the novel; "closer" is used an additional seven times.[22] Words, like people, like objects, can be extremely close, sometimes too close, but sometimes not close enough. And for all of the words frequently crammed onto the pages, Oskar's grandmother, whose sections use irregular spacing, narrates, "My life story was spaces" (176).

Like the images, spaces, and colors, even the literal events of 9/11 in *Extremely Loud and Incredibly Close* are representational rather than some kind of literary reenactment. Foer seems much more interested in the symbolic significance of 9/11 and the aftermath of trauma than in reestablishing what we believe we already know. Novels, unlike films that tout their basis in a true story, often contain a disclaimer on their Library of Congress publication data page: "All characters appearing in this work are fictitious. Any resemblance to real persons, living or dead, is purely coincidental." Instead of the usual warning, however, the data page for *Extremely Loud and Incredibly Close* features this caveat: "Letters attributed to real people in this novel are entirely fictitious, even if they seem real." Indeed, correspondences from cosmologist Stephen Hawking and Beatles drummer Ringo Starr appear in the novel. But the warning turns ironic, one of many ploys throughout the book. The letters do not seem real at all, with the fictional Hawking letting us "know that I read and save every letter, with the hope of one day being able to give each the proper response it deserves" (12), and Starr's appreciation for Oskar's "glorious letter and bulletproof drumsticks, which I hope I'll never have to use" (40).

Like that disclaimer, we should take Foer's incorporation of 9/11 into the novel's plot—Oskar's father, we learn, was killed in the collapse of the World Trade Center—as "attributed to real" events that are rendered "entirely fictitious." *Extremely Loud and Incredibly Close* is a modern folktale, like the story that Oskar's father tells of the "sixth borough" (13), set in a magical, symbolic doppelganger of New York City. Unlike 9/11's nonfiction, Stone's and Greengrass's true-story films, to say nothing of politicians or presidents, Foer is not interested in realism, despite references to towers, planes, and concluding flip-book of a falling man reversed, so that he rises back up to the top of the tower. Yet this lack of realism becomes, for me, the book's strength rather than a detriment. The plot of *Extremely Loud and Incredibly Close* feels provincial—consummate New Yorker Oskar has hardly left Manhattan, let alone New York City—and its focus on family life, separation of father from son, and ways in which 9/11 becomes about missing men and fatherhood place it squarely within the conventions of stories about, and after, 9/11.

Despite the limited locale, range of characters, and domesticity, however, the novel is not, as Susan Faludi says of *World Trade Center*, another American cultural presentation of 9/11 that "replicate[s]" but does "not delve." The novel does not replicate—its plot, about Oskar's search for a missing lock, is too farfetched to resemble a true story. It delves deeply into Oskar's psyche, but through literary irony: by way of Oskar's voice, readers come to understand Oskar better than he understands himself. And, after delving, the story rises—literally for the flip-book falling man in the novel's last pages, and emblematically for Oskar, who learns that, despite his father's death, he is not alone.

Extremely Loud and Incredibly Close opens with an unusual sentence—"What about a teakettle?" (1)—but then quickly develops the image into what will prove to be one of Oskar's many imaginary inventions: "What if the spout opened and closed when the steam came out, so it would become a mouth and it could whistle pretty melodies, or do Shakespeare, or just crack up with me? I could invent a teakettle that reads in Dad's voice, so I could fall asleep, or maybe a set of kettles that sings the chorus of 'Yellow Submarine' " (1). The first page continues to ask "what about . . .?" and "what if . . .?," inventing "little microphones" that play "the sounds of our hearts" (1); later, Oskar describes "a set of wedding rings, where each one takes the pulse of the person wearing it and sends a signal to the other ring to flash red with each heartbeat" (106). Oskar imagines "skyscrapers for dead people that were built down" and "a skyscraper that moved up and down while its elevator stayed in place . . . because if you're on the ninety-fifth floor, and the plane hits below you, the building could take you to the ground, and everyone could be safe" (3). During this internal monologue the reader learns that Oskar is "wearing heavy boots" because his father died, but we do not know that he died in the Twin Towers on 9/11 until much later. Thomas, Oskar's father, left a series of messages on the family answering machine, which Oskar then hides from his mother by replacing the machine with an identical model: "I knew I could never let Mom hear the messages, because protecting her is one of my most important raisons d'être" (68).

The circumstances of Thomas Schell's death change what we understand about the boy's fascinations. Oskar's inventions are not the overactive fancy of a precocious kid, but the anxious longing of a boy who has lost his father, leading to preoccupations with hearing his father's voice through a magical, Disney-esque teakettle rather than the recorded messages that he cannot bear; with the ability to hear, plainly yet symbolically, others' heartbeats; and with constructing death-proof skyscrapers.

We later find that Oskar has many fears: dirty bombs, public transportation, and walking over bridges (all on one page, 87), as well as phones, which obviously remind Oskar of what he calls "the worst day." In another time, for another child, these fears would seem extravagant, but in the aftermath of 9/11, they seem apt. Even the bulletproof drumsticks Oskar imagines for Ringo Starr are no joke; they demonstrate the boy's genuine concern for a fantasy father figure's safety, considering that, against all reason, John Lennon was assassinated in New York City. If *United 93* is rated R by the MPAA for "some intense sequences of terror and violence," *Extremely Loud and Incredibly Close* has no specific sequences involving terror, instead showing the ways in which post-9/11 fear is simply part of Oskar's cultural landscape.

Oskar's unique speaking style is not merely a literary device, either. Instead, his sentences demonstrate his fixation on the conditional—what would or could be, with "what if's or "what about's, and with the word "maybe." In keeping, when Oskar writes a letter, putatively from his mother, to his French teacher, he thanks her "for everything you have taught Oskar, particularly the conditional tense, which is weird" (51). The conditional is one way in which Oskar manages his grief. Oskar's very syntax reveals his wishes for what could have been—Thomas's occasion to the World Trade Center was a one-time event, not his everyday job. Oskar also overuses adverbs, especially the "extremely" and "incredibly" of the title, which crop up on many pages. "Extremely loud and incredibly close" becomes more than a reference to 9/11 itself, or Oskar's reaction to it. If the conditional represents Oskar's hopes, then the adverbs demonstrate the heightened states of awareness and fear that would lead him to feel as though nearly every action warrants the label of "extremely" or "incredibly."

With his favorite adverbs, Oskar speaks in certitude, as his mother informs him: " 'You sound just like Dad ... He used to say things like that'. 'Like *what*?' 'Oh, like *nothing* is so-and-so. Or *everything* is so-and-so. Or *obviously*. ... He was always very definitive'. 'What's "definitive"?' It means certain' " (43). In the style of the novel, the dialogue is compressed into a single paragraph, without discourse markers like "he said" and "she said," another way for the pages themselves to make words and characters appear "incredibly close." For now, the reader can see Oskar's ambivalence: in the era of terror, the circumstances of the world are conditional, yet his beliefs are absolute. He pines for what could be, yet he is fundamentally sure of what is.

Similarly, Oskar's diction relies on what are called nonrestrictive elements in grammar: "... which is a song by the Beatles"; "which is a

French expression I know"; "which is in Versailles, which is outside of Paris, which is in France," all in the opening paragraph (1). These elements make Oskar's sentences longer, embedding one idea into the next and allowing Oskar to demonstrate more and more knowledge and further precision in his descriptions, even as the effect on the reader is that of a sentence spiraling out of control. The same device that Oskar uses to manage his ideas instead demonstrates that he cannot exercise power over them. That Oskar pinches and bruises himself as well reveals that he controls what he can—his own body and its punishments—even as the bruising also demonstrates his feelings of guilt and powerlessness.

The plot of the novel mirrors Oskar's sentences: meandering, odd, and misleading, but ultimately revealing of Oskar's emotional state after 9/11, his fears, and his loss. Oskar spends most of the book looking for the lock that goes with a key he found in his father's closet. He does not know precisely what the lock will look like, or what it will open, but he remains certain that the key and lock will reveal something larger, some message, some kind of metaphor, about his father and himself. Yet he spends at least eight months investigating it, meeting and talking with strangers—mainly, people with the last name "Black"—before discovering the answer from Abby Black, only the second person he spoke to, who had left him a message eight months earlier. Oskar had not checked it because of his post-9/11 fear of the answering machine.

At first, the idea of a traumatized nine-year-old who self-injures traversing New York City alone, in the wake of 9/11, to knock on the doors of strangers, at best seems unlikely and at worst borders on heinous parental neglect. By the conclusion, however, to borrow from the title of Foer's previous book, everything is illuminated: Oskar realizes that his mother knew of his trips all along, that she "had talked to all of [the people I visited] before I had" (291), and that she had made sure that an adult always accompanied him. In a reminder of just how young Oskar is, despite that he often seems older, he realizes that "[i]t made sense that Ada knew I lived on the Upper West Side, and that Carol had hot cookies waiting when I knocked on the door, and that doorman215@hotmail.com said 'Good luck, Oskar' when I left, even though I was ninety-nine-percent sure I hadn't told him that my name was Oskar" (291). But the result is that the key unlocks someone else's mystery, involving someone else's deceased father. In sharing stories with the owner of the lock, Oskar finally reveals that he was unable to pick up the phone on the day his father called: "He needed me, and I couldn't pick up. . . . Are you there? He asked eleven times . . . Maybe he kept saying it to give me time to get brave enough to pick up. Also there was so much space between the times he asked" (301). Like his mother, Thomas's story is in spaces as well. Thomas and Oskar never unite—*World Trade Center*'s rescue, or even the connecting moment on the phone that concludes *United 93*—and Oskar cannot forgive himself. Reuniting the key with its lock cannot reunite him with his father, and the open lock seems to reveal little.

Yet the image of keys, doors, and locks—and the novel features many photographs of keys, doors, and locks throughout—is one of the most basic ways of understanding story itself. Every reader imagines that a story is a kind of lock in search of a key and that if the reader can provide the key, then the story will open up and make sense. Oskar begins with the key, a character in search of a story, and the key gives him one—just not the story he thinks he is looking for. What amounts to his search for his missing father becomes a kind of mystery, but, like most mysteries, it also contains red herrings, clues that are distracting or misleading. In the end, there could be no tidy resolution, even when the key found its lock. What would a definitive solution to Oskar's yearning have even looked like?

Like fictional children including Dorothy Gale and Harry Potter before him, or Katniss Everdeen in *The Hunger Games* and a reimagined Bruce Wayne in *Batman Begins*, Oskar wanders unaccompanied through strange lands (like Oz, or Queens), meets unfamiliar people, searches for special objects, and believes that he will, in some way, rescue his lost family. Of course, though, it is not the search, or the result, that will be the solution, but what the search represents. Oskar needed to search for his father, even as the book ends with Oskar's reconciling not his lost father, but his mother, who, like the answer to the mystery of the key, was there all along, waiting at home. Like Dorothy, Oskar could have gone home any time, but he had to find out for himself. He does not discover any grand message from beyond the grave, only the possibility of connecting with the people living around him. Oskar attempts to rescue his father, which is impossible. Instead, perhaps he rescues himself.

In that sense, perhaps his father did communicate with Oskar, if inadvertently. Oskar's pursuit of the lock is inspired by a game that his father invented in an early flashback: "I spent all day walking around the park, looking for something that might tell me something, but the problem was that I didn't know what I was looking for. I went up to people and asked if they knew anything that I should know, because sometimes Dad would design Reconnaissance Expeditions so I would have to talk to people" (11). The game's purpose, clear enough to the reader, was always to help the seemingly obsessive-compulsive or autistic Oskar[23] come out of his shell—or Schell, as it were. (Along with locks and keys, turtle imagery runs throughout the novel as well. Oskar has carried his house on his back the whole time.) There was never anything to find, only connections to be made. And by the end, Oskar connects: with Stephen Hawking, who finally gets around to writing a personal (and entirely unbelievable) letter back, citing Albert Einstein: " 'Our situation is the following. We are standing in front of a closed box which we cannot open' " (305). He connects with Ron, his mother's boyfriend, who, Oskar learns—rather late, because he never listened—has also lost his family. And of course, Oskar, who had been angry with his mother, unites with her, but also his grandmother, who reveals in her last letter that she never told her sister "how much I loved her." "Here is the point of everything I have been trying to tell you," she writes to Oskar. "It's always necessary. I love you, Grandma" (314). For all of its verbal vivacity, in the end *Extremely Loud and Incredibly Close* suggests that the most basic, banal, least-literary words turn out to be the only ones that matter, as the passengers in *United 93* understand too well.

Failing Marriage in Don DeLillo's *Falling Man*

The film adaptation of *Extremely Loud and Incredibly Close* (2011) further complicates what it means to represent 9/11, even a decade later. A film, unlike a novel, must of course depict actual events, real people that the viewer can see and hear. As a result, the film seems less fable-like than the novel, and without Foer's playfulness, it seems far more straightforward and serious. We lose the initial strangeness of the novel, in that the film feels familiar, linear, and overly literal. Like Oliver Stone, director Stephen Daldry wants to fit 9/11 into a recognizable genre, this time the quest. It no longer feels like a fairy tale even as it visually calls to mind an urban *Lord of the Rings*, with actor Thomas Horn, and his big, soulful blue eyes, substituting for Elijah Wood, and Max von Sydow standing in for Viggo Mortensen, his older, taller, more powerful protector. The key on a string around Oskar's neck becomes the new ring, and it serves the same narrative function. The key, like the ring, is a MacGuffin, to use director Alfred Hitchcock's term for an object designed to move the plot of a story along with minimal narrative explanation. To adapt the book's spirit, not just plot, the film needed to be strange, experimental, and cinematically discomforting. Daldry needed to make a film like *United 93*, but instead he made one like *World Trade Center*. The camera's images replace Oskar's voice on the page, without which Oskar seems less gifted and more troubled, pinching and bruising himself viscerally, visually, instead of verbally. It becomes the portrait of a post-9/11 traumatized child rather than an imaginary adventure that happens to take place in the real post-9/11 Manhattan.

The novel remains stridently a storybook, rather than the film's attempt at realism, through the very end. In the concluding pages of the novel, Oskar again looks at "the pictures of the falling body." "Was it Dad?" he wonders.

> Maybe.
> Whoever it was, it was somebody. I ripped the pages out of the book.
> I reversed the order, so that the last one was first, and the first was last.
> When I flipped through them, it looked like the man was floating up through the sky. (325)

Falling Man, the 14th novel by Don DeLillo, seizes upon the same powerful image, the way in which, in the picture, the falling man remains suspended in midair indefinitely, even as we understand that the human being caught in the image, terrifyingly, could not. Like *Extremely Loud and Incredibly Close*, *Falling Man* is what might be called a "9/11 novel"; turning again to the data page, *Falling Man*'s Library of Congress Cataloguing-in-Publication subject heading reads, "1. September 11 Terrorist Attacks, 2001—Fiction." Certainly the destruction of the Twin Towers and its aftermath generate the action and contemplation that follow. Yet in many ways, *Falling Man*, with its recursive story arc, dream-like language, and domestic focus, is not only *not* a 9/11 novel but barely a novel at all. Instead, as I previously suggested of Chuck Palahniuk, DeLillo uses the framework of fiction to expose its key terms' multiple meanings: "plot" as story, secret, and funeral; and "character" as fictional figure but also personal probity. In doing so, *Falling Man* begins with the concrete events of 9/11, but ends as a poetic mediation on the intertwined mysteries of love, language, and survival.

Despite the gravitas of writing about the falling towers, terrorism, and aftermath of September 11, 2001, *Falling Man*'s major events—the plot, such as it is—centers on Keith and Lianne's damaged marriage, after Keith escapes the collapse of the North Tower on September 11, 2001; their attempted and failed reconciliation; and the ways in which seemingly global phenomena affect them, and by extension, each of us, personally. By focusing on this fragile marriage, DeLillo lends names and particulars to the day that others, including the president at the time, referred to as unthinkable, unfathomable. At the same time, however, the novel emphasizes the everyday aspects of catastrophe, through stream of consciousness style and elevation of personal, subjective experience and language.

With his career interest in terrorists, New York City, and disaster, Don DeLillo could have invented 9/11 rather than the attacks influencing him. Yet unlike DeLillo's previous novels such as the sprawling *Libra*—like Oliver Stone's *JFK* but predating it, about a conspiracy to assassinate President Kennedy—and even bigger *Underworld*—considered by a *New York Times* authors and critics poll to be the second greatest novel of the previous 25 years[24]—*Falling Man* defies the obvious conventions of its premise. Counterintuitive to 9/11's global shock, *Falling Man* seems a modest novel, a family drama, and an unconventional love story. The systems and secrecy, the narratives and counternarratives, the scale and complex subplots that characterize DeLillo's previous work are gone. Like Stone, DeLillo seems to have traded in Kennedy-era conspiracy theories for a different way of understanding the post-millennial world. If *Libra* and *Underworld* ask how we got where we are, *Falling Man* asks, instead, What are we to do, now that the worst has happened? And even the "we" has shrunk—*Libra* and *Underworld* consistently implicate the reader in their schemes, making him or her witness to conspiracies as they unfold, silent accomplices to narrative connections and plots that, typical of DeLillo's novels, lead deathward. *Falling Man*, however, is less about 9/11 as the day that changed everything, the metaphor of collapse, although the book suggests that as well, as much as Keith and Leanne Neudecker's marriage as metonymy—an attribute that comes to stand for the whole event of 9/11—allowing for the imaginative extension of something closer to the reader's life onto the page. The challenge for novelists and filmmakers remains: how can they hope to capture the scale of 9/11 through only a handful of characters, without reducing the day's significance? DeLillo's characters, once again, illustrate specific people altered by the towers, at the risk of downplaying those who died or whose stories remain untold. At the same time, DeLillo challenges novelistic representations of characters by making them synecdochal more than symbolic, individuals affected by 9/11 who come to stand for all, in a way that the familiar tropes of *World Trade Center* do not develop.

Unlike *White Noise*, *Libra*, *Mao II*, *Cosmopolis* (discussed in Chapter 3), and DeLillo's other previous novels, which all build toward acts of violence, *Falling Man*'s destruction of the towers comes first, although it presumes a reader's familiarity to recognize it. The opening line, "It was not a street anymore but a world, a time and space of falling ash and near night," shows how catastrophe both shrinks and enlarges our scope, but it uses the indeterminate, ominous "it" to refer to New York City just as the shock of the attack registers but before the towers' collapse.[25] Recent history provides the reference for "it," but the next sentence's pronoun is personal—"He was walking north through rubble and mud and there were people running past holding towels to their faces or jackets over their heads" (3). This time, the context provides no direct antecedent, because for now, the specific "he," or even individual "people," does not matter. Disaster expands their world but diminishes their identity.

In these first two sentences, unlike Foer and his teakettle, DeLillo establishes the need to write about both the global scale of the attack and the personal level of its effect: the street as a world, the unnamed protagonist as anyone, or no one in particular. Later, one character, Martin Ridnour, himself a suspected former terrorist, makes the sentiment concrete, telling Lianne, the wife of the opening sentence's "he," "There's the event, there's the individual. Measure it. Let it teach you something. See it. Make yourself equal to it" (42). We need to know, he tells us, the event and the individual separately to understand them together. This dichotomy—street versus world, individual versus event, identity versus anonymity—characterizes the tension of the opening and the novel as a whole: suspended and static, freezing the moment of the fall for study, as trauma, reexamination, and lesson.

The embodiment of this tension arrives through the falling man of the title. He is not, as we may have assumed, Foer's jumper from the tower, although the confusion is deliberate. Rather, he is "a performance artist ... [who] appeared several times in the last week, unannounced, in various parts of the city, suspended from one or another structure, always upside downs, wearing a suit, a tie, and dress shoes" (33).[26] This imagery of suspension complicates the way in which 9/11 has routinely been interpreted. On the one hand, through its very premise as a novel about 9/11, it supports the media motif that 9/11 was the day when everything changed. But upon examination, the novel resists that reading. Life and history, unlike novels, have no deliberate plot, because they have no author.

The backdrop of 9/11, then, is very different from the "based on a true story" trope that usually informs historical fiction. It reminds us of our need to impose names and narrative to shape the world, but not always for the better. The novel's terrorists are the only characters with a firm belief in "the magnetic effect of plot. ... Plot closed the world to the slenderest line of sight, where everything converges to a point" (174). In contrast, the novel retells Keith's escape from the towers four different times, suggesting that only the repetition and retelling make it a narrative, not anything intrinsic about it. Like the novel itself, Keith's story presents a series of abstractions, sensations, descriptions, and vignettes. The novel's harrowing opening, the recurring narration of the same events, written and rewritten, becomes analogous to the repeated footage of the planes destroying the towers on television, and the way in which the trauma victim relives his pain endlessly, a point I will return to in Chapter 4.

A recap of the novel reveals the banality of the typical American life, even one that was directly affected by 9/11, as well as the limitations of plot itself: Keith Neudecker survives the collapse of the World Trade Center, but instead of going to his apartment or the hospital, returns to his estranged wife and son's apartment. While the event temporarily reunites them, the same spiritual restlessness that alienated them earlier divides them again. Through a coincidence, Keith meets and begins an affair with another World Trade Center survivor, and over the next few years he becomes a professional poker player. Interspersed in these fragmented details are the small and mostly underdescribed lives of Lianne; Lianne's mother; her mother's lover, Martin Ridnour, who may or may not have been a terrorist himself in the 1970s; the falling man performance artist; and Hammad, an imagined terrorist on the flight that took down the first tower.

Yet the summary is not the story. *Falling Man* undermines its linearity, which both begins and ends with the towers' fall, and the individuality of its characters, who are nearly impossible to visualize, seldom described, and routinely introduced by referenceless pronouns. In addition to the opening sentences, Chapter 2's first mention of a character begins with, "She's put down a book or magazine and a small pause settled around them" (7); we do not hear the name Keith, the man from Chapter 1, until page 10, or that "she" is his semi-ex-wife, Lianne, until page 10. Chapter 3 opens with the sentence, "He signed a document, then another" (15); Chapter 5, "He entered the park at the Engineers' Gate" (51); Chapter 6, "They stood on the entranceway" (77). The novel consistently leaves its pronouns without antecedents, in a way that challenges what we think of as characterizations.

Balancing this repetition of linguistic indeterminacy, however, is that each of the novel's three sections (not individual chapters) begins with a name: Bill Lawton, Ernst Hechinger, and David Janiak. Yet like the pronouns, each name proves more elusive than revelatory. The names are neither the antecedents for the pronouns that follow nor any of the characters' names: Bill Lawton is a mishearing of bin Laden by Justin, Keith and Lianne's son. Ernst Hechinger is a possible but unproven alternate identity for Martin Ridnour. And David David Janiak is the post-humously revealed name of the Falling Man artist, whose obituary reveals the facts about him but only obscures the truth of his intentions, in a fitting overlap with the novel that shares his title.

DeLillo is deliberately playing against fiction's convention of naming his characters right away. Each chapter illustrates the necessity yet futility of names, so important to George Bush's and the *New York Times*'s narrative of 9/11, which here do not help us to understand the individual and yet are all we have. The novel's relentless "he"s and, to a lesser extent, "she"s emphasize the primacy of the person, the way in which seemingly global phenomena affect individual people. In doing so, the reader must contemplate what we have been told repeatedly is the unnamable, unfamiliar nature of a nevertheless political attack, at the same time recognizing its familiar aftermath of pain, disappointment, and grief.

Falling Man is not, then, as concerned with politics as it is with the ways in which the most basic elements of storytelling—character, plot, and language—become epistemologically entangled—married, as it were—to falls of all kinds: the fall of the towers and the people who fell from the towers, of course, but also the way in which the collapse of Keith and Lianne's marriage is itself another kind of fall. Even as Lianne listens to her mother extrapolate on the geopolitics and theology of the attack—" 'These are matters of history. This is politics and economics. All the things that shape lives, millions of people, dispossessed, their lives, their consciousness' " and much more—when Lianne leaves,

> [s]he [Lianne] stood in the bathroom looking in the mirror. The moment seemed false to her, as scene in a movie when a character tries to understand what is going on in her life by looking in the mirror.
>   She was thinking, Keith is alive. (47)

For the novel and character alike, the conventional mirror scene—reflection as literal and figurative, of psychology trickled down to easy box office metaphor—is not just what "seemed false"; so does the overheated rhetoric of the conversation. There is no 9/11, for Lianne, apart from Keith, our first falling man, and Lianne, a falling woman. Politics, in the realm of the novel, is a straw man. *Falling Man* suggests that the falling marriage parallels the falling towers, the incomprehensible through the ordinary. The tragedy of the novel is not just the lives lost; it is the love lost, the marriage that crumbles like, or as a result of, the towers. But this equation does not diminish the tragedy of the towers' fall as much as elevate the pain of the failed marriage, the alienated young son, and their estrangement from the world.

But if 9/11 is a kind of vast metaphor for marriage, then perhaps marriage is itself metaphor as well. The narrative associations between marriage and the 9/11 novel, not just in *Falling Man* but in *A Disorder Peculiar to the Country*, *Netherland*, *Emperor's Children*, *The Writing on the Wall*, *The Good Life*, *The Mercy Seat*, and *Extremely Loud and Incredibly Close*, seems to have disappointed critics like Richard Gray. Yet DeLillo's novel is a kind of political marriage: the timely with the timeless, the personal with the political, the individual with the societal, the individual's trauma as the nation's and vice versa. 1997's *Underworld*, of course, expresses precisely these themes as well, through the novel's symmetrical arrangement and its running conceits of the baseball and the bomb, waste manager Nick Shay and artist of ready-mades Klara Sax, and many more. *Falling Man*, however, presents a true dichotomy: it is impossible to divorce the Neudeckers' plight from the fallen towers, just as the towers remain incomprehensible without a human story. They are flipsides, mirror images, simply inseparable, married.

A brief aside, a one-line joke, from DeLillo's 1991 novel *Mao II* provides further explanation for the 9/11 novel's preoccupation with marriage. In a novel with multiple love triangles and domestic deceptions that turn national and international, two characters look out over Manhattan: "Out the south windows the Trade towers stood cut against the night, intensely massed and near. The word 'loomed' in all its prolonged and impending force."[27] Interspersed in their dialogue, one character—it is never clear who, but it seems to be the woman, Britta—remarks, without context, " 'One has an antenna.' " " 'The male,' " says the other, presumably, the male, Scott.[28] The Twin Towers play a Zelig-like cameo throughout DeLillo's work, a kind of metaphorical mirror like the one *Falling Man*'s Lianne found overly determined. Elsewhere in *Mao II*, the main character Bill Gray calls them " 'harmless and ageless. Forgotten-looking. And think how much worse.' 'What', she said. 'If there were only one tower instead of two' " (40). He could just as well be talking about himself, his futility as an aging writer, and his own loneliness. In *Players*, bored, bourgeois couple Lyle and Pammy spice up their marriage by becoming enmeshed in a terrorist plot. Pondering her office in, of course, the World Trade Center, Tammy wonders, "If the elevators in the World Trade Center were places, as she believed them to be, and if the lobbies were spaces, as she further believed, what was the World Trade Center itself? What is a condition, an occurrence, a physical event, and existing circumstance, a presence, a state, a set of variables?" (48). She could just as easily be talking about her own existential doubt, the duality of the towers as Cartesian crisis of reality, the spacial as ontological. In *Underworld*, the Twin Towers are, in one section, the symbolic flipside to the Fresh Kills landfill, built upward rather than dug underground (like Oskar's invented towers), the beginning of production's arc rather than its end; in another chronologically earlier section, artist Klara Sax watches their construction and comments, " 'I think of it as one, not two ... Even though there are clearly two towers. It's a single entity, isn't it?' "[29] Here, as always in DeLillo's work, the towers are a marriage, two functioning as one. In a detail that DeLillo could have himself invented, when the first tower fell, the second fell shortly after, the grieving spouse who dies of shock and loneliness.

This elevation of marriage in DeLillo's novels runs counter to the usual critical assessments, as well as typical critique. Immediately after 9/11, book critic James Wood, for example, condemned DeLillo and other purveyors of what he (Wood) termed "hysterical realism" for writing "street smart" works that do not engage in "individual consciousness." Wood suggests that the idea

> that the novelist's task is to go on to the street and figure out social reality ... may well have been altered by the events of September 11, merely through the reminder that whatever the novel gets up to, the 'culture' can always get up to something bigger. ... If topicality, relevance, reportage, social comment, preachy presentism, and sidewalk-smarts—in short, the contemporary American novel in its current, triumphalist form—are novelists' chosen sport, then they will sooner or later be outrun by their own streaking material.[30]

Wood, I think, makes three mistakes: first, he assumes that novelists are not already aware of the problems of out-inventing life, a point that Philip Roth made in 1960, as discussed in the previous chapter. Second, he mischaracterizes DeLillo's previous works. But most importantly, seeing DeLillo as a political pundit in a novelist's clothing does not describe *Falling Man*—in fairness, written after Wood's attack—at all. Instead, DeLillo's language straddles the line between reader and character, creating a particular kind of stream of coconsciousness—not a Modernist, subjective interior as much as a liminal, linguistic space where reader and character, men and women, violence and redemption, prose and poetry exist simultaneously as possibilities.

Names and narratives impose order and recognition onto a world thrown into anonymity and anarchy. This need converges in Keith's and in Lianne's post-9/11 preoccupations. Yet even the order produced by Keith and Lianne's separation, that he "had his poker game, six players, downtown, one night a week. She had her storyline sessions, in East Harlem, also weekly, in the afternoon, a gathering of five or six or seven men and women in the early stages of Alzheimer's disease" (29), becomes a kind of fiction, a pattern established by the necessities of narrative need more than logic. For Keith, poker becomes a series of linguistic rituals designed to alleviate the randomness of the world:

> The dealer skimmed the cards over the green baize, never failing to announce the name of the game, five-card stud, even though it was the only game they now played. The small dry irony of these announcements faded after a time and the words became a proud ritual, formal and indispensable, each dealer in turn, *five-card stud*, and they loved doing this, straight-faced, because where else would they encounter this kind of mellow tradition exemplified by the needless utterance of a few archaic words. (99)

Not surprisingly, after surviving the attacks, Keith takes more and more comfort in the game, at the expense of all other aspects of his life. Similarly, Lianne's Alzheimer's patients "worked into themselves, finding narratives that rolled and tumbles, and how natural it seemed to do this, to tell stories about themselves. ... an intimacy of clean physical detail and dreamy reminiscence that had no seeming connection"; "They signed their pages with their first name and first letter of last name" (30). The patients' work suggests DeLillo's ambivalence toward plot: patients need to impose order to events in writing, since they no longer can in their minds, and to write their names as a way of reestablishing their waning sense of self. Their stories cannot establish real connections, and, thanks to Lianne, their signatures reduce them to incomplete pseudonyms. Pairing Keith and Lianne, DeLillo seems to suggest that in the aftermath of 9/11, we are all gamblers now, hoping to control our fates through arbitrary and trivial linguistic ceremonies, or worse, Alzheimer's patients, relying on dubious, repeated stories to allay the terrifying mysteries of our vanishing identities.

The "Falling Man" of the novel's title comes to represent this problem of identity. The title first seems to refer to the performance artist, but it also recalls the famous photo of the same name, as Lianne self-referentially understands: "Was this position intended to reflect the body position of a particular man who was photographed falling from the north tower of the World Trade Center, head first, arms at his sides, one leg bent, a man set forever in free fall against the looming background of the column panels in the tower?" (221). At the same time, the title's seemingly singular "man" seems to refer to all of the men of the novel: the performance artist, the suicide, the male victims of the attack, including those in *World Trade Center*, who have fallen spiritually and psychologically, and even the attackers, who, like the passengers on the plane and terrorists in *United 93*, fall from the sky.

Yet DeLillo is concerned less with the specific men of 9/11, Library of Congress to the contrary, than with the way in which the most basic elements of storytelling—character and plot—become linguistically and epistemologically entangled with falls of all kinds: the fall of the towers themselves, a fall from the past, and ultimately, 9/11 as a fall from grace that secularizes the biblical fall. The title's falling man could just as well refer to falling Man, with the dual acquisition of knowledge and death calculable to the precise moment between the strike on the first tower and the second. Addressing the way in which people reacted to the plane crashing into the first tower as an accident, Keith, again referred to as "he" for the entire duration of the exchange, remarks, " 'The second plane, by the time the second plane appears', he said, 'we're all a little older and wiser' " (135). The post-9/11 moment is postlapsarian: not just after the fall of the towers, but the very biblical fall of humankind, the acquisition of knowledge that comes with the price of mortality.

The end of *Falling Man* returns to its narrative beginning, suggesting that we must return to the traumatic moment in order to know it. So it seems fitting that the novel ends again replaying the scene of Keith's escape from the towers, not as a matter of plot—action, suspense, drama—or character—what the event reveals about him, and through him, all of us. Rather, it is DeLillo's own imagining of the events that makes them powerful. The scene is enacted again at the novel's end, just as it is replayed on television (134), but this time, the reader, too, is a little older and wiser. In a jarring single sentence, the story itself seems to crash, running from the hijacked plane directly into the towers in a single sentence:

> A bottle fell off the counter in the galley, on the other side of the aisle, and he watched it rill this way and that, a water bottle, empty, making an arc one way and rolling back the other, and he watched it spin more quickly and then skitter across the floor an instant before the aircraft struck the tower, heat, then fuel, then fire and a blast wave passed through the structure that sent Keith Neudecker out of his chair and into a wall. (239)

Yet at the same time, the transitional image of a water bottle, the same image used for salvation in *World Trade Center*, becomes the trivial detail that allows us to see the vastness of the catastrophe. Somehow, DeLillo has made the endlessly replayed crash unexpected and small.

In response to Martin's statement, "There's the event, there's the individual. Measure it. Let it teach you something" (42), Lianne says, "People read poems. People I know they read poetry to ease the shock and pain, give them a kind of space, something beautiful in language," she said, "to bring comfort or composure. I don't read poems. I read newspapers. I put my head on the pages and get angry and crazy."

Like the tensions between the event and the individual, the street and the world, and the rolling bottle and the crashing airplane, the would-be 9/11 novel seems poised to merge the reportage of journalism with the language of poetry. Yet in the novel's concluding descriptions, DeLillo is ready to show that Lianne's, and possibly our own, inclination toward newspapers is misguided. Instead, perhaps poetry can provide the possibility of contemplation. And indeed, the last pages are poetry:

> They came out onto the street, looking back, both towers burning, and soon they heard a high drumming rumble and saw smoke rolling down from the top of the tower, billowing out and down, methodically from floor to floor, and the tower falling, the south tower diving into the smoke, and they were running again.
>
> The windblast sent people to the ground. A thunderhead of smoke and ash came moving toward them. The light drained dead away, bright day gone. They ran and fell and tried to get up, men with toweled heads, a woman blinded by debris, a woman calling someone's name. The only light was vestigial now, the light of what comes after, carried in the residue of smashed matter, in the ash ruins of what was various and human, hovering in the air above. (246)

This description, with its inevitable refrain of falling, presents the paradox of beautiful yet elegiac language, and it lends itself more to poetic than narrative analysis. The letters on the page look like quasi-cryptograms, repeating and nesting, as one word transforms into another, just as the people in the street, and the day in history, are transformed. The first sentence rises and falls on its commas, running grammatically as its people run, while the staccato and harsh onomatopoeia of the second sentence reminds us of the blunt shock and damage. Finally, the last sentence, like a haiku—a form Lianne thinks of elsewhere—unites the descriptions of the previous lines, the clauses, like the voices, hovering, the sound, again like the voices, humming. In this way, *Falling Man* rescues 9/11 from the relentless mechanisms of plot, through a kind of poetic redemption. In the retelling, in the language, the fall cannot be reversed, as Oskar Schell attempts by reordering the images of his falling man, but perhaps we may be wiser.

If the novel resists the usual comforts of plot and character, perhaps instead *Falling Man* presents a novel in the form of poetry, or maybe a poem in the form of a novel, with its rapt attention to the mystery of language hand but also its comfort and revelation. It is about the balance between our stories and ourselves. And if we are to understand a moral purpose of the 9/11 novel, despite the volumes of journalism already published on the subject in the years since the attacks, perhaps we can see its power to show both Keith's and Lianne's separation from each other, and themselves, with their concurrent need for order and story. The plot of 9/11—the hijacking, the destruction—leads only to death, as DeLillo suggests of plots in *White Noise* and *Libra*. The role of art after 9/11 is to rescue the reader from plot's grim teleology. On a practical level, DeLillo can get away with subverting plot, thanks to the overarching shadow that 9/11 casts on the novel as a whole. 9/11 has become its own master plot. *Falling Man* relies on the ready-made terror and suspense of the day that we know so well, yet it resists the obvious conventions of the material, assuming a readerly familiarity onto which it can project the microcosmic lives of the Neudecker family and their acquaintances.

Falling Man, in its deliberation, largely eschews plot, while at the same time, DeLillo subverts what most people understand by the word *character*, in that pages often go by with no name or specific signifier to refer to the characters, only ambiguous, antecedent-less pronoun references. Disaster, DeLillo suggests, undermines the already capricious relationship—the marriage—of words and meanings, signifiers and signifieds. As Lianne thinks to herself, while she looks at Keith asleep, "She'd never felt easy about that term. My husband. He wasn't a husband. The word spouse had seemed comical, applied to him, and husband simply didn't fit. He was something else somewhere else. But now she uses the term. She believes he is growing into it, a husbandman, even though she knows this is another word completely" (70). Names and narratives impose order and recognition onto a world thrown into anonymity and anarchy, so Lianne struggles to find the word that will identify what Keith is to her.

Some of the relationships in these 9/11 novels end well. In *The Writing on the Wall*, Renata is poised to reconcile with her lover, Jack; the same is true for Hans and Rachel in *Netherland*. *Falling Man*, however, does not end with Keith and Lianne's reconciliation. Surviving the attack does not ensure that the marriage can be mended. In a sense, the novel does not conclude at all, not really; it instead narrates, for the fourth time, Keith's escape from the collapsing tower, a reenactment suggestive of neurosis or trauma, a pathological need to relive the shock endlessly, in keeping both poker's repeated rituals and Alzheimer's-related amnesia; the same outlets that Keith and Lianne turn to for relief instead become emblems of their suffering. *Falling Man* rescues 9/11 from the relentless mechanisms of plot and character, that old married couple of literary analysis, though a kind of literary rescue. In the telling, in the language, the fall nevertheless cannot be reversed, like the man imaginatively rising back into the towers at the end of Foer's *Extremely Loud and Incredibly Close* or even the rise and rescue of *World Trade Center*'s fallen men. Nor can the marriage be mended, unlike Schwartz's *Writing on the Wall* or O'Neill's *Netherland*. But in the reduced space between character and reader that *Falling Man* insists upon, perhaps we may nevertheless find meaning, and even beauty, again, after the fall.

CHAPTER 3

War on Terror: Our Monsters, Ourselves

From *Cosmopolis* (2012): Robert Pattinson looking vampiric as Eric Packer at twilight. (Entertainment One/Photofest)

In this chapter: *World War Z* (2006), Max Brooks; film adaptation (2013) directed by Mark Foster; *Twilight* (2005) and *New Moon* (2006), Stephenie Meyer; film adaptations *Twilight* (2008), directed by Catherine Hardwicke, and *New Moon* (2009), directed by Chris Weitz; *Cosmopolis* (2003), Don DeLillo; film adaptation (2012) directed by David Cronenberg. Additional discussion: *Frankenstein* (1818), Mary Shelley; adaptation (1931) directed by James Whale; *Dracula* (1897), Bram Stoker; adaptation (1931) directed by Tod Browning; *Avatar* (2009), directed by James Cameron.

World Trade Center, United 93, *and* Extremely Loud and Incredibly Close *all conclude with hope after their fallen towers, planes, and fathers. Even* Falling Man, *while ambiguous about whether Keith can overcome his trauma, ends in exalted language. Yet to critics' consternation, these works remain provincial, exploring only the domestic side of the war on terror. Other stories, however, have different approaches to their scopes and their hopes. This chapter will examine books and movies that treat terror in a very different way: through monstrous imagery and narrative. If the stories overtly about 9/11 examined crises of family and fatherhood while in some cases also challenging the conventions of storytelling, other kinds of stories were not explicitly about 9/11 but evoked its themes and images symbolically. New stories about zombies, like* World War Z; *vampires, like* Twilight; *and aliens, like* Avatar, *can be read in the context of a decade preoccupied by terror. At the same time, they allow us to rethink the ways that older monster narratives like* Dracula *and* Frankenstein *work—and even help us to read a seemingly nonmonster novel, Don DeLillo's* Cosmopolis, *as a post-9/11 Gothic. In the end, contemporary readers simply enjoy stories of terror too much and identify too strongly with our monsters, for something called a war on terror to prevail without a careful emendation of our monsters and ourselves.*

On August 28, 2006, the *Weekly World News*, "The World's Only Reliable Newspaper," as it bills itself, led with this headline: "Vampires Attack U.S. Troops: Army of undead taking over mountains of Afghanistan." The *Weekly World News* was better known for its placement at supermarket checkout counters (before it went online) and its improbable headlines than it is for its geopolitical reportage. And needless to say, the United States did not fight vampires in Afghanistan. Yet the fear that the facetious paper belies is real enough. The *Weekly World News*, for all its frequent absurdity, understood that, metaphorically, we have been at war with vampires all along. The "New Terror in

Middle East" that the subheading warns us of is not new at all, but rather, a sensationalized way to describe the terror that is already there. In the post-9/11 climate, the new invasion narrative of the terrorist—and, later, of the insurgent—follows the conventions of previous monster stories. For the modus operandi of the terrorist is nearly the same as the vampire's: both infiltrate, hide in plain sight, use capital against the capitalist, and eschew the light. The revision of this conflict has a name: the War on Terror.

Despite attempts to change the name—Iraq War, second Gulf War, war on Saddam, war on Islamic radicals, war on militant jihadism, war against islamofascism—the war on terror is the title that stuck. Although President Barack Obama, after employing the term himself, called for his administration to discontinue using it in 2009, the war on terror persists in our language.[1] And little wonder—it is archetypal, epic, sweeping, poetic, and unassailable. It leaves no room for ambiguity, no place for argument, no possibility for, say, a pro-terror position. Waging something called a war on terror is understandable: its rhetoric instantly turns nonbelievers into implicit enemy collaborators, renders criticism dangerous if not treasonous, enforces an incontrovertible Manichaeism of us against them, and encourages a desperate times, desperate measures elusion of the law. Best yet, the enemy can remain nameless, amorphous, and disembodied. When we declare war on terror, we declare war on something other than terrorists, as a result turning the enemy into something not just foreign, not just inhuman, but noncorporeal. No wonder the Bush administration chose the name, then stayed the course.

Yet it is equally understandable that the Obama administration wanted distance from it. Declaring a war on terror presents problems as well, not so much in the vagueness of the name, narrowed now to only "at war with al Qaeda," but in the implied narrative. The stories nearly always begin with the monster's creation or invitation—frequently, by the would-be hero himself. And the endings are even more troubling: even when the seeming subject of terror is defeated, the conflict forces the hero, the creator-turned-slayer, into acts of barbarity and conspiracy that eventually rival the monster's own. Or even worse, news of the monster's death is greatly exaggerated, so that, sometimes in the same form, sometimes transformed, the terror will return. By the end, contemporary audiences often sympathize more with the tale's monster than with its hero. If anything, in addition to finding our monsters terrifying, we grow to love them, and want to become them, more than ever in the era of terror.

The model monster slayer in the post-*Frankenstein*, post-*Dracula* world is no longer the heroic archetype of Beowulf, not since Mary Shelley endowed her monster with feelings and eloquence, and, later,

John Gardner's novel turned Grendel from an antagonist into leading role. Even the on-screen *Beowulf* (2007) revises the canonical poem by having its hero sleep with Grendel's mother, only to make amends for his transgression later through the visitation of another monster, perhaps the most archetypal of them all, the dragon. For it is the dragon, Christian symbol of evil, that was the allegorical model for monster slayer Saint George, who seems to have had little in common with his presidential namesake in the modern world rife with ambiguity. Now that Sean Connery voiced an onscreen dragon in *Dragonheart* (1996), a boy befriended one in *Pete's Dragon* (1977), and young adult fiction like *Dragon Rider* (1997) and *Eragon* (2002; adapted into a film in 2006) remade dragons in our own likeness, we no longer want them slain at all. Today's readers and moviegoers are ever more likely to sympathize with the monster as with the ostensible protagonist. After Boris Karloff infused his monster with human pathos in *Frankenstein* (1931), Anne Rice made her vampires sullen and sexy in *Interview with the Vampire* (1976), and Francis Ford Coppola romantically revised Dracula into a quasi-Shakespearean tragic hero in *Bram Stoker's Dracula* (1992), we understand that the line between human and monster is precariously permeable. A few exceptions aside, many contemporary horror fans do not root for monster slayers at all. Who today sympathizes with privileged malcontent Victor Frankenstein over his beautiful, hideous monster, even as recently revised for Showtime's Gothic series, *Penny Dreadful* (2014)? Or with Keanu Reeves's callow, bewildered Jonathan Harker over Gary Oldman's charismatic, insouciant Dracula in Coppola's retelling? In uncanny reversal, the real monsters in the remake of *Dawn of the Dead* (2004) are the humans, blowing up zombies' heads as part of a game, rather than the pitiful, inarticulate zombies themselves. Unlike humans, zombies have no choice.

World War Z and the Monstrous Tradition

Two very different approaches to using the zombie as an extended metaphor for the post-9/11 sensibilities of the 2000s and 2010s have emerged. The first moves far beyond the usual scope of the zombie film—and, as we will see, the 9/11 narratives described in the previous chapter—replacing the usual American small town, suburb, or rural setting with the whole world, recognizing pluralism and diversity of language and culture—as well as the likelihood that a real zombie threat could not be contained. Max Brooks explores the tensions between the street and the world (to borrow from the opening of Don DeLillo's *Falling Man*), the past and the future, and what is human and what is monstrous in *World War Z: An Oral History of the Zombie War* (2006). The second post-9/11 approach to zombies, however, resembles Oliver Stone's *World Trade Center*, beginning with the calm, routine day that soon gives way to urban pandemonium, repeating the generic conflict of the nuclear family in peril owing to a foreign threat, and separating the ordinary yet heroic father from his endangered wife and children so that he can rise to heroism and they can be reunited. Ironically, this reversal of *World War Z*'s nuanced, multiperspective, deliberately fragmented approach, this zombification of the conventional 9/11 domestic narrative, arrives in the film adaptation of Brooks's very novel, *World War Z* (2013).

The popularity of both book and movie is not surprising—the new millennium has produced what fans have called "the zombie renaissance," a term that nicely captures the era's high quality as well as zombies' own penchant for coming back from the dead. Alongside the success of *World War Z*, *The Walking Dead* has captivated comic readers and television viewers; *Zone One* (2011), by Colson Whitehead; *Pride and Prejudice and Zombies* (2009), by Seth Grahame-Smith (and Jane Austen); and *Warm Bodies* (2010; adapted into a film in 2013), by Isaac Marion suggest that zombie literature is becoming a viable genre. The *New York Times* divided the world into the figurative dominant personality traits of zombies and vampires, as though the Myers-Briggs test can now add a Z/V to its inventory of personality dichotomies.[2] At the movies, beyond the successes of *28 Days Later* (2002), *Zombieland* (2009), and continuous remakes of the seminal zombie films of George Romero, even a movie like *Contagion* (2011), while technically zombieless, has more in common with the film version of *World War Z* than *World War Z* has with its source novel. Both illustrate a plague that mysteriously spreads, causing society to come close to collapse as scientists scramble to find a vaccine. On the Zombie Movie Database, fans can look up, say, *Klown Kamp Massacre*, to say nothing of the thousands of other zombie websites, including a promotional page for *Zombieland* where viewers can "zombify" themselves.[3] How has it happened that the decade ushered in by a presidentially declared war on terror would lead to a monster resurgence—and renewed popular desire to become monsters?

Vampires had a long literary history even before Bram Stoker's legendary *Dracula* was published in 1897. Unlike the vampire, the humble zombie has no classic work of literature to draw upon, only film, which often tells its story in a very different way. This absence, however, proved to be an opportunity rather than a disadvantage. *World War Z*—the novel, for now—does not reflect its subject matter: it is smart and, after a suspenseful build-up, fast. But what is more, Brooks seems to understand how monster stories work, so that he can use these conventions, as well as break away from them. True to the word *zombie*'s African etymology—in the novel, the zombie plague is first referred to as "African Rabies"—*World War Z* presents the ultimate invasion narrative. What starts, in the novel, in China and Africa quickly turns global, for the boundaries of the world are even more permeable than they were in Bram Stoker's late Victorian era, when Dracula slipped from Transylvania to London aboard a ship. Like Dracula, the zombie represents the fear of the foreign invader. Zombies make nearly everything they touch unfamiliar, starting with borders and ending with the border between people and monsters. Through their invasion, zombies estrange their victims from their very humanity, which, as we will see, may be the monster's most frightening lesson for the war on terror.

The novel *World War Z* takes the form of a fictional "oral history." Chapters are separate stories, narrated in the tellers' own voices through interviews conducted and culled by an unnamed correspondent for the "United Nation's Postwar Commission Report."[4] Brooks can, in the monstrous tradition of the multiple voices that make up *Frankenstein* and *Dracula*, foreshadow, allude to, and withhold details and plot points until they are at their most poignant and scariest. Yet at the same time, this narrative technique allows for a wide variety in points of view, more like the epistolary novels—novels in the form of letters—of the eighteenth and nineteenth centuries, to which Shelley and Stoker were indebted. Unlike the typical zombie movie's frequently local scope—*this* city or suburb, town, or even house—*World War Z* does not privilege a single point of view. Instead, through the frame of its interviewer hearing the stories of many survivors after the war is over and the humans are left to rebuild their damaged world, it provides international points of view.

An early chapter provides the perspective of an Israeli intelligence officer who is the only official to believe the zombie threat in time: "I happened to be born into a group of people who live in constant fear of extinction. It's part of our identity, part of our mind-set, and it has taught us through horrific trial and error to always be on our guard" (32). The following chapter focuses on a Palestinian professor, however: "We thought," he explains, that the sudden Israeli policy of "voluntary quarantine" was "a Zionist lie" (37). We hear from an unnamed South African who describes "the Redeker Plan," which deliberately sacrificed some people to save others; we later learn that the chapter had been narrated by Redeker himself, his psyche broken from the gravity of his strategy (105–111). We are reminded of the things we take for granted, like the simple "bottle of peacetime root beer" with ingredients from all over the world (141–142). We even see the perspective of an Australian astronaut trapped in space, nearly helpless as he sees the world in turmoil below him: "Nobody had a better view of what was happening than us" (255), even as "watching what was happening on Earth ... made it almost impossible to have hope" (258). Brooks's zombies may not be real, but his humans certainly are.

World War Z's tapestry narration resembles *Frankenstein*'s surprisingly modern frame story or *Dracula*'s semi-epistolary form, but the book also resembles these stories in its meaning. *World War Z* is not, in the end, about zombies. It is about people, "the human factor," as the unnamed interviewer tells us right away (1, 3). And so we see stories of struggle and sacrifice. In telling them, the "Zombie War" evokes genocide, AIDS, civil war, nuclear strikes, massive displacement, totalitarianism, and more: the great catastrophes of the twentieth and early twenty-first centuries, ones that humans managed to create without any zombies at all. The novel also dramatizes millennial ambivalence toward technology. During the war on zombies, when cars and modern artillery fail, axe-like weapons ("lobos," or "lobotomizers") succeed. In near–wish fulfillment of reactionary political fantasies as much as would-be dystopia, America reverts to a premodern, quasi-colonial society (an image that the television series *Falling Skies* develops much further as well), while England and Japan begin relying on castles and museum-piece battle axes and ceremonial Samurai swords to protect themselves, reverting to a pretechnological, semifeudal states.

World War Z's ultimate success comes from using a fantasy fear, zombie proxies, to frame a thoughtful, political discourse about the real things that people fear most in the post-9/11 era, a fully realized, literary version of the *Weekly World News*'s vampire attack. Brooks's zombies become a multifaceted, even potentially poor-taste political allegory, using the zombie threat to evoke the Israeli/Palestinian conflict, South African apartheid, and, in other examples through the book, corporate greed and government ineptitude. Yet the incursion of zombies into real-life political conflict does not minimize those problems. Brooks's zombies are thoughtful, multifaceted allegories. If anything, the zombies themselves seldom appear on the page at all. *World War Z* becomes a fictionalized thought experiment, more about the ways in which humans respond to terror than about zombies themselves, whose responses throughout the book are, needless to say, predictable. The book also draws connections between the Zombie War and the real life war on terror, particularly in the way that "people wanted so badly to anthropomorphize the walking blight. In war, in a conventional war, that is, we spend so much time trying to dehumanize the enemy, to create emotional distance. We would make up stories or derogatory titles ... when I think about what my father used to call Muslims" (196). Zombies exaggerate but emblemize the American fear of an enemy that is not afraid to die, that cannot succumb to "shock and awe," as the bombing of Baghdad at the start of the U.S. invasion of Iraq was called, at precisely that time when suicide attacks were at their peak. As Bruce Hoffman writes in his book *Inside Terrorism*, "The years from 2001 to 2005 alone account for 78 percent of all the suicide terrorist incidents perpetrated between 1968 and 2005." "Terrorists," Hoffman continues, "have become increasingly attracted to suicide attacks because of their unique tactical advantages. ... [They] are devastatingly effective, lethally efficient, have a greater likelihood of success ... and are generally easier to execute than other attack modes."[5] Already dead, zombies are the ultimate suicide terrorists, an exaggeration and extension of American fears.

When asked about this comparison during a *Washington Post* live chat with fans, however, to some extent Max Brooks equivocated:

Question: it seems you draw a lot of parallels between today's war on terror methods and the zombie war. How close, however, do you compare the zombies to today's fundamentalist Islamists? i.e, unthinking, uncaring, irrational villains who kill for the sake of killing?

Max Brooks: The lack of rational thought has always scared me when it came to zombies, the idea that there is no middle ground, no room for negotiation. That has always terrified me. Of course that applies to terrorists, but it can also apply to a hurricane, or flu pandemic, or the potential earthquake that I grew up with living in L.A. Any kind of mindless extremism scares me, and we're living in some pretty extreme times.[6]

Brooks may be right to avoid drawing a direct line from real terrorism to his novel's zombie terror. His book is not a neat comparison, but rather a messy pastiche of many different war on terror developments in American and global life. And crucially, unlike *Frankenstein* and *Dracula*, *World War Z* does not end immediately after the death of the monster, instead providing a lamentation and equivocation fitting a post-9/11 monster story. For all of their inventions, the authors of the Victorian monster stories could scarcely have imagined how many people could die at the hands of humans, let alone monsters, in the wars of the twentieth century. *World War Z*'s death toll, framed not just after 9/11 but World Wars I and II, far exceeds the relatively few casualties of its Victorian counterparts. Like real victims of trauma, the survivors of the Zombie War are scarred, scared, and chastened. *World War Z* denies the reader an easy return to the premonster status quo: family in *Dracula*'s final chapter (the Harkers' marriage and children) or the film version of *Frankenstein*, toasting to the "house of Frankenstein" as the scheduled marriage is merely interrupted, rather than ruined, by the monster's presence. Instead, at the end of *World War Z*, one character concludes, "Yeah, we stopped the zombie menace, but we're the ones who let it become a menace in the first place" (334), a sentiment that feels more politically and psychologically fitting than a book about zombies has a right to evoke. Victor Frankenstein and Jonathan Harker admit to no self-recrimination or remorse.

World War Z, Avatar, and Prosecuting War

The film adaptation of *World War Z* met mixed reviews from fans of the novel, in part because it was not faithful to its source material. (The web-comic *The Oatmeal* humorously used a Venn diagram to suggest that all the film and book have in common is the title.[7]) In many ways, the film was less like *World War Z* than it was like *World Trade Center*, with its emphasis on separating a heroic father from the rest of the family. In *World War Z* film, Brad Pitt, once again charming and dangerous, plays an American named Gerry Lane, a seemingly normal stay-at-home dad, cooking breakfast for his daughters on a perfectly ordinary blue-sky morning. Suddenly, New York is under siege by mysterious forces, and only Lane, who turns out to be a UN investigator with vast military expertise, is plucked by helicopter to investigate and solve the cause of the zombie outbreak. More importantly for the audience, though, Lane must save his all-American family from the incipient undead hoards. That he must also spend the second half of the film in locations other than America, and save the world so that the film can earn its title, seems entirely subsidiary to saving his American wife and daughters. Scenes abroad are mere set pieces for crashing airplanes, running from zombies, and firing weapons, whereas, in contrast, the novel reminds American viewers and readers, habituated to the usual zombie (and, in *Twilight*'s case, vampire) story's provinciality, that in a real global conflict, we would need to care about more people than a typical point-of-view male hero and his female dependents. *Avatar* (2009), the highest grossing film of the 2000s, takes us even further: we must even care about monsters beyond our world—even when we are at war with them.

Avatar tells the futuristic story of humanity's quest for "unobtanium," a substance that will provide a solution to Earth's energy crisis. Unfortunately, it exists only on a distant planetoid called Pandora, whose atmosphere is deadly to humans, and which is populated by tall, blue natives called the Na'Vi. Scientists develop the "avatars" of the title—cloned bodies of the Na'Vi controlled by the minds of a biologically compatible human—to explore Pandora. After the death of his twin brother, paraplegic ex-Marine Jake Sully is reluctantly called in to operate his brother's avatar. But after being rescued and adopted by the Na'Vi, Jake joins forces with them when he learns that the humans plan to destroy the Na'Vi's "Hometree," central to their whole world's interconnected consciousness, in order to harvest the unobtanium.

At first, the film's plot seems like a science fiction version of Disney's *Pocahontas* (1995) or *Dances with Wolves* (1990), trading Indians for aliens, or *FernGully* (1992), in its environmental allegories. Yet even then, the metaphorical shift is powerful. The Cold War trope of science fiction movies like *Invasion of the Body Snatchers* (1956)—about aliens invading Earth by pretending to be us—reverses, becoming a version where humans are the extraterrestrial invaders and body imposters. *Star Trek*'s humanism, its exploration and seeking out new life, gives way to the contemporary realization that humans would treat new planets exactly the way in which Europeans treated the New World—by occupying them, seizing their natural resources, and treating their natives as expendable. Yet the post-9/11 context of the film allows us to consider more. In the era of terror, *Avatar* reads more like a parable of American, not British, cultural hegemony.

A plot summary excludes the way in which the film also uses many of the signifiers of the war on terror. The attack on the Na'Vi is called "shock and awe," President George W. Bush's phrase for the initial attack on Iraq, which *World War Z* appropriated as well. In language similar to what has become known as the Bush Doctrine, a military commander in *Avatar* says, "Our survival relies on pre-emptive action. We will fight terror, with terror." More than science fiction or a criticism of early American colonialism, the film sometimes seems like a straightforward morality play about the hubris of the Iraq war. "Unobtanium" and "Pandora" represent that which humans want but should not possess. (In Greek mythology, Pandora was the woman who opened the box releasing all of the sins into the world.) The occupation of Pandora is premised on Earth's need for cheap fuel, just as critics of the Iraq invasion maintain that the war was never about American safety and always about oil.[8] The film's plot pivots upon the symbolic loss of a twin, much like Lynne Sharon Schwartz's post-9/11 novel

The Writing on the Wall, a reminder of the loss of the Twin Towers that, wrongly or not, was used to mobilize the war in Iraq. The main character is an injured military man who is pressured into another tour of duty. Director James Cameron, who is Canadian, said he was "surprised at how much it did look like September 11. I didn't think that was necessarily a bad thing."[9]

Most crucially, of course, is that the Na'Vi, 10-foot tall cat-like creatures, are the object of the audience's compassion, not the humans—the Americans—who are repeatedly inhumane. In this science fictional retelling of the war on terror, the occupied, and the monsters, elicit only sympathy. Jake Sully opens the film physically and emotionally damaged, impersonating a monster. But in becoming that monster, he learns how to love, share, and commune with others and his surroundings. He becomes human. Rather than seeing the monsters as proxies for a war against terrorists, as it is possible to read *World War Z*, in *Avatar* Earth's military is transformed from *World Trade Center*'s rescuers to alien invaders. The film itself becomes a kind of avatar. If not quite a physical manifestation of a divine teacher, it at least attempts to retell the American opening of our Pandora's box of unending preemptive war and occupation—but this time, with a happy ending for the oppressed. The film never even addresses how Earth will cope without having obtained the unobtanium. It does not matter.

In late October 2006, then–Pennsylvania senator Rick Santorum compared the war in Iraq with a different film (and, of course, book series) about a war against monsters, *The Lord of the Rings*: "As the hobbits are going up Mount Doom, the Eye of Mordor is being drawn somewhere else. . . . It's being drawn to Iraq and it's not being drawn to the U.S. You know what? I want to keep it on Iraq. I don't want the Eye to come back here to the United States."[10] In his analogy, the United States could be engaged in a war only to protect the innocent from pure evil. Just three years later, millions of Americans celebrated a film that transformed a U.S. soldier into a monster so that he could fight humans—as the hero. *Weekly World News* to the contrary, the new terror in the Middle East did not come from vampires, or zombies, or orcs. On Pandora, it came from humans. In a war on terror, we cannot necessarily know which side we are on.

Rereading *Dracula* and *Frankenstein* after the War on Terror

World War Z's inspirations for an allegorical war on terror are, as I have mentioned, Bram Stoker's *Dracula* and Mary Shelley's *Frankenstein*. In addition to looking at the influence these seminal monster novels have on a reading of *World War Z*, I would also like to examine the ways in which the context of the war on terror can allow us to reread and rethink these novels as well.

Like Brooks's zombies, Dracula—from Bela Lugosi to Gary Oldman to *Sesame Street*'s The Count—is specifically foreign, an outsider, different. His strength, however, is not bound to the obvious monstrosity that Halloween costumes emphasize. The vampire's pointed ears, pale skin, and elongated fangs that Stoker mentions have been exaggerated well beyond the novel's brief description of "a very marked physiognomy": "The mouth, so far as I could see under the heavy mustache, was fixed and rather cruel-looking, with particularly sharp white teeth . . . His ears were pale and at the tops extremely pointed . . . The general effect was one of extraordinary pallor."[11] Dracula's power, we discover, instead lies in his physical similarity to us: Dracula is a monster that looks human. But he is not: he is an infiltrating parasite, inhuman and undead, and so he must take that which is most vital to us—our very lifeblood—and use it to nourish and sustain himself. By Stoker's late Victorian era, similar in many ways to our own condition in post-9/11 America, Britain had the ironic fear of, in the words of literary critic Stephen D. Arata, "reverse colonization."[12] Even as England had, in fact, dominated the world, by the end of the nineteenth century it was far more worried of being penetrated and attacked from the inside out by an alien force than it was concerned with its own outwardly fragile global hegemony. And so just as bad as his human appearance is the fact that Dracula can change shape, from wolf to bat to rats and even to mist, so that he can walk among us, hide in plain sight, and blend in.

Finally, and perhaps worst of all, the vampire gains strength when people do not believe in him. Empiricism and scientific skepticism are precisely what allow him to permeate the fabric of British society and thrive. He is safer, more comfortable in cosmopolitan London than in his native Transylvania, since the superstitious peasants there believe in him and recognize him for what he is, while sophisticated urbanites allow him greater safety, since he can walk unrecognized. London allows him to use the money unsavorily accumulated over the centuries to buy what he needs, sucking England of its blood literally and figuratively, its capital and its capitalists alike. Comparing Dracula to "monopoly capital," literary theorist Franco Moretti explains that Dracula's "ambition is to subjugate the last vestiges of the liberal era and destroy all forms of economic independence"; at the same time, however, "Dracula is thus at once the final product of the bourgeois century and its negation."[13] Like today's terrorists, who used America's permeable borders to slip in and then hijack America's own airplanes to destroy the World Trade Center, our greatest symbol of commerce, Dracula exemplifies capitalism's capacity to be destroyed from within by its very machinations.

At the same time, however, while *Dracula* does not use the now-familiar trope that the vampire must be invited before crossing a threshold, Jonathan Harker had arrived in Transylvania in order to facilitate the sale of London real estate to Dracula. In that sense, Dracula is not an invader as much as a deceiver. (Financial transactions are a key theme in the vampire story, as we will see later in this chapter in discussing Don DeLillo's *Cosmopolis*.) The threat of terror presents a monstrous paradox: the attempt to stop Dracula—and, by extension, terrorism—risks undermining the same foundations of freedom, tolerance, and secularism of the society it presumes to sustain.

As we see in the novel, Jonathan Harker, Abraham Van Helsing, Jonathan Seward, Quincey Morris, Arthur Holmwood, and Mina Harker attempt to stop Dracula. Their authority does not come from science, although Seward and Van Helsing are doctors, or from the law, although Van Helsing is conveniently also a lawyer, but from faith—not in God as much as in the idea of sheer, unmitigated evil. As Van Helsing asks Harker, "Will you not have faith in me?" (150), and later, foreshadowing the *X-Files*: "My thesis is this: I want you to believe" (172). Faith must trump reason, for turn-of-the century London's secular relativism and rationalism only help the vampire: " 'Ah,' " says Van Helsing, " 'it is the fault of our science that wants to explain all; and if it explain not, then it says there is nothing to believe' " (171). Precisely these same attitudes were under attack in post-9/11 America as abetting the terrorists, our own invisible, shape-shifting monsters who, in the imagery of the war on terror, use our freedoms and disbelief against us. Foreshadowing contemporary state classification, Van Helsing warns that " 'our toil [to kill the vampire] must be in silence, and our efforts all in secret; for in this enlightened age, when men believe not even what they see, the doubting of wise men will be his [Dracula's] greatest strength' " (279). In doing so, Van Helsing denigrates reason and candor as aid to the invader, even as these qualities are the hallmarks of the enlightened society he seeks to protect.

Yet at the same time, the contemporary reader of *Dracula*, or perhaps a contemporary viewer of Tod Browning's Universal Studios film adaptation from 1931, notices not just the monster's power and terror, but what the monster does to its victims. Yes, the vampire's kiss is like a sexually transmitted disease, infecting the victim by turning her into a creature just the same as Dracula, an image that *Twilight* will develop further. Yet the astute reader or viewer begins to understand that the vampire does not just create monsters by biting and transforming them. He also makes his victims into monsters by making them behave like monsters: they must defy laws, lie, break into private property, and kill. When Van Helsing and the others must destroy the monster that Lucy Westenra, beloved to all the men, has become, the scene in the novel is erotically brutal, reminiscent less of monster slaying than violent rape and disturbingly similar to images of the vampire's own attack. When Seward first sees the vampiric Lucy, he says, "At that moment the remnant of my love passed into hate and loathing; had she then to be killed, I could have done it with savage delight" (188). But that task falls specifically to Arthur Holmwood, Lucy's fiancé, who consummates their engagement by penetrating Lucy with a stake, in violent simulation of sexual intercourse and an imitation of the vampire's own pointed teeth taken to the source of blood and life, here the heart replacing the throat. Thus, after struck with the hammer and stake,

> the Thing in the coffin writhed: and a hideous, blood-curdling screech came from the opened red lips. The body shook and quivered and twisted in wild contortions; the sharp white teeth champed together till the lips were cut, and the mouth was smeared with crimson foam. But Arthur never faltered. He looked like a figure of Thor as his untrembling arm rose and fell, driving deeper and deeper the mercy-bearing stake, whilst the blood from the pierced heart welled and spurted up around it. (192)

More and more, the novel suggests that the men need to capture Dracula because of the effect he has on the women closest to them, even as it seems as though the men themselves commit the most egregiously described acts of sexualized violence. The men only track down Dracula, who has already fled from them, because Mina Harker has been bitten and her transformation has begun. Yet unlike the male heroes, Mina alone, despite trivializing and condescending treatment, understands that her burgeoning monstrousness—the fact that she is already nearly a vampire—is itself the key to finding Dracula. And when the men do find him, despite the reader's anticipation of a protracted battle, they dispatch him quickly and brutally, their mission accomplished. As Mina narrates, "But, on the instant, came the sweep and flash of Jonathan's great knife. I shrieked as I saw it shear through the throat; whilst at the same moment Mr. Morris's bowie knife plunged into the heart" (325). We accept this violence as heroic because we accept that

Dracula is a monster, that he had worse in store for the humans, and that it is the only way.

Yet part of the reason, I suspect, that the story has turned from potentially forgettable Victorian pulp into an archetypal and particularly American story, thanks to decades of movies, is our ambivalence at seeing the monster die, as well as our latent guilt toward his slayers' ultimate cruelty. To kill the monster, they must behave like monsters themselves. This point seems especially apparent in Browning's film: Bela Lugosi's performance is so suave and humanizing that his monster's death looks like xenophobic murder, less good triumphing over evil than a hate crime. Unlike in the novel, which at least describes the fight scene even if it is surprisingly brief, the film's Harker and Van Helsing sneak up on Dracula in his sleep, an imitation of the same monstrous tactic Dracula himself uses on his own victims. The death is off-camera, but the thud of the hammer forcing the stake into a man we had just seen at rest, followed immediately by Lugosi's disturbingly subdued moan, seems less cathartic than ambivalent. Dracula's death releases Mina from his spell, but the film's ending—just moments after Dracula's anticlimactic, undignified death—seems mixed as well: Jonathan and Mina ascend the castle's stairs, while Van Helsing, a foil to Dracula, stays behind, in the dark. Their foreign ally is left behind to clean up what is left of the equally foreign menace. Only the young and, it seems, native, are allowed to emerge from the crypt into the light, the nascent nuclear family reunited.

In the film, and returning to the novel, the monster does not directly make supposedly good people monstrous. It is their own attempt to stop the monster that makes them so. The heroes quickly turn fraudulent, including lying on Lucy Westenra's death certificate (137) and to the realtors (233). They seem heartless, abandoning Renfield to die, just as Dracula does. And, as the movie intimates, their impulses mirror the Count's; Harker hopes that Van Helsing's theory—that the vampire's body will disintegrate—proves correct, because he understands how criminal their actions seem: "the Count's body ... will soon after [his death] fall into dust. In such case there would be no evidence against us, in case any suspicion of murder were aroused" (290). Worse, Van Helsing, looking at the dormant female vampires he has come to destroy, fears that they are "so full of life and voluptuous beauty that I shudder as though I have come to do murder" (319), and later, that dispatching them "was butcher work" (320). To stop the monsters, they behave like monsters: violently and heartlessly, in secrecy and subterfuge, as outsiders and then infiltrators themselves. Only Mina seems to notice, and then only for a moment: "Everything that one does seems, no matter how right it may be, to bring on the very thing which is most to be deplored" (226). No wonder Hollywood, unlike Stoker, keeps bringing Dracula back: we want to see our antihero Dracula rise from the grave again, of course, but we also, I think, hope to redeem his would-be killers, to give them the chance to subdue the monster heroically rather than resorting to his own trade to stop him.

While Harker's work and his employer's avarice surely made Dracula's invasion possible, at least Harker did not create Dracula directly. That, of course, is the premise of the other prototypical monster narrative, *Frankenstein*. Predating *Dracula*, Mary Shelley's novel gives rise to the classic relationship between the monster and his maker. As most will know, whether they read the novel or saw the 1931 film or not, scientist Victor Frankenstein created a monster, in the most literal way imaginable: "After days and nights of incredible labour and fatigue, I succeeded in discovering the cause and generation of life; nay, more, I became myself capable of bestowing life upon lifeless matter"; he later reveals that "the dissecting room and the slaughter-house furnished many of my materials."[14] The reader who comes to the novel after seeing its film incarnations may be surprised by the absence of castles, laboratories, lightening, or many of the now-iconic images; the novel goes into surprisingly little detail of the creature's actual construction. Instead, the book suggests that while scientific creation gave the creature life, it did not make him into a monster. The creature, never named, believes that his abandonment made him horrible, not his frightening (and perhaps by today's standards, racial sounding) appearance: "yellow skin [that] scarcely covered the work of muscles and arteries underneath ... shriveled complexion ... straight black lips" (34). The creature's treatment forced him into deliberate acts of terror, not something intrinsic or essential. In contemporary jargon, it was nurture, not nature. Even the film, which at first seems to take the easy way out by having Frankenstein's assistant accidentally steal a criminal's "degenerate" brain instead of the healthy one, depicts the creature sympathetically. The viewer's compassion for the awkward creature, as mutely portrayed by Boris Karloff, remains the film's most striking feature.

If the monster's death in Browning's *Dracula* is disturbing, in James Whale's *Frankenstein* film it is even more so. And if Dracula's death resembles a premeditated murder, the creature's is like a lynching, building metaphorically upon the racialized physical description from the novel. In the film, unaccountably Southern-looking men scout the rural countryside with bloodhounds, ropes, and pitchforks, seeking the creature's death less for what he has done—as far as they know, no evidence links the creature to the girl Maria's drowning death—than what he is, or perhaps merely because they are drunk and following the aristocrats' orders. It is the scientist, first in his creation but especially in his treatment of the monster, who seems far more monstrous, despite his normal appearance and profession of best intentions.

As in the novel, Karloff's monster is rejected immediately after his creation. Yet seeing the time span in the movie—from conception to denunciation within seconds—rather than hearing it through Victor's point of view in the novel, the viewer cannot help but feel compassion for the creature. The camera, unlike the novel, functions as an outsider's eye, documenting Frankenstein's pathetic sense of his own victimhood at the expense of his hapless creation. Frankenstein never treats the creature like the infant he is, inexplicably expecting him to understand English and conventional human interactions. When the monster fails, as a newborn would, Frankenstein melodramatically turns from him and hides his face. Contrasting actor Colin Clive's self-involved drama as Frankenstein, Boris Karloff's minimalist facial expressions convey a wide range of feeling throughout the film: confused sadness at his rejection; frustration and rage at his torment by Fritz, the hunchbacked lab assistant; lascivious attraction toward Elizabeth, Frankenstein's fiancée; and desperation as the windmill to which he has fled is ignited. Yet for all their eloquence, his gestures can just as easily be read as inarticulate, unfortunately the way in which the film's other characters see them. Much of the novel's power comes from the reader's inability—because it is a book and not a film—to see the monster, who is indescribably horrible. The film by necessity depicts the monster, and the viewer paradoxically infers both the creature's meanings yet his helplessness in expressing them.

The creature's violence in the film thus seems accidental. Yet in the novel, Frankenstein continues to flout and rebuke the creature, until, desperate, the creature turns to violence. If readers had not seen him as a monster before, they may have no choice now. Victor professes the creature's evil from the beginning, referring to the "breathless horror and disgust [that] filled my heart" (34), calling the creature "the demonical corpse to which I had so miserably given life" (35). The creature, on the other hand, escaping his confines and learning to speak and read on his own, argues for a kindly nature that was turned evil by his creator's apathy and rejection. As he tells Frankenstein, "Remember, that I am thy creature: I ought to be thy Adam; but I am rather the fallen angel, whom thou drivest from joy for no misdeed. Every where I see bliss, from which I alone am irrevocably excluded. I was benevolent and good; misery made me a fiend" (66). Spurned again by his creator, this time in making the monster a mate, the creature seeks and murders those closest to his master. At this point the novel turns. Frankenstein becomes the pursuer, and it is the creature who is pursued, until, in the end, they both seem to perish, in ice, together: the reunion, attention, and metaphorical consummation that the creature craved all along.[15]

In both *Frankenstein* and *Dracula*, the Manichean division between good and evil blurs. A critical part of the terror narrative is the would-be hero's own role in creating or releasing the monster, not just in *Frankenstein* but continuing as a major plot point and theme of famous monster movies like *King Kong*, *The Silence of the Lambs*, *Jurassic Park*, *Aliens*, and many others. Critics have long noted the United States' role in this especially troubling aspect of the terror narrative: in supporting Saddam Hussein to use him against Iran, in funneling money to the mujahideen to wage a proxy war against the Soviets in Afghanistan, we created our own monsters, and then released them, only to resort to dangerous tactics ourselves in the attempt to extract justice. It is fitting, then, that Steve Coll's definitive book on the subject, subtitled *The Secret History of the CIA, Afghanistan, and Bin Laden, from the Soviet Invasion to September 10, 2001*, should be called *Ghost Wars*. Coll's title underscores the venture's clandestine, seemingly ethereal nature, while simultaneously referring to the "CIA-supplied Afghan rebels called ... *dukhi*, or ghosts."[16] At the same time, however, the title reinforces the way in which our past, monstrously and terrifyingly, haunts our present.

While George W. Bush has been compared, to the point of cliché, to the cowboy, this image has never been fully accurate, despite the Texas twang, cowboy boots, and Wanted Dead or Alive posture toward Osama bin Laden. The classic Western hero exhibits reluctance, even sadness, at resorting to violence. The cowboy operates as a liminal frontier figure, one who understands that, his foes vanquished, he has no place in the city. The ride-off into the sunset is an ambivalent victory, for the borders of the West are exhausted, and he can never enjoy peace. In the era of terror, Americans are more like monster slayers than cowboys. As writer Richard Devetak suggests, "One way of understanding the Bush doctrine, then, is to read it as a heroic fight against monsters"; Devetak, however, notes the way in which this approach specifically contrasts with those of John Quincy Adams, who, as Devetak puts it, "made explicit reference to the potential risks associated with chasing monsters."[17] But what neither Bush nor even Adams acknowledged was the complex narrative role—the dramaturgical dyad, the archetypal foil, the balancing alter egos—that the hero and monster must together play. (This book's final chapter will analyze heroes as well.) Like Frankenstein, we create our own monsters, and then cast them out. Yet, as in *Dracula*, we must also invite our monsters in. Perhaps, though, monster stories can guide us in life, since monsters, as creatures of the imagination, are inextricably bound to their stories.

Monsters frighten us, but they also break down the boundaries, and undermine the distinctions between inside and outside, in ways that we find not just entertaining but truthful and compelling. We must amend our monster stories, and our monsters. Yet "amending" suggests not just revision but putting back together, as well as making amends or atonement. We may or may not be able to negotiate with terrorists, but we must amend our monsters. We must put them back together again rather than take them apart or reincarnate them, for the monster's body, usually by definition, requires emendation. In amending our monsters, we heal ourselves. And in doing so, we can begin to make amends with terror, a phrase that here does not mean apologize as much as redress and balance, for, as readers, and perhaps even in life, we are always both our monster slayers and our monsters.

Yet as readers, we also create our own monsters, each time we open another narrative of terror for our own pleasure, each time we watch another monster movie, each time we reread a horror classic. As Mary Shelley famously wrote in her Introduction to the third edition of *Frankenstein*, "I bid my hideous progeny go forth and prosper" (173). And it—her monster and her book—certainly has. In one way or another, monsters make monsters of us all. As philosopher Friedrich Nietzsche memorably said, "Battle not with monsters, lest ye become a monster," so we had better tread carefully. We must come to terms with terror, not, as President Obama understood, declare war on it. Not only does terror always win, but we, as a readership, wouldn't have it any other way.

"You don't care if I'm a monster?": Loving Terror in *Twilight*

In the 2000s, readers have done even more than tolerate and accept their monsters: they have fallen in love with them. *World War Z* and *Zone One* depict terrorized survivors in a cadaverous landscape—in keeping with Cormac McCarthy's *The Road*, as I discuss in Chapter 5, and dystopian series *The Hunger Games*, in Chapter 6. But the biggest publishing success of the decade did not include zombies or even the usual postapocalypses of post-9/11 YA fiction and film. Instead, the best-selling new novel series of the 2000s was *Twilight*, which spawned five successful films. And while some critics have disparaged the writing style and implicit political messages of the novels, literary critic Milly Williamson points out that, since its beginnings, Gothic literature "was defined as a woman's genre, downgraded in the cultural hierarchy of the day because of the association with femininity, the irrational and the supernatural (which today is echoed in the critical reception of the *Twilight Saga*)."[18] Still, that a quartet of YA vampire novels could far outsell all novels of the zombie renaissance may seem surprising, given that our sense of terror seems more culturally aligned with the world represented by zombies, the post-9/11 sentiment that everything we think we know can disappear.

Both the film *28 Days Later* and the TV series *The Walking Dead* open in exactly the same way: a man awakens alone in a hospital bed after a coma to discover that all of his certainties—and, worse, nearly all of the people—have vanished, seemingly overnight, in the wake of a zombie apocalypse. The moment perfectly captures their in-between state of emergence, rather than emergency, where reality seems hazy and patients are prone to confusion. The end of the world in these stories, however, is no mere nightmare. Instead, they starkly dramatize the post-9/11 idea of a single day that changes everything. They represent a fantasy of destruction and the heroism of the man who would make it right. The castles and parlors of vampire novels, from *Dracula* through Anne Rice's *Vampire Chronicles*, with their combination of Gothic mysteries and debaucheries, seem far out of place in a culture preoccupied with overt destruction. *World War Z* author Max Brooks was asked about this shift during his live chat:

> **Question:** Where the Anne Rice vampire novels seemed to address the fear of death through intimacy (and the transmission of blood), zombie lit seems to reveal a fear of social breakdown due to environmental factors like a pandemic flu. Comments?
>
> **Max Brooks:** Anne Rice's vampires were sleek and sexy. And why not, the late 80s to 2000 were a very sleek and sexy time. People wanted to be vampires. They were cool. The times we were living in were cool. Not anymore. Just like vampires go hand-in-hand with some kind of elite, celebrity life, the zombie genre is deeply rooted in Armageddon.[19]

Twilight represents a very different fantasy, not the Armageddon of *World War Z* or *The Walking Dead*, but the beginning of the year in a new high school that *feels* like the end of the world. Its dramatic situation is very different from that of Dracula's Transylvania (or London) or the Vampire Lestat's New Orleans, and the way the story is told shifts as well. Bram Stoker's novel appears in the form of his characters' pieced-together journal entries, letters, recordings, and newspaper clippings, which, taken together, allow them to expose the vampire's secrets. Anne Rice's aesthetic invention reverses Stoker: her novels narrate the vampire's story from his own perspective, since the only perspective noticeably absent from the novel that bears his name is Dracula's own.

Stephenie Meyer develops the change in point of view further, by narrating the story through the eyes of an ordinary teenaged girl, the sole object, rather than perpetrator, of fear—although the series complicates this idea. If representing the vampire's point of view still seemed novel in the 1980s, by the 2000s, after Tom Cruise's mainstream Lestat and a decade of dangerous men ushered in by *The Sopranos*, it was more or less a given that the main character of a vampire story would be yet another ambivalent villain, a sinful yet sympathetic adult male. And in one sense, he still is: as Edward Cullen, *Twilight*'s centenarian vampire, tries to warn us, evoking rapper Eminem and *Breaking Bad*'s Jesse Pinkman," 'What if I'm the bad guy?' "[20] But despite the feeling of legions of fans, *Twilight* is not really Edward's story. Its lead, by contrast, is young, female, ordinary, and powerless—or so it seems.

Twilight belongs to Isabella "call me Bella" Swan, a 17-year-old girl who moves from Phoenix, Arizona, to Forks, Washington, to live with her father, a police officer, after her mother remarries. If Phoenix, like the mythical bird, represents fire and rebirth—and a nod to the Harry Potter Series—Forks is cloudy and wet, the perfect place for sun-averse vampires to conceal their identity, as the Alaskan vampires in the comic and film *30 Days of Night* similarly realize. (The vampires in *Twilight* also move between Washington and " 'somewhere in Alaska' " [21]). Arriving in Forks, Bella finds herself at a metaphorical fork in the road, a crossroads in her life. As the new girl in a new place, Bella has the frightening opportunity to make or remake her identity. Yet the first novel's Preface does not begin chronologically, briefly flashing forward (as we figure out when we turn the page and begin the novel proper) to what seems to be Bella's death—a Chuck Palahniuk–like, recursive beginning-at-the-end opening for what some readers think of as a teen romance. The still-unnamed narrator thinks, "I knew if I'd never gone to Forks, I wouldn't be facing death now. But, terrified as I was, I couldn't bring myself to regret the decision. When life offers you a dream so far beyond any of your expectations, it's not reasonable to grieve when it comes to an end" (1). Her crossroads seems to lead right to death, but, as we later understand, it instead leads her to undeath. In folklore, people who had committed suicide were buried at the crossroads, under the belief that the unsettled soul of the deceased may cause the body to come back to life, and the intersection would confuse it. In other versions, a grave at the crossroads was the closest that the unredeemed death could come to any kind of cross-like grave marker. Still other folktales say that the crossroads is the place to make a deal with the devil. In Forks, Bella's path diverges, her soul becomes unsettled, and she makes a deal with her own devil. But more than anything else, forks are sharp eating utensils, a signal that the novel will be about many intersections, but especially the intersections of different hungers.

Soon after her move, Bella meets Edward Cullen, " 'gorgeous, of course,' " a new friend explains, "' but don't waste your time. He doesn't date. Apparently none of the girls here are good enough for him' " (22). But instead of ignoring her, Edward reacts unexpectedly violently to her; Bella sees that "his black eyes [were] full of revulsion. . . . The phrase *if looks could kill* suddenly ran through my mind" (24). Like the couples in Jane Austen's novels, which Bella adores (147–148), Bella and Edward's relationship begins with a misunderstanding that distances them, even if, say, *Pride and Prejudice*'s Elizabeth Bennet is not under the first impression that Mr. Darcy wants to kill her. Of course, Edward does not want to kill Bella—not exactly. Instead, we learn that Edward is attracted to Bella as a woman, but also as prey for his vampiric appetite. As he tells her, co-mingling sex and death, " Your number was up the first time I met you' " (175). Like *Dracula*'s Jonathan Harker, Bella figures out that Edward is a vampire, with his "impossible speed and strength," "inhuman beauty," "the way he spoke . . . that better fit the style of a turn-of-the-century novel than that of a twenty-first-century classroom. He'd skipped class the day we'd done blood typing. He hadn't said no to the beach trip till he heard where we were going. He seemed to know what everyone around him was thinking . . . except me" (137–138). But unlike Dracula, Edward and his clan are self-proclaimed "vegetarians," hunting animals instead of humans: " 'I don't want to be a monster,' " he concedes to Bella (188). And of course, after their conversation, "a few certainties become evident" to Bella: "First, Edward was a vampire. Second, there was a part of him—and I didn't know how potent that part might be—that thirsted for my blood. And third, I was unconditionally and irrevocably in love with him" (195).

Despite its emphasis on the terrifying side of love, *Twilight*, like *World War Z*, like Edward's mannerisms, echoes pre-twenty-first century novels, from Jane Austen to *Jane Eyre*, with Mr. Edward Rochester—older, more powerful, wealthier, harboring secrets—playing Edward to Bella's prototype, the original Plain Jane. *Jane Eyre* itself seems indebted to a number of fairy tales, from Bluebeard, about an aristocrat who kills his wives and hides their bodies, to, less horrifically, Beauty and the Beast. Like fairy tales and other young adult literature, including *The Hunger Games*, *Twilight* focuses on adolescent conflicts of first love, romantic triangles, and the need to belong to a community while at the same time wanting to stand out as an individual. When Bella first sees the family of teen vampires at school, even before she understands what they are, she thinks, "I felt a surge of pity, and relief. Pity because, as beautiful as they were, they were outsiders, clearly not accepted. Relief that I wasn't the only newcomer, and certainly not the most interesting by any standard" (22). Vampires or not, these are the reasonable thoughts of any new girl on campus. Here, these seemingly everyday conflicts are rendered through the fantastic, and the monstrous.

As legions of *Twilight* fans—Twihards—know, Edward is not even the only handsome monster vying for Bella's affection. The most famous love triangle in 2000s pop culture, developed further in the later novels, became the rivalry between Edward and Jacob Black, who is a Forks native, Quileute Indian, and werewolf. The vampire versus werewolf war, similarly dramatized in the *Underworld* films, is nowhere to be found in folklore or *Dracula*, where vampires and wolves are kin. Yet this monstrous opposition works symbolically well on film, a supernatural version of the old romantic convention of a woman who has two men pining for her, each suitor representing opposite personality types. *Pride and Prejudice* pits Fitzwilliam Darcy—lacking social skills but warm and intelligent—against George Wickham—smooth and charming on the surface but conniving beneath. *Jane Eyre* foregoes a marriage of convenience from placid, spiritual St. John Eyre Rivers because she has known Edward Rochester's passion.

At least Stephenie Meyer evenly matches Bella's beaus—Wickham and St. John never really stood a chance. Jacob, however, is (almost) a fair contestant for Edward. Jacob is earthy and down to earth; Edward, refined and arrogant. Jacob works on cars; Edward plays the piano and holds Harvard degrees. Jacob is young—even younger than Bella, while Edward is not really 17 years old, having had the entire twentieth century to hone his romantic game, so much so that he's bored with humans—*none of the girls here are good enough for him*—except, of course, Bella. Crucially, and perhaps troublingly, Edward can seem cruel and capricious in his affections, repeating a pattern of getting close and then vanishing, raising and then crushing Bella's spirit, as opposed to faithful Jacob, always there for her. Edward may not want to be the bad guy, but he is a pure pop culture bad boy; Jacob is less a wolf than man's (or woman's) best friend. In the films, which emphasize the rivalry, Robert

Pattinson's Edward and Taylor Lautner's Jacob are conspicuous visual foils, with Pattinson pallid, aloof, angular in feature and cat-like in movement, coldly patrician, ethereal, and melancholy. Lautner is dark haired and olive complexioned, obviously pleased around Bella and noticeably peeved with Edward, usually shirtless and exposing his gym-sculpted muscles, exuding excitement.

Jacob's lycanthropy perfectly embodies adolescent malehood, as it has throughout movies from *I Was a Teenaged Werewolf* (1957) to *Teen Wolf* (1985, revised for television in 2011 after the success of *Twilight*). Films such as *An American Werewolf in London* (1981) visually dramatize the horror of the changing body—the hair, the elongations—and powerful new cravings that represent a monstrous version of normal male puberty. But Edward is no wolf and no true adolescent: he is a more-than-adult man who remains forever in the body of a beautiful boy, an undead Peter Pan. True to the adage, Jacob's nice guy finishes last. Bella, and Team Edward fans, choose Edward—he is unfathomable, yet he finds *Bella* mysterious. In the conventions of storytelling, Jacob's warmth and loyalty work against him. Edward's appeal, like that of Darcy and Rochester, lies in his very inscrutability, his cageyness. Jacob is permanently friend-zoned.

But why does Edward choose Bella? She is self-deprecating, describing herself as "ivory-skinned, without the excuse of blue eyes or red hair . . . slender, but soft somehow, obviously not an athlete. . . . I looked at my face in the mirror as I brushed through my tangled, damp hair. Maybe it was the light, but already I looked sallower, unhealthy" (10). While Bella sees herself as mousy and clumsy, Edward craves her as an alcoholic would "the rarest, finest cognac." Shifting analogies to make Bella seem less overtly drinkable, she becomes "exactly my brand of heroin" (267–268). While Edward understands that he's " 'the world's best predator' " (263), in reversal he sees Bella as " 'some kind of demon, summoned straight from my own personal hell to ruin me. The fragrance coming off your skin. . . . I thought of a hundred different ways to lure you from the room with me, to get you alone. . . . I had to run out, to get away before I could speak the words that would make you follow. . . . You would have come', he promised. I tried to speak calmly. 'Without a doubt' " (269–270). From his own perception, Bella, not Edward, is the monster, the one who, for Edward, has all the power. The predator feels like prey. Edward is tempted, in keeping with the apple on the first edition's cover and its epigram from Genesis 2:17. But as the scene makes perfectly clear, his bloodlust is an allegorized sexual lust. (HBO's *True Blood*, adapted from the *Sookie Stackhouse* novels by

Charlaine Harris, provides an adult-themed, fully sexualized version of the same premise.) Edward is horrified of what Bella does to him, and frightened of what he could do to her. The language of sex and death, Sigmund Freud's opposing drives of *eros* and *thanatos*, intersect, as they do in *Dracula* and throughout the vampire mythos. Sex is not life affirming or procreative; it is equated with death, and the fear of sex is inextricable from the fear of death. As a generation of teens has been told, the only form of safe sex in *Twilight* is abstinence, even as Edward and Bella crave each other.

For millions of readers, Bella is exactly their brand of heroine. Like her presumed audience, Bella is a voracious reader: "I kept my eyes on the reading list my teacher had given me. It was fairly basic: Bronte, Shakespeare, Chaucer, Faulkner. I'd already read everything" (15). But beyond the primal attraction to her scent and body, Edward is attracted to Bella because *he* cannot read *her*. She, not he, is the mystery—or they are mysterious to each other. Bella laments, " 'My face is so easy to read—my mother always calls me her open book'. I frowned." " 'On the contrary,' " Edward tells her, " 'I find you very difficult to read.' " Bella thinks, "Despite everything that I'd said and he'd guessed, he sounded like he meant it. 'You must be a good reader then', I replied. 'Usually'. He smiled widely, flashing a set of perfect, ultrawhite teeth" (50). The book reader meets the mind reader.

Yet in some ways, with only a vague physical description and little sense of Bella's interior life despite the voluminous first-person narration, audiences may find Bella difficult to read as well. This blankness, however, becomes much of her appeal to readers, who can easily imagine themselves in her position and fanaticize about being perfectly loved and chastely desired. Bella's blankness is, for others like book critic Laura Miller, a weakness: Bella "is purposely made as featureless and ordinary as possible in order to render her a vacant, flexible skin into which the reader can insert herself and thereby vicariously enjoy Edward's chilly charms."[21] While critics may deride the character, Bella's unreadability is as appealing to *Twilight*'s readership as it is to Edward. He does not love Bella despite that he cannot read her mind; he loves her because he cannot. And Bella does not love Edward despite that he is a vampire. She loves him because he is one, his ultrawhite teeth a reminder of his handsome menace. In an interview, Stephenie Meyer was asked, "Edward is so perfect—you've ruined regular men for a lot of teens. Do you feel bad?" She responded, "Oh, a little bit, I guess. I just wanted to write for myself, a fantasy. And that's what Edward is."[22]

If *World War Z* is primarily a book about fears with elements of wish fulfillment—that humans can ultimately come together to stave off the undead threat—as a fantasy Edward represents Meyer's, and her reader-ship's, wishes but also their fears. Beneath its surface themes of love and maintaining control of one's desire, *Twilight*, in keeping with its monsters, is also a novel about terror. Unlike zombie and interpersonal conflicts of the multinational cast in *World War Z*, *Twilight*'s war on terror is internal, waged within, and between Edward and Bella. It collapses the global scale of *World War Z* back to the personal, domestic, and matrimonial of the 9/11 novels. The *Twilight* series demonstrates the ways in which people can desire yet fear that which seems foreign or different. On the one hand, vampire Edward represents the ideals of the literary tradition of courtly love: he places Bella on a pedestal, and the relationship is illicit and erotic, exalting yet not to be consummated (at least not for thousands of pages). Edward is also consistently described as beautiful—he even sparkles, rather than bursting into flame, when exposed to sunlight, which explains the clandestine Cullen clan's preference for overcast Forks.

While it's tempting to see *Twilight* as an update of a fairy tale, with its semi-absent mother and pre-Victorian gender dynamics, and as opposed to a more culturally specific, contemporary story, it's worth considering that, despite Bella's name, Edward is both the beauty and the beast. Bella falls and stays in love with Edward very much because of his appearance, not because she must learn to see past it. In fact, that she may see past his pleasant appearance is another of Edward's fears. Edward thinks he's a monster, and he both wants and does not want Bella to see him as such. For Bella and Twihards, Edward is honorable and loyal, yet to detractors these same traits make him seem obsessive and manipulative. Bella, meanwhile, as the point-of-view character, seems in narrative control yet spends much of her narration wondering what Edward sees in her, while the novel's plot sets her up as a dependent cypher for repeated rescue.

In the films, the visual line between courtly lover and monstrous stalker blurs quickly. When Edward sneaks into Bella's room at night, the image of the vampire staring over a sleeping teen can be read as comforting or creepy; when he disappears upon her waking, he seems to have more in common with Dracula than with Darcy. In *New Moon*, when Edward leaves Bella, in contrast to the courtly love ideal (although he says it's for her own good), the novel uses single-word chapters "October," "November," "December," and "January" amidst a sea of blankness on the page to signify Bella's existential and narrative emptiness.[23] The film shows a hazy gray scene of her spiraling depression, the falling pages of the calendar dissolving over Bella as she wiles away the months alone in her room. After discovering that danger allows her to imagine Edward's voice, Bella continuously puts her life in jeopardy: "I thought briefly of the clichés, about how you're supposed to see your life flash before your eyes. I was so much luckier. Who wanted to see a rerun, anyway? I saw *him,* and I had no will to fight . . . Why would I fight when I was so happy where I was?" (361).

As the series continues, Bella suffers for her love: physical injuries, like the ones that conclude the first novel, but also an increasing desire to become a vampire like Edward, a desire—along with her intertwined sexual desires—that he will not give in to until much later. In the end, their passion is difficult to disentangle from their pain, a literary, vampiric version of sadism and masochism. In *Twilight*, Edward confesses to Bella that he "couldn't live with" himself if he ever hurt her: "You don't know how it's tortured me" (273). In *New Moon*, Bella wonders, "Was I trying to push myself into a zombie stupor? Had I turned masochistic—developed at taste for torture?" (159). With their shared sense of torture, their behavior could be considered a form of terror, but here, the pain is married to their passion. It is no surprise, then, that the next publishing sensation after *Twilight* would be *50 Shades of Grey*, an erotic exploration of bondage and discipline and dominance and submission from a man called Christian, and that it originated as *Twilight* fan fiction. Author E. L. James, perhaps even more than Stephenie Meyer, understood that feelings pleasure through pain—inflicting and receiving—may be the true underlying attraction between Edward and Bella, and they may also explain readers' and viewers' love for Edward's monstrosity.

Robert Pattinson, David Cronenberg, and Don DeLillo: The Vampire Capitalism of *Cosmopolis*

Cosmopolis (2003), by Don DeLillo, does not seem to have much in common with *World War Z* or *Twilight*. It does not feature any monsters at all. A brief plot summary makes the book seem mundane: a super-rich, young-ish man takes a day-long limousine ride across Manhattan to get a haircut at his childhood barbershop. With its cold, artful prose, the novel seems firmly in the category of literary fiction or postmodern literature. On the other hand, Don DeLillo—author of *Falling Man*, discussed in Chapter 2—seems a postmodern writer with unpostmodern sensibilities. In retrospect, after director and screenwriter David Cronenberg's 2012 film adaptation, the connections to the uncanny and undead seemed clearer. Near the end of *Cosmopolis*, billionaire capitalist Eric Packer is confronted by former employee Benno Levin, who believes that Packer has ruined his life. Brandishing a gun, Levin tells Packer, "Anyway you're already dead. You're like someone already dead. Like someone dead a hundred years. Many centuries dead."[24] For all of its talk about the future, *Cosmopolis* is not futuristic. Despite DeLillo's essay title, discussed in Chapter 1, it is not set "in the ruins of the future." Although it takes place "[i]n the year 2000, a day in April," a date that for a century served as cultural shorthand for the future, *Cosmopolis* is not about the year before 9/11. Rather, DeLillo presents the reader with a post-9/11 revision of the Romantic-era Gothic novel.

David Cronenberg understood the right actor to star in *Cosmopolis* was *Twilight*'s Robert Pattinson, whom viewers would already see as perfectly personifying the twenty-first-century film vampire. Like his near namesake Edward Cullen, Eric Packer is haunted and haunting, detached from humanity, and out of time. Eric Packer's apartment, his building, even his view of New York City seem less the title's cosmopolis—a city inhabited by people from many different countries—than a nineteenth-century Gothic tableau ripped from the pages of a Victorian penny dreadful: "It was all nighttime down at the river, half night, and ashy vapors wavered above the smokestacks on the far bank" (6). Yet like all movie vampires, Eric Packer displays a tension between his eerie sense of disembodiment and his exaggerated lusts of the body. His vampire has none of Edward Cullen's unvampiric restraint. Exercising to the point of "six percent body fat" (111), he always wears sunglasses when he is not inside his cork-lined, hearse-like limousine. Rats, literal and figurative, follow him wherever he goes. He is insatiable, perpetually prowling for food (" 'I'm hungry for something thick and chewy' " (17); "He ate quickly, inhaling his food. Then he ate her food" [18]) and sex (" 'You do actually reek of sexual discharge' [72], his semi-estranged wife, Elise Shifrin, deadpans). He even finds their intersection, as he looks at his wife in a restaurant and thinks, "He wanted to bite her lower lip, seize it between his teeth and bite down just hard enough to draw an erotic drop of blood" (73). He is so preternaturally smart that he seems to have experiences before they happen, which explains his success in the financial market. When sex is not enough and he asks his bodyguard Kendra to use her stun gun on him, we understand that he is so frozen to human feeling that only the defibrillating action of the weapon can bring his deadened heart to life. Attempting to talk to Elise, he makes statements like, " 'This is good. We're like people talking. Isn't this how they talk?' " (119). The conversation reveals how little they know each other, but also how difficult it is for Packer to conduct anything resembling natural human interaction.

Visually, cinematically, Eric Packer comes bundled with all of the film tropes of the Hollywood vampire. In the novel's opening lines, we learn that Eric Packer has been awake all night. The language immediately reveals his hubris and skewed perception—not that he cannot sleep, but rather that "[s]leep failed him" (5). Similarly, Packer imagines that "[w]hen he died he would not end. The world would end" (6). Monstrously solipsistic, Packer declares his unnatural immortality right away. As his limousine creeps along the streets, he seems to distance himself from the "others high and slick with fingernails from vampire movies, long, fanged, and frescoed" before declaring his affinity with them by telling adviser Jane Mellman, " 'I didn't sleep last night' " (41).

The notion of vampires—even metaphorical ones, as alive and well, so to speak—in today's world has of course become its own contemporary literary genre. Yet perhaps it goes without saying that DeLillo is after something very different from *Twilight*, to the dismay of Robert Pattinson's fans, according to these (typical) Amazon.com DVD reviewers: "As much as I like Robert Pattinson, this was the worst movie I've ever watched. Wanted to throw away DVD afterward," and "I love Robert Pattinson. . . . I loved all the Twilight movies . . . but Cosmopolis is . . . not a movie so much as a long nightmare in which every word is measured and every character represents something heavy. . . . Even Pattinson, who is very handsome in his business suit, isn't enough to make me want to watch this again." Pattinson fans hoping for a love story, or even a story, certainly set themselves up for disappointment. While DeLillo, Cronenberg, and Pattinson deliver a post-9/11 critique of techno-capitalism, the novel's neo-vampire imagery allows it to delve into the interconnectedness of death, time, and language.

Cosmopolis seems a post-9/11 novel and precursor for 2007's *Falling Man*, even as it once again cements Don DeLillo's reputation for prescience. DeLillo's previous novels like *Players*, *Mao II*, and *Underworld* had analyzed the World Trade Center's significances, as discussed in the previous chapter, but by *Cosmopolis*, the description of Eric Packer's apartment building seems more somber: it "was nine hundred feet high, the tallest residential tower in the world, a commonplace oblong whose only statement was its size" (8). Later, a description of the New York skyline turns elegiac, mourning the towers' loss by ironically displacing them into the future:

The bank towers loomed just beyond the avenue. They were covert structures for all their size, hard to see, so common and monotonic, tall, sheer, abstract, with standard setbacks, and block-long, and interchangeable, and he had to concentrate to see them.

They looked empty from here. He liked that idea. They were the last tall things, made empty, designed to hasten the future.

They were the end of the outside world. They weren't here, exactly. They were in the future, a time beyond geography and touchable money and the people who stack and count it. (36)

At least five years ahead of schedule, *Cosmopolis* also forecast that the global financial network, as seemingly untoppleable as towers themselves, could be brought down by a hubristic day trader. Packer spends much of the novel betting against the *yen*: "His actions ... were causing storms of disorder. He was so leveraged ... that the whole system was in danger" (116). DeLillo also depicts a protest, anticipating the Occupy Wall Street movement—ideas that seemed unlikely in the initial shadow of 9/11. But more than being ahead of its time, as analyses of the novel usually contend, the novel looks backward. Eric Packer at first seems a familiar literary type, lifted from *The Bonfire of the Vanities* by Tom Wolfe or *American Psycho* by Bret Easton Ellis. Yet he is less a Master of the Universe or a materialistic murderer than the uncanny embodiment of Karl Marx's monster metaphor in *Capital*, restated in *Cosmopolis* twice—"A specter is haunting the world—the specter of capitalism!" (89, 96)—as well as the idea's continuation, which *Cosmopolis* leaves out: "Capital is dead labor, that, vampire-like, only lives by sucking living labor, and lives the more, the more labor it sucks." Eric Packer is a capitalist vampire beyond Marx's Industrial Age imagination, beyond controlling the means of production but the production of capital itself, earning billions of dollars by manipulating even more billions. Stoker's Dracula relied on feudal aristocracy and time to amass his coins—time really is money—but capitalism takes away the need for either. *New Moon* casually mentions that "Edward had a *lot* of money—I didn't even want to think of how much. Money meant next to nothing to Edward or the rest of the Cullens. It was just something that accumulated when you had unlimited time on your hands and a sister who had an uncanny ability to predict trends in the stock market" (13). Packer doesn't even need time. In Marxist vampiric manner, he makes money by siphoning and leveraging other people's money, one form of currency against others, his wealth amassing entirely on a computer screen. But despite the book's seeming investment in currency, in every sense of the word, DeLillo calls attention to things that exist out of time, and beyond time—even beyond the normal scope of life and death.

Eric Packer seems less interested in humanity's mortality than the virtual lives and deaths of words and things. Everything Packer sees seems to him out of time, or its very language is out of time, even his beloved towers: "He took out his hand organizer and poked a note to himself about the anachronistic quality of the word skyscraper. No recent structure ought to bear this word. It belonged to the olden soul of awe, to the arrowed towers that were a narrative long before he was born" (9). Packer sees an entire obsolete belief system entombed in the single word. Like the skyscrapers, the novel's key images supposedly occupy the future, or the past, but never the present. And like the bank towers, which appear empty to Eric Packer but are surely not, it can seem as though DeLillo's novel is devoid of three-dimensional human presence as well. If Max Brooks wanted to include "the human factor" in his book about zombies, DeLillo's narration reveals the monstrous appetites of humans.

The skyscraper is not the only architectural misnomer: "The word office was outdated now. It had zero saturation" (15), and "he knew these devices [his security officer's earbuds] were already vestigial. They were degenerate structures. Maybe not the handgun just yet. But the word itself was lost in blowing mist" (19). Packer wonders, " 'Why do we still have airports? Why are they called airports?' " (22). Later, when his personal physician arrives, Eric Packer's mind goes "blank except for some business concerning the pathos of the word satchel" (42) and, in proto-vampiric imagery, wonders "why stethoscopes were still in use. They were lost tools of antiquity, quaint as bloodsucking worms" (43).

In his actions and language, Eric Packer harbors a deep ambivalence about the human body, which he extends into the realm of human interaction with technology. Even money is meant to exist in streamlined code, not in the cluttered corporeality of bodies, bills, or banks: "He was thinking about automated teller machines. The term was aged and burdened by its own historical memory ... part of the process that the device was meant to replace. It was anti-futuristic, so cumbrous and mechanical that even the acronym seemed dated" (54). Communication systems as well become part of an antiquated notion of modernity that the postmodern Packer has long abandoned: "It was time to retire the word phone" (88), and "He saw a police lieutenant carrying a walkie-talkie. What entered his mind when he saw this? He wanted to ask the man why he was still using such a contraction, still calling it what he called it, carrying the nitwit rhyme out of the age of industrial glut into smart places built on beams of light" (102). The decade since the novel was published has certainly borne out Packer's predictions: the last thing people do on their phones is talk, and that is when they are even still referring to it as a phone, as opposed to a cell or a mobile. Yet after reading *Cosmopolis*, those words seem well past their expiration dates, just as Eric Packer notices that "[e]ven the word computer sounds backwards and dumb" (104).

People no longer use their phones for phonetic sound or computers for computing.

Packer relegates the naming systems of skyscraper, office, airport, and phone—nouns as synonymous with the events of 9/11 as they are with the twentieth century itself—to the sarcophagus of dead nomenclature. So his own obsolescence is, of course, his worst fear, revealed even more explicitly when he witnesses the funeral of Sufi rapper Brutha Fez, where Packer imagines himself as "the powdered body in the mummy case, the one they've all lived long enough to mock" (136). Although blind to the dead body before him, Eric Packer sees dead things and dead language everywhere. Yet in death they are at least inert and harmless, mere annoyances to Packer's ultramodern worldview. Mummies are not vampires—that is, sustaining unnatural, undead existence by preying on the blood and energy of the living. After putting a pie in Eric Packer's face, "pastry assassin" Andre Petrescu says of himself, "But I am kicked and beaten so many times I am walking dead" (143). But he too is no vampire. For that, of course, we need Eric Packer himself.

Shortly after declaring the word *computer* dumb, Packer's adviser, Vija Kinsky, explains to Eric, "People will not die. Isn't this the creed of the new culture? People will be absorbed in streams of information. . . . Computers will die. They're dying in their present form. They're just about dead as distinct units. A box, a screen, a keyboard. They're melting into the texture of everyday life" (104). Again, the novel seems prophetic, in that most people don't think much of the boxless, keyboardless supercomputers in their pockets that we anachronistically still call phones. But in a monstrous inversion, things and words will die, or their corpses will remain semi-animated even after their death, but people no longer will.

Similarly, as Eric sees Brutha Fez's hearse, a foil for his own limousine, roll down the street, "He wanted to see the hearse pass by again, the body titled for viewing, a digital corpse, a loop, a replication" (139). Technology, unlike life, is controllable, subject to the whim of the person wielding the remote control. Yes, the body may die, but the image will live in perpetuity. If DeLillo was concerned about the televised replays of the Zapruder film's Kennedy assassination in *Libra*, then the digital age has exponentially greater potential for truly endless replication. As Packer thinks after seeing the televised death of Arthur Rapp repeated, "He could see it again if he wished, any time, through scan retrieval, a technology that already seemed oppressively sluggish" (34).

But in true vampire fashion, this kind of techno-ontological undeath is to be feared as much as desired, for it seems as though Packer may already be dead throughout the novel we are reading, when, in the first section narrated by Benno Levin, we learn that "[h]e is dead, word for word" (55). Like *Pulp Fiction*'s Vincent Vega, who appears alive because of non-linear narration, Packer may have been killed before the novel begins, and *Cosmopolis* is told entirely in flashback. Rereading the novel, readers must wonder: is Eric Packer dead all along? While Eric reserves this description for his hated rival, the president of the United States— "He was the undead. He lived in a state of occult repose, waiting to be reanimated" (77)—it seems much more applicable to the person who is alive in some chapters but possibly dead in others. Of course, Benno Levin makes a highly unreliable narrator, one whose word we should not take for granted, or even word for word. We have no way of knowing whether Eric Packer is a dead man walking, or being driven, throughout the novel, or even dead at the end, but this very indeterminacy is part of his literary, if not literal, undeath.

Late in the novel, Eric discovers "three hundred naked people sprawled in the street . . . Of course, there was context. Someone was making a movie" (172–173). Stripping what was left of the clothing he had shed and lost throughout the day, Eric Packer decides to "lay down among them" (174), finally, and paradoxically, experiencing his most human, and humane, moment of communion and deepest connection he will feel toward his wife, who is also in the mass: "He felt the presence of the bodies, all of them, the body breath, the heat and running blood, people unlike each other who were now alike, amassed, heaped in a way, alive and dead together" (174). The bodies are not aloft in the towers, but together, on the ground, the specter of death but the reality of life.

This powerfully cinematic and potentially self-referential scene does not appear in the film adaptation. Yet in other respects, writer and director David Cronenberg seems a natural partner for DeLillo's novel, having previously adapted the seemingly unfilmable *Naked Lunch*, by William Burroughs, and *Crash*, by J. G. Ballard. As literary critic and book reviewer Cornel Bonca writes, when *Cosmopolis* "first came out in 2003, it was regarded by most reviewers, myself included, as a disappointment," but he rightly concludes that the film may give "renewed life and attention to a novel that tells us more about this culture's hurl into the future than we want to know."[25] Like DeLillo, Cronenberg has a particular ambivalence toward the automobile. *Cosmopolis*, then, brings together DeLillo's, Cronenberg's, and maybe America's obsessions: cars, guns, money, and power.

Unlike DeLillo, Cronenberg has long been fascinated with the intersections between technology and vampirism. Cronenberg began his career with straightforward, vampire-influenced films, including *Shivers* (1975), about a scientist who develops blood-sucking parasites that trigger uncontrollable sexual desire in the host; inevitable mayhem ensues, featuring a climactic scene in a parking garage. *Rabid* (1977) is about a woman injured in a motorcycle accident who develops a stinging, blood-sucking fistula in her armpit. While the vampirism of *Cosmopolis* is far more subtle, Cronenberg's other recurring trope, from his vampire films and *The Fly* to less fantastical movies like *A History of Violence*, is transformation.

Yet here, *Cosmopolis* fits more clearly into DeLillo's body of work and less comfortably with Cronenberg's, as it is never clear whether, or how much, Eric Packer learns or changes through his long day's journey for a haircut. When Packer learns of a "credible threat" (107) to his life, he seems different: with the possibility of death now real and palpable, as opposed to the amorphous, existential dread that produces his daily physicals, "[n]ow," he thinks, "he could begin the business of living" (107). Or is this just another declaration of vampirism, of life after death? In any case, he does not behave any differently. Similarly, the death of Brutha Fez, unlike the deaths of Arthur Rapp and Nickolai Kaganovich ("Your mind thrives on ill will toward others. So does your body, I think. Bad blood makes for long life … He dies so you can live" [82], Vija Kinski explains), seems to move Eric: "He wept violently" (139). Yet we soon wonder whether the pain is feigned, another example of Eric's self-absorption, since "[h]e wept for Fez and everyone else here and for himself, of course" (139). Even after the funeral, and after merging with the bodies, and his wife, in the film scene, Eric Packer seems unchanged. Like the antecedentless pronouns that begin many of *Falling Man*'s chapters, Packer is another of DeLillo's familiar flat characters, capable of keen and wry observations about the world but never about himself. As Benno tells Eric before he plans to kill him, or actually kills him, since we can never know, "You're not a reflective man. … Time for a philosophical pause. Some reflection, yes" (187). But again in true vampire fashion, Eric is not capable of reflection.

Cornel Bonca suggests that Christian Bale "would have been perfect for Eric Packer." But the *American Psycho*–era Bale that Bonca envisions has turned into a *Dark Knight Rises*–era Bale—an action hero, or anti-hero, but a method-acting master and established alpha male leading man, too physically imposing, too expected, for the ethereal weirdness of DeLillo's prose and Cronenberg's vision. Pattinson's casting resembles David Fincher's at-the-time risk with Brad Pitt in *Fight Club*: Pitt, like Pattinson, seemed less in keeping with the adaptation's social satire and more like the thing the film was satirizing. Yet instead, like Pitt, Pattinson brings an artless, rather than method, self-assuredness to the part. His ready-to-wear materialism and superficiality, his remoteness and lack of emotional range and register—the precise qualities his critics most disparage—become assets in playing Eric Packer. He even seems out of control and frightened by the end, when menaced by Benno Levin's gun, which is more likely than Bale's perpetual imperturbability or even DeLillo's Packer, who, on paper, never loses his icy cool. Without a solid physical description to go on—just that he is 28 years old, gym fit, and possessing supernatural powers of sexual seduction and market speculation—*Twilight*'s Robert Pattinson easily carries his vampire fame readymade into the part of Eric Packer. And viewers' strong identification of Pattinson with Edward Cullen—another anachronism, over a century old in the trim, sparkly body of a muscular 17-year-old—cements the metaphor that vampirically conceals itself within the pages of a postmodern novel supposedly about the future.

The film trailer for *Cosmopolis* refers to the movie this way: "Finally, the first film about our new millennium." DeLillo has suggested he had the idea for *Cosmopolis* "just about the time that the market was beginning to flatten out, which was spring 2000. I then realized that the day on which the action occurs would be the last day of the era—the golden age of cybercapital, with booming global markets and rampant dreams of individual wealth."[26] But undeath transcends beginnings and endings, and the year 2000 remains a mythic but ultimately arbitrary number. At the end of the film, as Paul Giamatti's Benno Levin holds the gun to Packer's head and the film abruptly cuts to black, Robert Pattinson's Eric Packer is again vampirically left suspended between life and death, undead, the final moment of the murder endlessly deferred, never to arrive. He does not die, and the world does not end. But the novel, and movie, must, even if the war on terror rages on under new names and guises.

CHAPTER 4

We Have to Go Back: Television's *Lost* after 9/11

From *Lost*, Season 1, "Pilot" (2004): Dominic Monaghan as Charlie, amidst the literal and symbolic wreckage. (ABC/Photofest)

In this chapter: *Lost* (2004–2010), created by Jeffrey Lieber, J. J. Abrams, and Damon Lindelof. Additional discussion: *Survivor* (2000–present), created by Charlie Parsons; *Heroes* (2006–2010), created by Tim Kring; *24* (2001–2010), created by Joel Surnow and Robert Cochran.

Novels and film were not the only media to incorporate signifiers of the 9/11 attacks into fiction. On television, the series Lost *borrowed familiar imagery—a plane crash, catastrophe, the conflicts of unity among a diverse group of people, torture, and the terroristic threat of an unknowable enemy. In doing so,* Lost *explored post-9/11 conflicts between the individual and the community, freedom and security, and faith and distrust. Unlike novels or films, however,* Lost's *continued, serialized approach, as well as its propensity for nonlinear, nonchronological approaches to storytelling, allowed it not just to respond to America's initial post-9/11 atmosphere of fear but also to metaphorically reflect America's changing attitudes about the ensuing war on terror and post-9/11 economic downturn.* Lost *becomes a multilayered narrative response to community trauma: the wish to remember, coupled with the compulsion to relive, and repeat, with psychological desire—and, thanks to science fiction, possibility—to "go back."*

The television show *Lost* debuted in September 2001. It revolved around a group of strangers haphazardly thrown together with little more than the clothes on their backs. Despite individual differences, they needed to work together to escape from their unknown location— somewhere unspecified in the Pacific—to find their way back to America.

But wait, fans must be thinking: *Lost* debuted in 2004. And it was more much complicated, and far less clichéd, than my summary. Yet everything in the above paragraph is true, except perhaps for the first word, "the." The *Lost* I'm describing is not *the Lost*—it was a reality TV show with the same name, developed to compete against other early 2000s hits like *Survivor*. This forgotten *Lost* was canceled just a month into its run, in part because of legal and logistical challenges following the attacks of September 11, 2001, but mostly because network executives believed that the "real-life terrorist attacks would lure viewers away from faux reality entertainment shows," including the now-forgotten *Amazing Race*, *The Mole II*, and *The Runner*, each also ill-fatedly introduced in September 2001.[1]

Yet the similarities, beyond the name alone, between these two *Lost*s may be revealing in retrospect. For while the first, failed *Lost* may have seemed too topical in the immediate aftermath of 9/11—who wanted to see more threatened Americans or a show about people sneaking into the country?—the second *Lost*, the one that viewers came to know, love, and follow through six intense seasons, may have been more of its time than people have acknowledged. When *Lost* premiered, its most distinctive features seemed to be its desert island genre mash-up—*Castaway* meets *Gilligan's Island* meets *Survivor*—now infused with the unusual particulars of life on *this* outlandish island. Yes, they faced the practical problems of food, shelter, medical care, and potential rescue, and the ethical issues of leadership and cooperation, but mostly they—and by extension, viewers—were fascinated by the metaphysical mysteries of healed paralysis, resurrections, polar bears, and, of course, the smoke monster.

And then there were, of course, the characters—their personalities, conflicts, development, redemptions, and in many cases, even their deaths. Their variety seemed as indebted to 2000s-era reality television as the island premise, replacing *Survivor*'s influence for that of the *Real World*'s cast-to-clash archetypes: the straight man, the hothead, the druggie, and the bad girl, along with novel additions that even reality TV would not have touched: a pregnant woman, a prepubescent boy, a paraplegic (as we would discover), a couple that speaks no English (or so we thought), an older (interracial) couple, semi-incestuous step-siblings, an ex-Republican Guard Iraqi torturer, an obese bilingual schizophrenic (although supernatural explanations would supersede psychological ones), and many more.

Yet now, beyond setting, characterization, and even story, two interconnected aspects of the show seem most striking in retrospect. First, the style: fractured and fragmented use of time and narrative, shifting perspective, and, seemingly straight from the theories of Jacques Derrida, a constant deferring of meaning through constantly differed story lines. Second, the philosophical and psychological implications that this style bears on America in the 2000s. Taken together, the changing narrative devices—flashback, flash-forward, time travel, and "flash sideways," as *Lost* fans referred to the alternate story line of Season 6—mirrored the ways in which *Lost* gauged and updated the fears—and, in Freudian reversal, desires and wish fulfillment—of a country reeling from its worst terrorist attack in history and the launch of two wars across the ocean, yet at the same time the ways in which these plights were experienced, by most Americans, as television.

Lost in America

While most of the critical attention to *Lost* has focused on its inventive and compelling visual style, a few critics have also noted the relationship between its storytelling and its cultural relevance. As J. Wood, in *Living*

Lost: Why We're All Stuck on the Island, explains, "Lost performs a very necessary function: It gives a narrative (and a safety-distant context) to a real-felt sense of trauma. By giving these abstract ideas a tangible narrative with a beginning and ending each week, that sense of terror is contained by the show, and this become something that might actually be manageable."[2] Or, as Mikal Gilmore explains in a *Rolling Stone* piece barely longer than this quotation, *Lost*'s characters "are lost in their times—which is to say they are lost in our times, the uncertain reality of post-9/11. Planes hurtled from the sky that morning in 2001 and brought with them fear and irresolution; we now live with an unanticipated horror at our center. Like *Lost*'s survivors, we can't forecast the turns that horror will take, and we can't immediately fathom our own part in it."[3] Finally, writing in *Slate*'s TV Club, Seth Stevenson echoes Gilmore: "When the show debuted in 2004, I think it was pretty clearly influenced by the post-9/11 context. An airplane no longer controlled by its pilots. A bewildering, catastrophic incident. Community forming in the wake of tragedy. Ben Linus, with his sinister methods and veiled motives, called to mind the paranoia of the anthrax-in-envelopes days."[4]

Yet Stevenson, like me, seems reluctant to use the word "allegory," with its suggestion of a single or true meaning behind its emblems; unlike for Plato, whose famous "Allegory of the Cave" is intended to have a single, symbolic meaning, *Lost*'s cave can have many meanings—or sometimes a cave is just a cave. Despite—or perhaps, because of—its sheer length as a serial narrative and its concomitant intricacies, *Lost* has consistently been too elusive and ambiguous for such direct equivalencies. Rather than eschewing such similarities, however, Chadwick Matlin, responds to Stevenson with further specifics, even using the word "allegory":

> Seth, if you want to talk about *Lost* as a reflection of its times, I'm more than eager. I can deliver a dissertation on how *Lost*'s time-travel season was written during a U.S. election that revisited the past as it looked into the future. I can wax philosophic on how this season's dual-timeline approach corresponds to an administration that has changed everything and nothing in Washington, and a viewing public that doesn't know which narrative to believe. And then there's Ben Linus, the best allegory for the Wall Street debacle television has provided. Ben built his power on a foundation of lies and deceit. It was followed by an inevitable crash and then (a potential) resurrection.[5]

While Matlin does not quite deliver that dissertation, quickly shifting to the ways in which *Lost* has not changed and other topics, I want to emphasize his reading of *Lost* as an expression of our increasingly relativistic world, a common post-1960s lamentation but one that deserves reiteration after 9/11. Viewers, especially of a show steeped in the paranormal from the beginning, could be expected to accept continuously updated, retroactive explanations and continuously revised continuities. The same cannot be said of an invasion of Iraq based on erroneous intelligence, suspicious treatment of prisoners and detainees, and an economic meltdown that treated mortgages the way *Lost* treats story lines—constantly shifting, constantly differed and deferring. Again and again in the 2000s, viewers, and Americans in general, have been told that everything we thought we knew previously turned out to be mistaken and that no one could have foreseen the current crisis. After 9/11, *Lost*—as well as reality TV and a number of other shows, films, and novels—allowed fans to find pleasure, rather than dismay, in narrative twists, surprises, reversals, and shifting justifications. The good storyteller, unlike the good leader, is entitled to be—*must* be—a good liar.

Even so, this emphasis on context, *Lost* as a political parable, risks reducing the show to a cardboard morality play, and *Lost* is indisputably top-notch television. It is more than highbrow soap opera, the now-familiar tangled yarns of love triangles, betrayals, amnesia, coincidences, and returns from the dead, this time tricked out with philosophical name-dropping and postmodern bells and whistles. But as Wood and *Slate*'s writers suggest, context does matter, and certainly some of *Lost*'s success was due to its being the right show in the right place at the right time, a way for Americans to experience what felt like the escapist thrills of fantasy and science fiction but may also have provided a safe psychological and narrative outlet for the genuine trepidations gripping America. *Time* magazine concluded that the 2000s were the worst decade in American history (not even just recent history), vacillating between calling it "the Decade from Hell, or the Reckoning, or the Decade of Broken Dreams, or"—no surprise—"the Lost Decade."[6] If the name "The Lost Generation had not already been coined by Gertrude Stein to describe the writers, artists, and expatriates unmoored by the pointless carnage of World War I, then that label would surely suit the generation to come of age after 9/11.

Indeed, as Gilmore and Stevenson suggest, *Lost*'s premise, imagery, sustained conflicts, and mysteries that bordered on conspiracies borrowed overtly from representations most frequently associated with 9/11: the premise of the plane crash itself, from the Pilot episode through the concluding overhead image of the last episode, The End, through the show's recurring conceits of Iraq, torture, air marshals, paranoia, the ways in which people from different backgrounds alternately mistrust each other and band together, the presence of infiltrators and Others in our midst, and the tensions between faith, reason, and coincidence. The airplane, for 9/11, and for *Lost*, came to symbolize the delicate, porous intersections between people the world over, perhaps a narrative convenience to bring disparate characters together, a contemporary version of John Ford's *Stagecoach*—or even Chaucer's pilgrimage in *The Canterbury Tales*.

The airplane—for 9/11, for *Lost*, and building on the image from Chuck Palahniuk's *Survivor*, whose title just predates the TV show but creates a nice coincidence—also represents opposition and paradox: freedom versus security, strength versus vulnerability, destinations versus luminal spaces, separation versus connection, closeness versus distance. And certainly 9/11 itself represents the greatest kinds of things lost—the lives lost, of course, but also the missing persons flyers that covered New York City after the attacks, evident in the novels and films of 9/11, even the moral direction and post–Cold War stability lost. *Lost* managed to embody each, but with the safe, requisite distance of a familiar, even corny, island conceit. If Manhattan was too obvious an island setting, if the first *Lost*'s reality TV was too close to home, then *Lost*'s unnamed, unclaimed island could provide the appropriate outlet for our post-9/11 fears and our desire ultimately, not to be lost but to be found—or, perhaps, to escape.

Yes, *Lost* is more than life-after-9/11's requisite components reshuffled, despite its preponderance of plane crashes, an island, torture, and a hiding, shape-shifting presence that kills people: the smoke monster is the ultimate force of terror on the island. Much of the show's resistance to allegory stems from its equal resistance to Manichean separations of good and evil: who on the island is unambiguously good—or evil? Otherwise, *Lost* would more closely resemble other TV shows of its time, *24* and *Heroes*. *24* explicitly addresses post-9/11 fears of terror, providing wish fulfillment in its straightforward solution: masculine muscle, the autonomous hero who single-handedly foils the unequivocal terrorists' plots. *Heroes*, despite its sci-fi trappings, squarely places the possibility of a human-made disaster in New York City at its center. Only unlike in life, our heroes will stop the disaster before it is too late, a trope I will develop in Chapter 7. Like *Lost*, both shows complicate chronology and narrative. In addition, like the movies *Crash* (2004) and *Babel* (2006), *24*, *Heroes*, and *Lost* all suggest significant links between seeming strangers, the ways in which the world after 9/11 seems smaller, more connected, and closer—for better and worse, as a result. But *Lost*'s moral complexity is greater; unlike *24*, the only bomb on *Lost* is detonated by our heroes, not ostensible terrorists. And the only plane to crash was the one metaphysically hijacked by the Lostaways (as fans referred to the characters), who knew that their presence would cause the plane to crash on the island without knowing whether the other passengers would suffer collateral damage.

Lost's treatment of 9/11 imagery, however, does more than play narrative games, or even just create fear and suspense. Instead, *Lost*'s distinctive narrative features, combined with its 9/11 tropes, create a kind of wish fulfillment that balances the show's mystery. The fantasy amidst the fear is crystallized in Jack's exhortation during the finale of Season 3 that "We have to go back," a statement that, appropriately enough, applies retroactively to Seasons 1 and 2 and foreshadows 4, 5, and 6, as we will see.

Up until Season 3, *Lost* had alternated between a narrative present on the island and recurring flashes into an individual character's past. We *did* have to go back—to the characters' lives before the fated plane crash. *Lost*'s flashbacks, in its post-9/11 context, like the plane itself, supports the notion that the show's narrative structures were not separate from or incidental to its thematic tensions—rather, it epitomized them. Our characters, like us, could understand the crisis of the present only by delving into the past. Writing in *Newsweek* just a month after the 9/11 attacks, Fareed Zakaria asked, "Why Do They Hate Us?" without needing to provide a specific pronoun antecedent in his title for "they." Yet he also knew to preface his subsequent analysis this way: "To the question 'Why do the terrorists hate us?' Americans could be pardoned for answering, 'Why should we care?' The immediate reaction to the murder of 5,000 innocents is anger, not analysis. Yet anger will not be enough to get us through what is sure to be a long struggle. For that we will need answers. The ones we have heard so far have been comforting but familiar."[7]

Lost, in this sense, is completely unlike its desert island forebears. It was far less concerned with getting its castaways off the island than in understanding, epistemologically, how and why they wound up there in the first place. As the mysteries of the island unfolded, the flashbacks provided further and further evidence of furtive connections and coincidences between the characters. Several proved solvable and concrete, such as Jack and Claire's shared parentage. Others were explained much later, by introducing Jacob and his quest for candidates. Still others, like the meaning and import of the Numbers, were never resolved at all. Taken together, though, this accumulation of correlations, represented by the consistent juxtapositions between past and present, began to suggest an unlikely combination of concerns, concerns that again mirror *Lost*'s time: religion, paranoia, conspiracy, and quantum physics. For the believer, like John Locke and Mr. Eko; for the paranoiac, as Hugo, Desmond, Rousseau, and others have at times seemed; for the con man and the plotter, as Sawyer, Ben, and Charles Widmore have at times been; for the quantum physicist, like Marvin Candle, Eloise Hawking, and Daniel Faraday, everything happens for a reason, everything is significant, and everything is connected.

Of course, everything happens for a reason, everything is significant, and everything is connected for three other groups as well: gifted storytellers, their most avid fans, and die-hard conspiracy theorists. *Lost*'s flashbacks proved the best narrative device to merge plots of every kind—narrative plots, conspiracy plots, and funeral plots—as many major characters, beginning with Boone, began to die or disappear. This intersection between *Lost*'s form and content—flashback as editing and as metaphor—was striking even in the Pilot, a title that for any other show would be the generic term for the test episode but here becomes a kind of dark, even ironic, allusion to the plane crash, an early introduction to death (the actual pilot of the Pilot dies horrifically), or even to the key theme of *Lost* in general: who, metaphorically or literally, is flying this plane? (Thankfully Lapidus survived the submarine explosion, or no one would have gotten off the island at the series' end.) Put in other ways: Who is the group's leader: Jack, Sawyer, or Locke? Whom will Kate choose: Jack or Sawyer? Who are the Candidates—and who will inherit Jacob's role? Who is in control: Jacob, the Man in Black (or, as I like to call him, UnLocke), or Charles Widmore? Who truly understands the island: again, Jacob, Man in Black, Widmore—or Eloise Hawking, Daniel Faraday, or Desmond Hume? And finally: who will be found, who will remain, and who will die? Even as the series progressed, from the flashbacks seemingly necessary for the sake of developing mysterious connections toward the revelation that those connections suggested Jacob's hand, or touch, behind them, by the end Jack emerges as the final volunteer—succeeded, finally, it seems, by Hugo. *Lost*'s initial premise may have been similar to its same-named, ill-fated reality-TV counterpart and *Survivor* knock-off, but so is its conclusion: Who remains on the island? Who goes home? And what is the reward? *Survivor*'s goal, to remain last on the island, now seems even more applicable to *Lost*. And in the aftermath of 9/11, questions of power and control could be played for *Survivor*'s bathos or *Lost*'s pathos.

Past, Present, and Future

As flashbacks changed to a literal attempt to go back, and then to time travel and flashing sideways, each season's new alternate story lines, time lines, and constantly postponed but evolving discoveries, the cliffhangers and thrills that the show is famous for, continued to suggest our post-9/11 yearning to go back and remake, go back and fix, that which in life remains stubbornly in the past. In the end, both our suspense and our satisfaction come from the characters' ability to keep going back—back narratively, psychologically, chronologically, and geographically—even as, or precisely because, in real life, as viewers, we cannot. Each season still maintained what might be thought of as its ongoing present, the saga of the survivors stranded on the island. But while the first seasons alternated between that narrative present and flashbacks that delved into the particular past and interior of one individual character per episode, the show switched gears and pulled a remarkable storytelling stunt for the finale of Season 3: that what viewers initially experienced as a flashback turned out to be a flash forward, the future after the castaways have been recovered. In this reversal, the show ushered in a powerful new narrative conceit, but also a powerful new post-9/11 metaphor.

The present-to-flashback structure was inventive, unusual for TV, and extensive, if still a reasonably common literary and film device. Jack's Season 3 pronouncement, however, provided the satisfying confusion and excitement of a perfect twist. Having exhausted the flashback—and flashbacks within flashbacks, a televisual version of the pluperfect tense in grammar—it then shifted, and surprised the audience again, by flashing forward in time: that we were seeing something other than what we thought we were seeing, but we knew that only in retrospect.[8] Bearded, alcoholic Jack is trying to go back to the island from which he had spent the first two seasons trying to escape. And as the country's attitude toward 9/11 shifted, so did *Lost*'s metaphor: we had been desperate to heal, to recover, and come together, but also to declare war and exact vengeance on someone, anyone.

In the confusion overlapping *Lost*'s debut and continuation, perhaps America—ironically or appropriately, depending on one's political persuasion—became nostalgic for the immediate aftermath of the trauma. As TV political personality Glenn Beck described in his "9-12" website, "The 9-12 Project is designed to bring us all back to the place we were on September 12, 2001. The day after America was attacked we were not obsessed with Red States, Blue States or political parties. We were united as Americans, standing together to protect the greatest nation ever created."[9] (The website's recurring references to America's Founding Fathers suggest a desire to travel back in time even farther.) Beck, despite crocodile tears to nonpartisanship, takes this notion of having to go back to its reactionary extreme. As fiction, however, *Lost* is more subtle and supple: the plane crashes of 9/11, like the crash on the island, has become our post-millennial primal scene, our national and narrative shock, and as a country, as a group of characters, we yearn to return to the site of the trauma in order to relive it, even as its repetition does not ease, and may even exacerbate, the pain.

In Season 3, post-island Jack is a textbook case of posttraumatic stress disorder, experiencing all of its key symptoms, from "feeling emotionally numb" and "difficulty maintaining close relationships" to "overwhelming guilt or shame" and "self-destructive behavior, such as drinking too much." The key symptom, however, ahead of each of these, is "[f]lashbacks, or reliving the traumatic event for minutes or even days at a time."[10] The cinematic and psychological overlap of the word "flashback" is illuminating, and the return to the island makes the flashback palpable, but *Lost* did not truly exploit the chronological ambiguities and instabilities attendant to an age demarcated by a symbolic date (9/11, of course) until its characters began to travel through time in Season 5. By then, the show was very different from where it had begun. The multiple time lines of flashing backward and forward were no longer narrative devices but literal renderings of multiple and simultaneous time lines, the main story line aware of the other. With this shift from metaphorical time travel-as-storytelling device to literal time travel-as-science fiction, the implication shifted as well. With the characters of *Lost*, the world in 2008 was no longer the post-9/11, post-Iraq invasion of *Lost*'s 2004 Pilot. Instead, the characters, like the world, were wondering what exactly they had gotten themselves into, and the majority of Americans voted for change. Time travel, unlike mere flashback, allows not just for psychological reenactment of trauma, but of its wish fulfillment, an existential do-over, a way to rewrite and re-right the past in order to alter the present.

As viewers versed in time travel could have predicted, though, the return to the past proved no more lasting a solution than the return to the island: "we have to go back" creates the problem of infinite regress. There is always more "back" to go back to, as *Lost* proved in the seasons that followed the pronouncement, going back to 1971, Richard Alpert's 1867, even Jacob's childhood about 2,000 years ago. Going back—to the island, in flashback, and through time travel—answered little. Instead, it allowed *Lost* to continue to defer its questions, enlarge its histories, and deepen its mysteries. Viewers, in turn, saw less wish fulfillment and correction than further fragmentation and paradox. In keeping, Season 5 ended with the final manifestation of multiple time lines. The attempt to detonate an atomic bomb—in historical homage to our pre-9/11 anxiety—to alter time, expunge the trauma, and go back not to 9/12, as Beck would have it, but something like earlier in the day on 9/11, did not erase the plane crash as much as it seemed to create an alternate time line. In doing so, we seemed to leave the world of the flashback, flash-forward, and time travel, to enter that other mainstay of science fiction and comic books, the alternate time-stream, the What If? scenario. Appropriately, the signals between worlds shifted from a fade to black to a fade to white, with an accompanying sound of white noise reminiscent of an airplane's ascent. The sound becomes a reminder of the way in which the castaways first found themselves lost and yet another link to 9/11, when airplanes first represented the means by which Americans exercise the global freedoms of their borders but then the vehicles that hijackers used to turn those symbols against the (equally symbolic) World Trade Center and Pentagon buildings.

Writing in 2006, David Hastings Dunn analyzes the ways in which *Lost* reflects 9/11, but he seems equally to anticipate the ways in which the series would escalate its fantastic elements:

> The series deliberately asks us to suspend disbelief, as if to ask whether the central scenario is any less plausible than the 9/11 attacks. After all is the world that the 48 survivors inhabit any less weird and threatening than our own? For as is soon apparent this is not your usual story, in the same way that 9/11 changed the narrative of what we understood to be a normal hijacking, LOST has changed the narrative of the disaster epic. This is no ordinary plane crash, there is no rescue and they have been transported to an entirely different place. Nor is there any planned end point to the story or the experience. There is no rescue, no reckoning and there appears to be no understanding because the enlightenment project has run aground. Each revelation instead reveals more hidden layers of questions and weirdness.[11]

What Dunn saw as "a different place" and "more hidden layers of questions and weirdness" had only just started, given that we had not yet traveled through time, into alternate universes as posthumous existential vestibules (or limbo, or whatever fans decide to call Season 6), or discovered Jacob and the Man in Black's relationship. Yet at the same time,

Season 6 seemed strangely less ambiguous and veered closer to a post-9/11 war on terror Manicheanism of Good and Evil that the show had previously avoided. The power struggles between the morally intricate Jack and Locke, as well as with the even more morally compromised, and complex, Sawyer, Kate, or Sayid, seemed to move toward the straightforward duality of golden-boy Jacob and his black-clad, unnamed brother vying to control both the island and its inhabitants. The final movements toward resolving the show's mysteries in many ways also seemed to narrow its complexity. Even as *Lost*'s alternative time line returned its characters to 2004, we were getting farther away from 2001; entering its terminal descent, *Lost* needed to check its existential baggage to prepare for departure.

The End

This move toward philosophical simplification after seasons of moral complexity is understandable. For the finale, *Lost*'s writers almost seem to be taking a page from a classic of literary criticism, Frank Kermode's *The Sense of an Ending*, first published in 1966. Kermode sees narrative ends as inextricably linked to our sense of impending apocalypse: "fictions," Kermode says early on, "whose ends are consonant with origins satisfy our needs."[12] The conventions of story dictate a beginning and an ending, for every "Once upon a time," a "Happily ever after." Kermode goes on to suggest that "one has to think of an ordered series of events which ends, not in a great New Year, but in a final Sabbath" (5). Kermode thus relates the endings of all stories to the endings of all things: narrative endings as death, but also death itself as a narrative ending. As he elaborates, "the End is a fact of life and a fact of the imagination.... As the theologians say, we 'live from the End', even if the world should be endless" (58). *Lost*'s The End provides the same sense of finality, the same sense of an ending: the end of the series, presented specifically as an apocalypse, a Rapture, where all of the (main) characters have died and ascended to a new spiritual place.

The finale in retrospect again presents a title as straightforward as the Pilot, but as well implies a dark ambiguity, since the episode, in keeping with Kermode, marked the parallel ends of the TV series, the story, and each character's life. Faced with the final revelation of the flash-sideways world, Jack meets his father, back from the dead once again, to ask, of his friends, but also presumably of himself, "They're all dead?" Christian Sheppard, his overtly allegorical name never previously uttered aloud (here with sarcastic surprise, by Kate—" 'Christian Sheppard'.

Seriously?"), responds, "Everyone dies sometime. Some of them before you, some of them long after you," telling Jack that their world "is a place that you all made together so you could find one another. The most important time of your life was when you were with these people. That's why you are all here. No one does it alone Jack. You needed all of them and they needed you. ... To remember and to let go."

We, like Jack, come to learn that the final season's flash-forwards were less alternate reality in which the plane never crashed than a purgatory-like dream sequence, in which each character had amnesia and needed to relive a meaningful moment from the island in order to remember who they were. In this way it reverses—and not via time travel—Season 3's traumatic need to relive and reenact, positing the notion that the Lostaways—like all of us suffering from loss—should not necessarily move forward, or backward, or forget it entirely, but rather "remember and let go."

And yet this advice, in the end, seems less about 9/11, whose mantra is still Never Forget, than it is Christian's advice to fans of *Lost*, about to lose their series and characters in a way that even resurrection and the afterlife cannot correct. The last season, then, was self-consciously and self-reflectively about television itself, away from the 9/11 allegory that began it. Indeed, the last scene of The End seems in keeping the flash-sideways of Season 6, much of which was more self-referential than expository. The Side World, until its characters' self-consciousness, could have existed as its own television drama. But it was the intertextual references and reversals that made it resonate with fans: see Sawyer as a cop, in keeping with his LeFleur security persona rather than his grifter ways; see Ben conspire, but when the stakes are for leadership of a high school, not the Others; imagine Jack with a son, able to rework his own father/son problems, and Locke with a wife, Hugo with unambiguous good luck, and more. At the same time, as Seth Stevenson suggests in *Slate*, "What if each week's mainland storyline tackled a different film/television genre?," noting that Sawyer's episode was a buddy cop show, Locke's a *Married With Children*-like sit-com (thanks to Katey Sagal's casting), and Ben's "a demented Saved by the Bell"—to say nothing of the upcoming horseback and flowing hair period romance (Richard) or swords and sandals epic (Jacob).

For nearly all of Season 6, the side world inspired further *Lost*-ian conjecture and mystery: it seemed to show what could have been, the alternate reality popular with so much science fiction, where the removal of the pivotal event—the plane crash—creates the famous butterfly effect. In other ways, the side world was more a parallel than alternate world,

a place to reenact and reengineer the coincidences that originally connected the castaways. But even more than a way to emphasize the foils
between island and sideways worlds, Season 6 has been about television
itself, a *Lost* version of past shows such as *Doctor Who*, *Quantum
Leap*, *Voyagers*, and the more recent *Journeyman*. Perhaps this self-
referentiality is in keeping with what J. Wood noted earlier about the
series: "The *Lost* audience is following the narrative the same way we
witnessed the events of 9/11—on TV, with repeated viewings, and more
in-depth analysis later in the press and on the Internet."[13] Perhaps, with
its trademark close-up of the eye that opened the Pilot and so many of
the early episodes, *Lost* has always been about itself, and about television,
just as 9/11 must be understood as the real, palpable, physical event that
took over 2,000 lives, affected millions more, and brought down the
World Trade Center. It is also the event as captured on camera, and
rebroadcast, and reenacted, and analyzed, as television. Indeed, the vast
majority of Americans, even New Yorkers, have only experienced the
attacks, and the name—"9/11," "September 11"—as television. But even
then, we would still have to go back, for the only way to understand it is
through the kind of analysis and reflection that comes after—not "back."

Yet if The End were only about itself and about television, a ploy to
stitch the cast reunion that followed on *Jimmy Kimmel Live* directly into
the series itself, it also suggests that the survivors are not, and were not,
able to change the past and that the past on the island, their time together,
however terrible at times, is not something that they should want to forget. Perhaps in the end, and The End, we are all lost after 9/11, all castaways struggling to find each other, and ourselves. Perhaps we should
not wish to return to the past or lament the inability to change our fate—
the bomb that concluded Season 5, it seems, failed. Rather, we must
remember, even celebrate, the time we have with those who matter most
in life, since viewers, unlike the castaways, cannot know what will come
afterward.

In retrospect, then, *Lost* has been a show about our post-9/11 fears and
wishes, and about the ways in which narrative and television can best represent them. But perhaps it also was not so different from the question
posed by that first, failed *Lost*'s foray into reality TV: who makes it
home? In the end, Hurley, despite his bad luck, and Ben, despite his
treachery, remain. Lapidus, Miles, Richard, Sawyer, Kate, and Claire
managed to escape—for good, it seems, this time. But in the sideways
time line—which of course turned out not to be sideways as much as
post—everyone, eventually, leaves their island, so to speak. Yes, we have
to go back: return to the island, flash back, time travel—and now,

posthumously, reunite in The End. But we can also go back anytime, to *Lost* and to 9/11, now that the series has concluded and the anniversaries of the attacks continue to accumulate, by watching and thinking about their mysteries again, as thoughtful viewers and close readers, eyewitnesses open to reconsideration, rumination, and thought even now that *Lost*'s eye has closed.

CHAPTER 5

9/11 Did Not Take Place: Apocalypse and Amnesia in Film and Cormac McCarthy's *The Road*

Tribute in Lights, a visual representation of erasure, absence, and loss. (Eduard4us/Dreamstime.com)

In this chapter: *Memento* (2000), directed by Christopher Nolan; *Mulholland Drive* (2001), directed by David Lynch; *Eternal Sunshine of the Spotless Mind* (2004), directed by Michel Gondry; *The Road* (2006), Cormac McCarthy. Additional discussion: *Cloverfield* (2008), directed by Matt Reeves; *War of the Worlds* (2005), directed by Steven Spielberg.

Lost played with framing and temporal narrative devices to represent the problems of traumatic memory and recovery, but a number of films responded very differently. While, of course, many Americans have not forgotten the Twin Towers, in some ways, popular culture has tried to forget. The films under consideration, in their political implications and cinematic aesthetics, represent America's post-9/11 ambivalence, mixed wishes and fears, of forgetting the recent past. Erasure and amnesia become the flipside of the initial 9/11 and imagery—the repeated footage and nonstop coverage. In its attempt to anesthetize America's wounds, or to redeem its suffering, popular culture is eradicating the towers' very image. In doing so, film, rather than healing, runs the risk of completing their destruction. Running counter to the destruction of memory, Cormac McCarthy's novel The Road *presents a dystopic America, whose biggest threat is not terrorists, zombies, or smoke monsters, but the possibility of losing touch with the past and one's identity.*

On September 10, 2001, Americans had two favorite kinds of action movies: special effects–laden depictions of New York City's gratuitous destruction and special effects–laden discoveries, preferably involving gratuitous destruction, that our perceived reality is simulated and unreal. Although the director of *Independence Day* (1996) and *Godzilla* (1998), Roland Emmerich, tried to repeat New York's devastation in *The Day After Tomorrow* in 2004, critics and audiences would not have it. Who by then could feel as though Manhattan's destruction would be a fear, or even an anti–East Coast wish? It had come to pass. Who could feel as though *The Truman Show* (1998) and *The Matrix* (1999) contributed a new truth, that American safety and complacency were tenuous illusions? That, too, had come to pass. Instead, in the years immediately following 9/11, Americans intuitively moved from both genres' operative narratives, a compulsion to uncover the truth—about alien menace or techno-conspiracy—to a desire to forget it. Cultural theorist Slavoj Zizek writes that television responded to the national trauma with "the compulsion to repeat and *jouissance* beyond the pleasure principle: we wanted to see it again and again; the same shots were repeated ad nauseam, and the uncanny satisfaction we got from it was *jouissance* at its purest."[1] But on film, the compulsion to repeat took a new form: toward depicting, and thus mirroring, the traumatic amnesiac, who simply, and dangerously, forgets.

The 2000s may be remembered, or forgotten, as the decade of the amnesia movie, even as it is not formally recognized as a category at all. Two of Jim Carrey's post-*Truman* dramatic efforts, *The Majestic* (2001) and *Eternal Sunshine of the Spotless Mind* (2004), involved characters who have their memories erased. Time may have proven Zizek's pronouncement hasty. Yes, the attacks of 9/11 enacted, and thus undermined, apocalyptic film fantasies of aliens destroying New York or men discovering that their happy reality was an artificial construct. But in the aftermath, Americans moved from a desire to repeat 9/11 to a desire to forget 9/11, to erase it from consciousness and memory. The terrorists may have destroyed the towers, but immediately after 2001, popular culture, through erasure and amnesia, seemed bent on annihilating their emblematic existence, even their history. But as this chapter will argue, the best of the amnesia movies also offer a warning against letting the past disappear. And in *The Road*, Cormac McCarthy, with a few years' hindsight, has rewritten the apocalyptic imagery of pre-9/11 fantasies as an elegiac, chastened mediation on the balancing nature of forgetting and faith, and of terror and storytelling.

Erasing the Past

Immediately after 9/11, erasure as symbolic destruction seemed eerily literal: HBO's "Sex and the City" digitally removed the towers from its introduction;[2] Chock Full o' Nuts Coffee removed its small, signature skyline from the bottom of its cans;[3] "The Simpsons'" Twin Towers–themed episode, "The City of New York vs. Homer Simpson," was temporarily pulled from syndication; trailers and posters for *Spider-Man* showing the towers were shelved; and *Serendipity*, *People I Know*, *Zoolander*, *Men in Black II*, and *The Time Machine* reshot scenes to circumvent the towers or cut scenes deemed egregiously destructive to New York City.[4] *Collateral Damage*, *The Heist*, and *Sidewalks of New York* pushed back release dates.[5] Finally, while the establishing shot of New York in *Maid in Manhattan* indeed depicts a tower-less Financial District, the movie poster substitutes the inoffensive Empire State Building for the standard filmic skyline that has dominated images of Manhattan since the 1970s. Of course, this erasure makes sense. As Max Page writes, filmmakers "claimed that they were simply trying to avoid offending and disturbing audiences unnecessarily. It seems equally likely that filmmakers worried that the sight of the towers would detract from the narrative and undermine the escapist pleasure that is the essence of Hollywood films."[6] Consumers may have had little appetite for a reminder of the towers with their coffee, or for the memory of the towers to intrude, in their absence, upon the American Cinderella fantasy of *Maid in Manhattan*.

But the deletions reveal more than mere good commerce, or good sense. Through these cuts, the towers intrude in their absence, as erasure always leaves traces of the original. As Gayatri Chakravorty Spivak writes in her Translator's Preface to Jacques Derrida's *Of Grammatology*, the seminal text of deconstructive criticism, her

> predicament is an analogue for a certain philosophical exigency that drives Derrida to writing "sous rapture," which I translate as "under erasure." This is to write a word, cross it out, and then print both the word and deletion. (Since the word is inaccurate, it is crossed out. Since it is necessary, it remains legible.) . . . In examining familiar things we come to such unfamiliar conclusions that our very language is twisted and bent even as it guides us.[7]

In this sense, 9/11 represents an act of destruction and deconstruction, twisting the familiar into the unfamiliar and violently demonstrating the ways in which the destruction of the towers, like the crossed-out word, only calls attention to its former existence.[8] Art Spiegelman's September 24, 2001, *New Yorker* cover, and later book cover, superimposing black towers against black background, illustrates this point: erasure creates absence, certainly, but also ensures its own paradoxical presence, as eloquently suggested in Spiegelman's book title, *In the Shadow of No Towers*. Similarly, "Tribute in Light," the 2002 spectral display of high-wattage lamps that now annually pays homage to the Twin Towers, wrote their intangible, luminescent outlines over the erased towers like a palimpsest—an ancient document on which the original writing has been erased and replaced with new writing—emphasizing not what is there, but what formerly existed underneath.

In his introduction to the 2002 collection *Film and Television after 9/11*, Wheeler Winston Dixon suggests that "in this bleak [post-9/11] landscape of personal loss, paranoia, and political cynicism, American culture has been forever changed," and despite the propensity to use movies as escapism, "one salient fact remains: the memory of 9/11 can never be obliterated from the American national consciousness."[9] But Dixon's familiar "we will never forget 9/11" maxim runs counter to what movies after 9/11 have depicted: Americans seemed desperately nostalgic, desperate to forget the present, and wanted desperately to go back—to borrow from *Lost*—to a prelapsarian September 10, the time before the fall, when Americans were free to enjoy their fictional apocalypses without fear or guilt. But unlike *Lost*, time travel—whether narrative or science fictional— was not the answer. Amnesia was.

With all of the "never forget" rhetoric surrounding 9/11, how can such amnesia be possible? While politicians, the architects of the new World Trade Center, and victims have not, of course, forgotten the Twin Towers, Americans, bumper stickers to the contrary, may wish to. Even in 9/11's immediate aftermath, Art Spiegelman saw the divide between New Yorkers, who had no opportunity to forget 9/11, and the rest of the country, for whom New York was only ever a celluloid simulation ripe for destruction:

> Only when I traveled to a university in the Midwest in early October 2001 did I realize that *all* New Yorkers were out of their minds compared to those for whom the attack was an abstraction. The assault on the Pentagon confirmed that the carnage in New York City was indeed an attack on America, not one more skirmish on foreign soil. Still, the small town I visited in Indiana ... was at least as worked up over a frat house's zoning violations as with threats from "raghead terrorists." It was as if I'd wandered into an inverted version of Saul Steinberg's famous map of America seen from Ninth Avenue, where the rest of the known world ends at the Hudson; in Indiana everything east of the Alleghenies was very, very far away.[10]

Yes, politicians have continuously used the attacks for political posturing; most famously, Joe Biden referred to then-presidential candidate Rudolph Giuliani's entire rhetorical repertoire as "a noun and a verb and 9/11." But at best, in keeping with Zizek, turning "9/11" into a repeated mantra has made it an empty signifier. At worst, in keeping with this chapter, Giuliani, other politicians, and some Americans have, in fact, forgotten about 9/11, epitomized by Giuliani's remark that "[w]e had no domestic attacks under Bush; we've had one under Obama."[11] Journalist Dan Amira goes further, saying, "There is a strange amnesia permeating the Republican ranks lately," including Giuliani, Dana Perino, and Mary Matalin, each of whom "seems to be jumping on the '9/11 never happened or at least not on Bush's watch' bandwagon."[12] The gap between remembering the date and agreeing about the nature of an event's cultural, historical, and political significance has grown even vaster in the past decade. For a few years, amnesia became the new apocalypse: a version of the end of the world.

~~Erasing~~ Forgetting the Past

Giuliani and Spiegelman to the contrary, however, Americans traumatized by the attacks could not easily gain comfort in merely erasing or deleting images of the towers. The only symbolic recourse remaining, then, was to erase the memories of the trauma. And forgetting is precisely the trope that cinema embraced after 9/11. Amnesia has long been a dubious film scenario, so much so that "the Screenwriters Guild went so far as to prohibit amnesia as a plot device."[13] Yet amnesia's new form seems different—post-9/11 films do not use amnesia to exemplify American archetypes of rebirth, youth, or lack of history. As Terrence Rafferty suggests, amnesia is the downside of "one of the most unshakable American values: our conviction that we should be free to invent ourselves, and reinvent ourselves, at will."[14] Instead, the best of these movies discordantly center on the loss of a morality that accompanies loss of memory, and by extension, the loss of identity. Writing just before 9/11, Jonathan Lethem began to observe this upcoming urgency in his introduction to *The Vintage Book of Amnesia*: "Amnesia appeared pulsing just beneath the surface, an existential syndrome that seemed to nag at fictional characters with increasing frequency, a floating metaphor very much in the air. Amnesia, it turned out when I began to pay attention, is a modern mood, and a very American one."[15]

Amnesia as a concept and plot device went on to shape and inspire at least 30 post-9/11 releases, many with top actors, writers, or directors: Jim Carrey in *The Majestic*, Tom Cruise in *Vanilla Sky*, Guy Pearce in *Memento*, Matt Damon in three *Bourne* movies, Ben Affleck in *Paycheck*, Halle Berry in *Gothika*, Finnish director Aki Kauronaki's *The Man Without a Past*, Woody Allen's *The Curse of the Jade Scorpion*, Adam Sandler in *50 First Dates*, Pixar's *Finding Nemo*, Brian Singer's two *X-Men* films as well as *X-Men III* and *Wolverine*, Ashton Kutcher in *The Butterfly Effect* and *Dude, Where's My Car?*, David Lynch's *Mulholland Drive*, screenwriter Charlie Kaufman's *Eternal Sunshine of the Spotless Mind*, Quentin Tarantino's *Kill Bill: Vols. I* and *II*, Denzel Washington in *The Manchurian Candidate*, Julianne Moore in *The Forgotten*, Milla Jovovich in *Resident Evil*, Robin Williams in *The Final Cut*, the documentary *Unknown White Male*, Liam Neeson in *Unknown*, Daniel Craig and Harrison Ford in *Cowboys and Aliens*, and Nick Cassavetes's *The Notebook*.[16] *The Notebook* is unusual, in that the amnesia was brought on by Alzheimer's disease. But its exception underscores the problem: amnesia, an exceedingly rare condition in non-elderly people, has likely occurred more frequently on film in the past decade than at any time in real life.

Of course, several of the films, most notably *Memento* and *Mulholland Drive*, cannot be thought of as conscious reactions to 9/11, and neither can Lethem's analysis. Analyzing the amnesia trend, *New York Times* film critic John Leland says that while "it may be tempting to relate them to Sept. 11, the movies were all conceived years before, during the economic boom, which produced waves of collective amnesia."[17] Instead, Leland connects the films to irrational market exuberance, fixation on status, and the fluidity of identity that accompanied the technological capitalism of the late 1990s, when the films were conceived and shot, rather than in the after-effects of September 11, 2001, when they were screened and reviewed. Leland's analysis fairly and, I think, correctly identifies the conditions under which the films were made. But by the time the films emerged, were viewed, and were available for cultural interpretation, the context had, crucially, changed. Had the movies not appealed to viewers' newfound psychic vulnerability, they may have failed and, perhaps appropriately, been forgotten. Instead, *Memento* and *Mulholland Drive* have become cult classics, and Hollywood, as always, took notice. The films' reception remains more salient than their geneses.

In place of the chronological, and certainly in place of the scientific, since "the overwhelming majority of films that portray amnesia do so in a grossly inaccurate fashion," I would substitute the semiotic and the metaphorical.[18] Indeed, James Gorman writes that amnesia films "may seem realistic, but they are really fairy tales. ... An old-time Freudian might take these movies as public dreams and look for a hidden wish. What it would be is clear. Enough! Enough collecting of information. Enough creation of new records."[19] While Gorman does not connect amnesia to 9/11, his point echoes Zizek, who, in his analysis of the pre-9/11 movies that destroyed New York, writes: "[T]he unthinkable which happened was the object of fantasy, so that, in a way, America got what it fantasized about, and that was the biggest surprise."[20] Zizek's "fantasy," the not-so-hidden wish, is renewed but revised through the amnesia imagery. Annihilating civilization is not enough. Instead, amnesia represents the will to annihilate even the memory of civilization. Gorman's "Enough!" rejects technology or bureaucracy, but it also represents a wish to escape psychology, history, and even narrative itself. The prevalent amnesia imagery turned the pre-9/11 apocalypses inside out; rather than destroying the external structures of civilization, the new films destroyed its internal frameworks.

Even so, the amnesia plot device is, of course, nothing new. Soap operas have used it for decades as a slipshod way to bring back written-off characters, explain narrative inconsistencies, or create cheap thrills. Pulp mystery and harlequin romance novels use it routinely as well, for its obvious and readymade drama. But many of the new films are different: together, they represent a post-9/11 ambivalence, the mixed wishes and fears of forgetting the recent past, and the final extension of post-9/11 desire to erase the towers from posters, screens, and coffee cans, to the desire to erase the towers from our collective memory.[21] And the best of these films, *Memento*, *Mulholland Drive*, and *Eternal Sunshine of the Spotless Mind*, do not just use amnesia as a high concept; in addition, they construct a cinematic language of the amnesiac experience, and this visual and aural aesthetic of amnesia places the viewer into the amnesiac's perspective. Lethem's analysis of amnesia in fiction clearly applies to these films: "I had in mind a fiction that, more than just presenting a character who'd suffered memory loss, entered into an amnesiac state at some level of the narrative itself—and invited the reader to do the same. Fiction that made something of the white spaces that are fiction's native habitat or somehow induced a dreamy state of loss of identity's grip."[22] Even genre films like *Paycheck* and the *Bourne* sequels withhold key information, functioning like the third-person limited perspective in a novel, so that the viewer knows only as much as the characters do, and often even less. September 11 may not have been the end of irony, as some pundits hastily predicted, but it challenged dramatic irony: the venerable literary device, where viewers connect and understand that which characters cannot, seems notably absent from amnesia pictures. Instead, the viewer is forced to identify with the amnesiac's plight, confusion, and struggle for comprehension. The ruined topography of pre-9/11 apocalypses turned inward, to the shattered setting of the mind.

In keeping, after beginning with a murder literally in reverse (shooting a double exposure of a backwind), *Memento*, directed by Christopher Nolan (who would go on to make the *Dark Knight* movies), constructs its narrative through fragmented alternation between chronologically backward episodes in color and forward-moving scenes in black and white, continuously reenacting various beginnings and endings. The viewer, like the amnesiac protagonist Leonard Shelby, understands the unending shock and dislocation of memory loss. Leonard spends the film attempting to track down the man who murdered his wife and inflicted the injury that stole his memory, but he must rely on Polaroids, Post-It notes, and even his own tattoos in order to have any sense of where, or even at times who, he is. In keeping with the low-tech hijacking of planes in 9/11, Leonard uses reliable but primitive pre-digital devices, resorting even to his own body as a repository of information. Writing on the body becomes a last refuge against a mind that refuses to accept the indelible; tattoos literally keep Leonard from being a *tabula rasa*, here a state of ignorance over innocence. The film's fragmentation coalesces at the end, which is really the story's beginning, when the viewer finally understands that Leonard may know himself even less well than he, or we, thought.[23]

Mulholland Drive, directed by David Cronenberg, before *Cosmopolis*, is visually and narratively confusing as well—the viewer is left unsure of its main characters' identities, the scenes' chronology, and even whether sequences are dreams or reality. After the opening's car accident, a beautiful woman is left unsure of who she is. Calling herself Rita, based on a poster of Rita Hayworth, she is discovered and cared for by another woman, Betty, a saccharine aspiring actress new to Los Angeles. Together, they attempt to piece together Rita's mysterious identity. Like *Memento*, *Mulholland Drive* seems to put the end at the beginning, forcing the viewer to reconcile the film's final act, in which it seems as though Rita's amnesia, as well as Betty's earnest innocence, may be a dream, sexual fantasy, or projection. Using frequent blurs, ambient sub-bass noise, and surreal juxtaposition, the visual and sonic aesthetics of the movie attempt to recreate the amnesiac experience, and the viewer frequently feels as lost as Rita does, by design.

Of all the recent amnesia films, *Eternal Sunshine of the Spotless Mind* is the most visually reminiscent of 9/11 itself. Jim Carrey's Joel undergoes a procedure to erase his memories of ex-girlfriend Clementine, after discovering that she has done the same of him. Like *Memento*, the film begins near the end, although the first-time viewer has no way of knowing this: it seems to show Joel and Clementine's first meeting but actually reveals their post-amnesia reunion. Through flashbacks within flashbacks, the viewer witnesses the memory erasure from inside Joel's head, so that, as in *Mulholland Drive*, voices are out of synch with mouths and various buzzes and muffling effects obscure dialogue. But in addition, people, like words, disappear in blurs, fog and water darken backgrounds, and, most disconcertingly, buildings shake, collapse, and crumble. The destruction of matter signifies the destruction of memory, and viewers understand that this renewed demolition of New York (even if it is upstate New York, *Spotless Mind*'s location), unlike in *Independence Day*, within the movie is representational rather than literal. But it was the symbolic as well as literal destruction of New York that 9/11's terrorists sought. If these films' characters emblemize our need to forget, they also bring to the surface our repressed posttraumatic turmoil. And in the place of disintegrating buildings, *Spotless Mind* (as well as *Paycheck*) shows images of brains on computer screens, with lit-up neurons targeted and obliterated, along with metaphorical or hypothetical buildings collapsing.

In his essay *Requiem for the Twin Towers*, cultural theorist Jean Baudrillard suggests that

> although the two towers have disappeared, they have not been anni-hilated. Even in their pulverized state, they have left behind an intense awareness of their presence. No one who knew them can cease imagining them and the imprints they made in the skyline from all points of the city. ... By the grace of terrorism, the World Trade Center has become the world's most beautiful building—the eighth wonder of the world![24]

Despite his powerful rhetoric, the luminous, numinous efforts of "Tribute in Light," or Art Spiegelman's sublime work, however, Baudrillard, like Zizek, spoke too soon. The towers' symbolism is endan-gered, overpowered by the culture's need to erase and forget. Baudrillard's own, more contentious conclusion about the first Gulf War, published in 1995, now seems more applicable to the fall of the Twin Towers. At the time, he wrote:

> There is no interrogation into the event itself or its reality; or into the fraudulence of this war, the programmed and always delayed illusion of battle; or into the machination of this war or its amplification by information, not to mention the improbable orgy of material, the sys-tematic manipulation of data, the artificial dramatization ... If we do not have practical intelligence (and none among us has), at least let us have a skeptical intelligence towards it, without renouncing the pathetic feeling of its absurdity.[25]

If Baudrillard still maintains that the criterion for symbolic or actual existence of an event is "interrogation into the event itself or its reality," or "the programmed and always delayed illusion of battle," or "its ampli-fication by information," or "the systematic manipulation of data, the artificial dramatization," or "practical intelligence," or even "skeptical intelligence," then 9/11 never took place. If, thanks to the disappearances of images, the towers never existed, then they never fell. If all traces of the towers are erased from memory and culture, if moviegoers and Americans are metaphorical and metaphysical amnesiacs, then the sym-bolic violence of this amnesia and erasure completes the work of the ter-rorists. For their goal, as Baudrillard implies, was not just to demolish the towers themselves, but to destroy the towers' very significance. It is now our own unwillingness to bear witness to the towers that is annihilating them, expunging them of their posthumous symbolism.

Our hope to forget is forgivable. Just as we found comfort in the apocalyptic imagery of *Independence Day* and *The Matrix* for depicting our simultaneous worst fears and dearest wishes, or maybe dearest fears and worst wishes, we now find comfort in the wave of amnesia, with films that allow us to escape the twin prisons of identity and chronology. What's more, the movies replicate but ultimately reverse one of the most insidious and pervasive fears in the post-9/11 world, discussed earlier in Chapter 1: that the terrorists lived in America and held jobs, and then one day were activated, the word equally applicable to terrorist cells and time bombs. Amnesia films invert this anxiety. *Memento*'s Leonard, formerly a mild-mannered insurance assessor, suddenly becomes capable of detective work, gunplay, and murder, with no explanation; *The Bourne Identity*'s Jason Bourne discovers amazing fighting abilities unbeknownst even to himself; in comic-book films *X-Men* and *X2*, Hugh Jackman's Wolverine possesses superhuman healing abilities, an unbreakable metal skeleton, and retractable claws but no clue about how he became this killing machine—or anything before his mysterious trauma. Later sequels reveal that Bourne and Wolverine were created to be American right-wing quasi-terrorists themselves, reversing the reality of the 9/11 suicide bombers in heroic American fashion: we can all wake up from our everyday lives and routine normalcy capable of detective work, superheroics, and killing, but crucially as an autonomous, heroic individual unattached to a government or even an ideology, working only to solve the personal, existential mystery of who we really are.

Like this reversal of moral alignment, perhaps the amnesia films may be less interested in erasing than in warning us, like *Hamlet*'s Ghost, to remember. In their dénouements, the best of these films do not ever espouse amnesia as much as alert us to its dangers. Like the best film apocalypses, they function as cautionary tales rather than exemplars, correctives for, rather than perpetrators against, destruction, in this case, of memory. Even as they embody our post-9/11 wish to become, in Gore Vidal's disparaging phrase, a "United States of Amnesia," they demonstrate amnesia's ultimate harm.[26] While some, like *Paycheck* or *The Majestic*, with their hackneyed happy endings, imply that amnesia is bliss, opportunity, or resurgence, more serious films self-consciously challenge their own cinematic assertions. In *Memento*, viewers discover that Leonard is incapable of true revenge; instead, in keeping with his former profession, he is using his condition to release himself of any moral accountability, since he remembers neither vengeance nor any crimes committed toward his ends. Indeed, like Leonard's impotent but dangerous retribution, our post-9/11 war on terror—even now, after the moniker has been discarded—may be by definition a war without end, as we moved from Afghanistan to Iraq, with Libya or Pakistan or Syria or Iran on the horizon even after the death of Osama bin Laden. Our 9/11 retaliation may be doomed to be as short lived and continuously deferred as Leonard's revenge. In *Mulholland Drive*, after much confusion, by the end it seems as though Rita's amnesia really is part of Betty's fantasy, one of starting over sexually, romantically, and personally. And in *Eternal Sunshine*, Joel realizes that he needs his memories, despite as well as because of their pain. While he and Clementine understand that their reconciliation may be doomed because it failed the first time, they venture on nonetheless. The pleasures of life and love are more valuable than the ignorant safety of amnesia. Like *Eternal Sunshine*'s memory erasure, these amnesia movies seem a way to ease our collective pain and embody our collective desires. Instead, though, the surprise endings of *Memento* and *Mulholland Drive* depict the dark consequences of amnesia, while *Spotless Mind* suggests its corrective: faith. Perhaps the new American wish and fear is not the complete destruction of time. Warning about the danger of individual and collective amnesia, the films depict specific memories as visible, discrete, separable, and destroyable entities in the mind, substituting vanishing neurons for *Independence Day*'s demolition of New York and *The Matrix*'s ravage of reality.

Yet in the end, the films' amnesias differ medically, not just metaphorically. *Memento* depicts anterograde amnesia: the inability to remember ongoing events *after* the incidence of trauma; *Mulholland Drive*, retrograde amnesia: the inability to remember events that occurred *before* the incidence of trauma. *Spotless Mind*'s electronic targeting of specific memories remains science fiction, although perhaps not for long.[27] Their warnings, thus, are different but equally important: if we as a culture, like Rita, forget everything that happened before the trauma, we are childlike, helpless ciphers for whatever delusion or fantasy those in power choose to impose upon us. But if we forget all that occurs after the trauma; if, like Leonard, we live in a perpetual present; if we lose our ability to form a new future, and by extension a new understanding of the past, then we will be forced, futilely and forever, to relive our suffering. Rita loses her consciousness; Leonard, his conscience. Americans in the aftermath of 9/11 seem in danger of losing both. And if we do, then that loss would be far worse than merely losing our collective memory, or even losing the world, as we have on film so many times. Unlike memory, which in real life, although not in movies, is frequently recovered, or buildings, which are nearly always rebuilt, obstacles to One World Trade Center to the contrary, consciousness and conscience are delicate, precious, and irreparable. Life after 9/11 has been painful, even excruciating. But like Joel of *Spotless Mind*, we must not only reject amnesia; in addition, we must cherish our memories, even our pain. Despite that Clementine reminds Joel that "you will think of things" that he won't like about her and that "I'll get bored with you and feel trapped because that's what happens with me," in the end, we must emulate Joel and Clementine's reply and agree to press forward:

"Okay."
"Okay."

The Road ~~to~~ from 9/11

Not surprisingly, as the decade progressed, amnesia set in with filmmakers and audiences. Yes, Roland Emmerich's *The Day After Tomorrow* (2004), title to the contrary, appeared too soon, but a score of superhero movies and television shows (the *Spider-Man* and *Batman* franchises, *Heroes*), *The War of the Worlds* (2005), *I Am Legend* (2007), *Cloverfield* (2008), and Emmerich's next attempt, *2012* (2009), did not. Whereas in the immediate aftermath of 9/11, movies displayed atypical sensitivity, by 2005 it was safe for Hollywood to destroy New York, and the world, once again. Writing independently of any Hollywood trends—independently, it would at first seem, of anything—Cormac McCarthy published *The Road*, a book that would go on to win the 2007 Pulitzer Prize for fiction. At first glance, the novel seems in keeping the postapocalyptic resurgence of the above-named films, the old fears of a postnuclear holocaust renewed in the aftermath of fresh disaster. Its main conceit—the plight of solitary survivors in a ravaged world—was already well worn by 1981's *The Road Warrior*, let alone by *The Road*, decades and dozens of dystopian narratives later.

But context is crucial, and the shadow of no towers envelops the novel. Of course, just as *Cloverfield* and the rest are not "9/11 movies" in the manner of *World Trade Center* or *United 93*, *The Road* is not a "9/11 novel" in the sense of Don DeLillo's *Falling Man* of Jonathan Safran Foer's *Extremely Loud and Incredibly Close*, each discussed in Chapter 3. McCarthy certainly does not depict the events of the attack on New York or Washington, D.C.; refer to the escape or death of anyone trapped in the World Trade Center; or connect his world in any clear or linear way with America in the 2000s. As Richard Gray suggests, though, "[I]t is surely right to see *The Road* as a post-9/11 novel, not just in the obvious, literal sense, but to the extent that it takes the measure of that sense of crisis that has seemed to haunt the West, and the United States in particular, ever since the destruction of the World Trade Center."[28]

Moreover, the novel clearly displays the apocalyptic tropes of the post-9/11 world: its imagery of the dazed and traumatized man, walking amidst blackened ash and amorphous organic and inorganic debris; its consistent sense of looming, impending, but mostly nameless terror; the haunted vision of a crippled America; and the renewed emphasis on hope, struggle, masculinity, and family that characterized sentiments in America after the attacks. And unlike the aliens, monsters, supervillains, and zombies that infest film's postapocalyptic imagination, humans themselves represent the worst blight, even amidst McCarthy's ruined landscape. *The Road*'s America is despoiled, but even more troublingly, most of its few survivors are morally contaminated as well.

More importantly, however, like *Memento*, *Mulholland Drive*, and *Eternal Sunshine of the Spotless Mind*, *The Road* consistently emphasizes the danger of forgetting one's personal and national past, balancing the dual danger of apocalypse and amnesia. In fact, the unnamed man and his son's physical peril distracts them from the moral danger of their impending, and maybe inevitable, cultural amnesia. As the man explains to his son early in the novel,

> Just remember that the things you put in your head are there forever, he said. You might want to think about that.
> You forget some things, don't you?
> Yes. You forget what you want to remember and you remember what you want to forget.[29]

The man's combination of cliché with antimetabole emphasizes the way in which Zizek's televisual repetition of trauma may not be at odds with the amnesiac's compulsion to forget: people may repeat some elements of the past and suppress others, with the unfortunate likelihood that they will repeat the harmful and suppress the valuable. *The Road*'s intersections between trauma, memory, and redemption thus function as an ethical and literary response to the shock of 9/11, even more than its apparent warnings of disasters environmental or eschatological. Even referring to "the man" and "the boy" underscores the novel's central preoccupation with forgetting, along with the novel's early detail that the man "hadn't kept a calendar for years" (4). While other novels (including *Fight Club*) and movies (for example, Clint Eastwood's Westerns) deliberately do not name their main characters, *The Road* goes further: only one character, Ely, is ever named at all.[30] The lack of proper names certainly suggests McCarthy's allegorical intentions, as other critics have explored.[31] Yet it is not that the characters do not have proper names; rather, their names are under erasure, representing a forgotten past, and by extension lost future, as well as a present in which names no longer serve any purpose. At the same time, the lack of names, like the amnesia movies, continuously forces the reader into the sustained acceptance of narrative ambiguity.

In an interview with *Rolling Stone* magazine, unusual for the reclusive writer, McCarthy describes his experience of becoming a father again:

> Soon after, in 2001, [McCarthy] was visiting Tennessee when the attacks of 9/11 unfolded. Being a septuagenarian dad in the modern age is sobering. "When you're young and single, you hang out in bars and don't think about what's going to happen," McCarthy says. "But in the next fifty years when you have kids, you start thinking of their life and the world they have to live in. And that's a sobering thought these days."
>
> McCarthy began to wonder about the future facing his boy. "I think about John all the time and what the world's going to be like," he says. "It's going to be a very troubled place." One night, during a trip to Texas with John, McCarthy imagined such a place. While his son slept, McCarthy gazed out the window of his room and pictured flames on the hill. He later decided to write a novel about it; *The Road* is dedicated to his son. While McCarthy suggests that the ashcovered world in the novel is the result of a meteor hit, his money is on humans destroying each other before an environmental catastrophe sets in. "We're going to do ourselves in first," he says.[32]

9/11 looms in the background of the novel's genesis, because the attacks, unlike McCarthy's extratextual meteor strike, actually occurred. And while Gray notes that "many reviewers of the book referred to the setting of *The Road* as post-nuclear," unlike *Dr. Strangelove* at the beginning of the Cold War and *The Day After* near its end, *The Road* never explicitly names, discusses, or even mentions the cause of the catastrophe—not as human-made atomic fallout (Gray observes that "there are no signs of radioactivity, and none of the characters suffer from radiation sickness") and certainly not meteors.[33] This decision starkly contrasts the majority of pre-9/11 postapocalyptic movies. The catastrophe is supposed to establish the narrative—say, the war and subsequent plague that kill almost everyone in *The Omega Man*. Or the true cause of the catastrophe must reveal itself in the climax: the surprise that "Soylent Green is people!," or in *Planet of the Apes,* that "I'm back. I'm home. All the time, it was . . . We finally really did it," to cite Charlton Heston's dystopias alone. In *The Road,* the cause, or discovery at the end, is irrelevant and, like the characters, never named. Perhaps it has been forgotten. The novel is not interested in dystopia's usual historical urgency, political commentary, or straightforward adventure. Instead, the book lyrically but discordantly dramatizes the suspended state of an amnesia-like perpetual present: "Like the dying world the newly blind inhabit, all of it fading slowly from memory" (18).

The novel channels the raw shock and suffering after 9/11, the fear of and for the future, and recasts it as a poetic rumination on the stripped-down existence of the man and his son. Certainly other post-9/11 apocalypses draw upon the same semiotics of the attacks. Steven Spielberg's *War of the Worlds* revises the director's earlier broadmindedness toward aliens in *Close Encounters of the Third Kind* (1977) and *E. T. the Extraterrestrial* (1982). Now, aliens are attackers, even as the action, like the film version of *World War Z,* focuses almost entirely on the family drama of Tom Cruise's estranged daughter and son. The film borrows more from 9/11 than from H. G. Wells, using the now-familiar media imagery of the 9/11 attacks: the New York cityscape under siege, the plane crash (with water bottles), the missing persons posters, the dust and paper of bodies and buildings enshrouding everything. But *The Road* is very different from *War of the Worlds* or, in another example, *Cloverfield.* As Stephanie Zacharek suggests, "*Cloverfield* harnesses the horror of 9/11—specifically as it was felt in New York—and repackages it as an amusement-park ride. We see familiar buildings exploding and crumpling before our eyes, and plumes of smoke rolling up the narrow corridors formed by lower-Manhattan streets, images that were once the province of news footage and have now been reduced to special effects."[34] McCarthy's novel takes the opposite approach: no explosions, no falling men or falling buildings, and any plumes of smoke are relegated to the archetypal, burned-out image of "the road," which here has little in common with "lower-Manhattan streets." The book is no amusement-park ride: not the brief, safe, and wordless thrill of simulated physical excitement, but a slow, emotionally painful linguistic reflection on what the end of things would mean not just for humans, but for our humanity.

Literary critic John Cant writes, "*The Road* is a literary return, a retrospective on the author's own previous works, a re-viewing of his own work that offers a different perspective to that of the young man whose vision was structured by the oedipal paradigm that we find in . . . *Suttree* and *Blood Meridian.*"[35] But while Cant then analyzes the novel primarily in terms of its "poetic language and expression of profound ideas,"[36] the main theme of the novel is *itself* "return" and "retrospective," the wishes and fears of remembering and forgetting in a dying world. Indeed, a concordance of all the pages in *The Road* that use the words "memory," forms of "remember," or forms of "forget" threatens to run nearly as long as the novel itself. Yet the ways in which it evokes memory suggests a man who needs his past and his memories even as he finds them painful and futile. Returning to his old house, the man finds "[a]ll much as he remembered it" (26). Later, he tells the boy "old stories of courage and justice as he remembered them" (41). While lost, "[h]e tried to remember if he knew anything about it or if it were only a fable. In what direction did lost men veer?" (116–117). Before scouting and leaving the boy, "[h]e thought about waking him but he knew he wouldn't remember anything if he did" (118–119). Setting up camp, he thinks, "It was as long a night as he could remember out of a great plenty of such nights" (125).

Yet the most troubling description comes when, finding a deck of cards, the man tries

> to remember the rules of childhood games. . . . Sometimes the child would ask him questions about the world that for him was not even a memory. He thought hard how to answer. There is no past. What would you like? But he stopped making things up because those things were not true either and the telling made him feel bad. The child had his own fantasies. How things would be in the south. Other children. He tried to keep a rein on this but his heart was not in it. Whose would be? (54)

The only thoughts worse than the memories are the fictions we create in memory's absence. With the man's—and the world's—past nearly gone, there can be no future. The opposite of memory here is not forgetting; it is "making things up," "fantasy," or falsehood.

In keeping with Cant, readers of *The Road* will notice the hallmarks of McCarthy's earlier style: the poetic turns of phrase, frequent use of fragments, and unusual word choices, all exemplified by this sentence on the opening page: "Their light playing over the wet flowstone walls" (3). And as McCarthy's readers have come to expect, no dialogue is rendered using quotation marks. Certainly, unnamed characters, lack of quotation marks, missing apostrophes ("wont," "cant"), and frequent sentence fragments are not unique to *The Road*, much less to McCarthy. Yet this minimalist rhetoric, derived from writers like Ernest Hemingway and William Faulkner and developed throughout McCarthy's body of work, here becomes a powerful symbol within the larger context of this particular novel and its response to 9/11. Here, the characters, and the world, have been reduced to their most spare. As the duo scavenges for ever-scarcer food supplies (17, 29, 158, 181, and *passim*) or drops of oil (136), McCarthy also uses his words and punctuation marks as though they might soon run out. Similarly, his idiosyncratic vocabulary choices here feel less like poetry and more like makeshift devices, as though he were using the only word left in his verbal shopping cart, just as the man "went through the drawers but there was nothing there that he could use. Good half-inch drive sockets. A ratchet" (6).[37]

Like everything in *The Road*'s barren world, punctuation marks and words have been laid waste, reduced to their bare minimum, so that some sentences are a single word or a handful of words, while others run commaless powered by their own rolling inertia: "He pushed the cart off the road and tilted it over where it could not be seen and they left their packs and went back to the station" (7). Apostrophes after the apocalypse seem wasteful. The lack of quotation marks is even more ominous: even the novelist, it seems, lacks the power, the memory, to recreate words as the characters spoke them. The best we can hope for, in this world, and possibly ours, is the imperfection of indirect discourse, the approximation of what people said based on our fallible and waning memories. *The Road*'s style and language, for what it provides as well as what it withholds, presents the perfect medium for its bleak, terrifying, but ultimately redemptive story.

Not surprisingly, perhaps, despite the awards and critical accolades, *The Road* was voted by online readers the most depressing novel of all time, over Sylvia Plath's semi-autobiographical novel about suicide, *The Bell Jar*, and Elie Wiesel's *Night*, about Nazi atrocities.[38] Throughout most of *The Road*, life seems hopeless, except for the man and boy's bond. Even then, the man is burdened by his memories; the boy, by his amnesia-like ignorance:

Did you have any friends?
Yes. I did.
Lots of them?
Yes. Do you remember them?
Yes. I remember them.
What happened to them?
They died.
All of them?
Yes. All of them. (60–61)

Yet at the end of the novel, despite the man's death, the boy survives and is found by a full family. Just as the man hoped, "Goodness will find the little boy. It always has. It will again" (281). And so when the new unnamed man, the possible adoptive father, finds the boy, the boy asks,

Are you carrying the fire?
Am I what?
Carrying the fire.
You're kind of weirded out, aren't you?
No.
Just a little.
Yeah.
That's okay.
So are you?
What, carrying the fire?
Yes. (283)

As Amy Hungerford observes, "It is hard to decide whether the boy's light is nothing or everything."[39] Clearly, many readers fear it means nothing. Yet the light, the fire, is a clear-cut symbol that the man, the boy, and the new family are, in a refrain repeated as though for light and heat throughout the novel, "the good guys" (77, 103, 129, 137, 140, 115, 184, 245–246, 278, 283). Fire and light also seem straightforward images of divine wisdom and hope, whether that divinity is Prometheus and his gift to humankind, the Hebrew Bible's Creation story, or Jesus saying, "I am the light of the world." And McCarthy's fire and light can be each of these. Certainly a novel that begins in a cave and refers to fire dozens of times pays homage to Plato, author of the most allegorical cave of all. Like "the man" and "the boy," the language feels allegorical, as though McCarthy were less interested in the road than the spiritual journey. Yet I am not ready to accept mere allegory. The novel, unlike Plato's Allegory of the Cave or Medieval morality plays, forces the reader to identify emotionally and often viscerally with the man's struggle and danger, and with his fervent, animal love for his son. For an allegory, the novel—unlike, for the most part, Lost—painfully details the minutiae of physical survival: keeping alive, staying sheltered, finding food, protecting oneself from the elements and bands of marauding cannibals, and moving on. The fire in the novel, then, is God, hope, light, and wisdom. But in the aftermath of 9/11, when physical and metaphysical seem inextricable, sometimes the fire means fire: "He threw the branches on the fire and set out again" (96); "He kept a fire going" (237), and many other instances. The fire may be a metaphor, but it is not an allegory; unlike allegory, metaphor balances relationship between the literal and figurative. The novel as a whole, then, is also not, like *War of the Worlds* or *Cloverfield*, an apocalyptic allegory for 9/11. It is a moving, multilayered metaphor not easily reduced to post-9/11, Manichean oppositions, even its own George W. Bush–like oppositions of good guys and bad guys. It is terrifying but, in the end, like the best apocalyptic tales, strangely comforting. When the man reassures the boy that "I'll be back and then we'll have a fire and then you wont be scared anymore" (72), the boy believes him, and so, within and beyond the novel, do we.

Yet if the fire must be more than fire, and surely it must, then it is not just spirituality or sanctity: it is also memory. When the man sees "a forest fire making its way along the tinderbox ridges above them . . . , [t]he color of it moved something in him long forgotten. Make a list. Recite a litany. Remember" (31). And thus when, in the end, the boy is assured that the new people—a nuclear family of father, mother, little boy, and little girl—are "good guys" and "carrying the fire," the narrative shifts to the boy's perspective for the first time: "I'll talk to you every day, he whispered. And I wont forget. No matter what. Then he rose and turned and walked back to the road" (286). Perhaps this ending is too conventional or conservative for some readers. Yet I believe that McCarthy's moral urgency, represented by both the boy's survival and memory, rescues what seems like a postwar on terror Manicheanism of "good guys" and "bad guys." Richard Gray sees as the conclusion's "sheltering confines of American myth" as "deeply unconvincing."[40] Instead, I would suggest that the original, evocative, and elegiac language, rather than its plotline, allows readers to move beyond apocalypse and toward McCarthy's literary and spiritual redemption.

This final series of tensions—originality and formula, life and death, past and present, end and beginning, memory and forgetting—even more than soot-stained, solitary figures amidst broken buildings and landscapes, evokes McCarthy's, and film's, ultimate narrative response to 9/11. And in one of the novel's last quotation mark–less dialogues, the new man and the boy, exactly like *Eternal Sunshine*'s Joel and Clementine, assure each other that it's "okay":

And can I go with you?
Yes. You can.
Okay then.
Okay.

Still, McCarthy does not end the novel here, or with the boy's quiet eulogy. Instead, the novel concludes with its own tribute to the dead world, one far beyond any potential misgiving about the novel's seemingly conventional conclusion: "Once there were brook trout in the streams in the mountains" (286). But despite the poetry, the fish can never return, and there is no "happily ever after" to close the "Once there were . . ." construction. The world represented by the "vermiculate patterns" on their backs would "not be right again. In the deep glens where they lived all things were older than man and they hummed of mystery" (287). Life after the apocalypse can never return to its previous bliss, if such a state ever really existed. But we can take comfort in knowing that time, in its attendant mystery, exists independently of human loss or memory. There can be no return to September 10, no uncomplicated erasure, no painless amnesia. Nor should there be. But in *The Road*'s postapocalyptic world, or perhaps our own post-9/11 one, saying "okay" to our past, present, and future is good enough. We'll have a fire and then we wont be scared anymore.

CHAPTER 6

Bedtime Stories after the End of the World: Coming of Age in a Future of Fear

From *The Hunger Games: Mockingjay, Part I* (2014): Jennifer Lawrence as Katniss Everdeen, self-possessed even when the world is catching fire. (Lionsgate/Photofest)

In this chapter: *The Hunger Games* (2008), *Catching Fire* (2009), and *Mockingjay* (2010), Suzanne Collins. Additional discussion: *The Hunger Games* (2012), directed by Gary Ross; *Catching Fire* (2013), directed by Francis Lawrence; *Mockingjay—Part 1* (2014), directed by Francis Lawrence; *Harry Potter and the Sorcerer's Stone* (1997), J. K. Rowling; *The World's End* (2013), directed by Edgar Wright; "A Hunger Artist" (1922), Franz Kafka.

In the 2000s, The Road *may be the exception: a postapocalyptic novel intended primarily for adult readers. This chapter analyzes the ways in which Young Adult (YA) fiction of the 2000s has radically shifted from the pre-9/11 beginnings of the* Harry Potter *series, which imagined a secret, magical world, to the post-9/11 dystopian settings of* Hunger Games, *where children and teens live under martial law and perpetual danger. By 2008 through 2010, the years of* Hunger Games' *publication, the disaster of 9/11 had become more distant, especially to a readership that may have just been born around 2001. Yet its world, and similar connected fictions of postmillennial YA dystopia, is less of a reaction to 9/11 itself than it is to the cultural climate of fear ushered in by a decade of ensuing wars, the Great Recession, and cultural divisions. Despite their darkness, though, perhaps these novels, like* The Road, *offer the possibility of hope and justice.*

In a single movie screening at the start of 2015, I saw trailers for a *Mad Max* remake, about dystopian life after the end of the world as we know it; *San Andreas*, featuring Duane "The Rock" Johnson, a giant earthquake, and the end of the world; *Insurgent*, the sequel to *Divergent*, a YA dystopian series based on the novels, themselves indebted to another YA series, *The Hunger Games*; *Avengers: Age of Ultron*, about a robot creating a dystopia by taking over the world; a new *Terminator* film, about robots creating a dystopia by taking over the world; and *Chappie*, about robots that may or may not take over an already-dystopian world.

Even the music of the millennium is a pop apocalypse, indebted to Prince's 1982 Cold War injunction to party like it's 1999, if about a decade too late or a thousand years too early for Justin Bieber, who sings, "We gonna party like it's 3012 tonight" in "Beauty and a Beat" (2012). Reagan-era metal and punk certainly incorporated end-of-times imagery— Black Sabbath's "Die Young" or The Circle Jerks' "Live Fast, Die Young," both released in 1980—but these groups provided underground dissonance for rebellious subcultures. The years from 2010 to 2014 have featured more mainstream top 40 songs extolling young lives cut short than any period since the 1950s and early 1960s, with its teenage death classics like "Teen Angel" (1959), "Tell Laura I Love Her" (1960), and "The Leader of the Pack" (1964). In "Teenage Dream" (2010), Katy Perry sings, "We can dance, until we die/You and I, will be young forever," while also in 2010 Rick Ross (with Kanye West) released "Live Fast, Die Young." In "Die Young" (2012), Kesha sings, "So while you're here in my arms/Let's make the most of the night like we're gonna die young," while fun. sings, "Tonight/We are young/So let's set the world on fire/We can burn brighter than the sun" (2011). One Direction keeps the sun imagery while dialing the death down in "Live While We're Young" (2012), singing, "Let's go crazy, crazy, crazy 'till we see the sun," while Icona Pop's "I Love It" (2012) plays up gleefully destruction: "I crashed my car into the bridge/I watched, I let it burn . . ./I don't care/I love it." The apocalyptic imagery reaches its apotheosis with Imagine Dragons' "Radioactive" (2012): "I'm waking up to ash and dust/I wipe my brow and I sweat my rust/I'm breathing in the chemicals/I'm breaking in, shaping up, then checking out on the prison bus/This is it, the apocalypse/Whoa." Whoa indeed. All of it is parodied by mock-rock band Steel Panther in "Party Like Tomorrow Is the End of the World" (2014): "Get crazy!/Rob a bank or hijack a plane/We got nothin' to lose . . ."

We are living in dystopian times. In less than a decade, Edgar Wright, Simon Pegg, and Nick Frost, responsible for *Shaun of the Dead* (2004), developed that film's local zombie outbreak to full-blown apocalypse in *The World's End* (2013). *Shaun of the Dead*, as the title implies, is an affectionate yet effective satire of the genre, a "zom rom com," or zombie romantic comedy. But *The World's End*, in which aliens replace everyone in the English town of Newton Haven with an adolescent android version of him or her, toward eventual world domination, is not a parody. Like *The Stepford Wives*, the replacements in *The World's End* suggest a conspiracy, but one that is youth driven rather than gender driven. Both *Shaun of the Dead* and *The World's End* orchestrate scenes of synchronized body movements, but *Shaun* wants viewers to see that, in our habits and conformity, humans are like zombies even before they are transformed into them, while the choreography in *The World's End* shows the opposite. Here, Gary King and his friends are coolly independent of everyone except for fellow members of their own crew, with whom they have found their community. No one wants to be a zombie, but when presented with the chance, nearly everyone in Newton Haven gives themselves up to be replaced by mechanized "blanks"—the term coined when Gary and his friends cannot think of a name for them—because, unlike Gary, they are already blank. The Blanks simultaneously represent the beauty and possibility—the blank expanse—of youth and technological progress, but at the expense of one's humanity, wrapped in a narrative of Gary's midlife crisis of getting older and missing the glory days of his never-finished pub crawl.

Iconoclast Gary rejects the prospect of being a Blank, literally and figuratively. Throwing off the shackles of middle class and middle age, Gary and his mates get drunk, fight, and tear up everywhere they go, yet they are clearly the heroes, despite the occasional pep talk about needing to grow up. When the aliens leave Earth and send humanity back to a pre-technology dark age, Gary gets to relive his reckless adolescence, accompanied by young Blank versions of his old friends. The ironic ending suggests that youth, or at least arrested development, becomes an asset in postapocalyptic times, a sentiment shared by the similarly named, similarly dystopic comedy *This Is the End*, which came out in the same year. Unlike *The World's End*, the majority of dystopian films and novels in the 2000s and 2010s, like the songs above, were not aimed at adults, but rather, at teens and preteens. And their messages seemed the same: about the dangers of adults and growing up, and the intertwined fears of social rejection and death. And ironically, they all universally espouse the virtue of nonconformity. Yet as bad as it is to grow up, the dystopian stories aimed at young adults, unlike *The World's End*, do not glorify being young at all. In *The Hunger Games*, Katniss Everdeen, like fun, like the incendiary concluding image of *The Road*, sets the world on fire. And it is terrifying. But Top 40's alternative, dying young, is even worse.

Nearly all of the post-9/11 novels, films, and television shows discussed so far can fall loosely under the mantle of dystopia. If a utopia, derived from Greek, is a good place, then at its simplest, a dystopia is its opposite, a bad place.[1] The primal scene of 9/11 on the opening page of Don DeLillo's *Falling Man* is only understood as the streets of New York after the Twin Towers fall later in the novel. As a cold opening, it could set up nearly any urban postdisaster scene—terrorism, a zombie apocalypse, or a future in which the totalitarian government destroys its districts at will, where everything, even mundane paper, is rendered dangerous and uncanny: "The roar was still in the air, the buckling rumble of the fall. This was the world now. Smoke and ash came rolling down streets and turning corners, busting around corners, seismic tides of smoke, with office paper flashing past, standard sheets with cutting edge, skimming, whipping past, otherworldly things in the morning pall."[2] The explosions and cults in the novels of Chuck Palahniuk, the desiccated sites of *World War Z*, the desert island of *Lost*, the unexplained environmental ravaging of *The Road*, each demonstrates that the end of times—like "the year

2000" in DeLillo's *Cosmopolis*—is upon us. Or worse, that the end has already happened, and these stories all take place in the aftermath. Fiction after 9/11, whether it addresses the fall or not, remains, to borrow from Art Spiegelman, in the shadow of no towers.

Yet these examples stand apart from popular culture's biggest end-of-the-world phenomena, what might paradoxically be called the New Dystopia of the 2000s and 2010s. What may be most striking about this dystopian resurgence in fiction and film is its intended audience: with its teen protagonists, it is aimed squarely at young adults. Like previous literary dystopias such as Aldous Huxley's *Brave New World* (1932) and George Orwell's *1984* (1948), *The Road* is a book that adults may find scarier and more upsetting than teens. Its allegorical father and son, attempting to survive the entwined threats of starvation and predation, may overlap thematically with the stories of the New Dystopia. But *The Road* is clearly narrated through the emotions of the father, at least until the very end, and its terrors are principally parental: not just one's own death, but the failure of a father to protect his child. As novelist Benjamin Percy puts it, "Reading this book [after the birth of my son] put me in a mindset that made me particularly vulnerable to the subject matter. *The Road* is ultimately about a father sacrificing everything for his son—keeping on and surviving despite a nightmare landscape, and only for his son's sake. I felt plugged into that current in a way that I don't know I would have if not a father."[3]

Percy's "current" comes from the same post-9/11 fear that President Bush articulated in his December 2001 speech, which continued to shape the national narrative about terror: "September 11th, 2001—three months and a long time ago—set another dividing line in our lives and in the life of our nation. An illusion of immunity was shattered. A faraway evil became a present danger. And a great cause became clear: We will fight terror and those who sponsor it, to save our children from a future of fear."[4] Like the father in *The Road*, like any decent parent, really, the symbolic father of the country wanted to "to save our children from a future of fear." Adults like Benjamin Percy aspire to be the father in *The Road*: selflessly saving their children from harm and horror. But what if, like abusive parents, the adults in charge of "our children" are not their saviors, but the very source of terror? What if, a series like *The Hunger Games* seems to ask, it is the abusive adults who need to be saved? Instead of saving children, the New Dystopian novels rewrite the *bildungsroman*—the coming-of-age novel—as a literal rather than figurative fight for identity and survival, so that, first, our children must save themselves, and then they must save their world. Yet even President Bush's possessive "our" children no longer seems apt. Katniss struggles throughout *The Hunger Games* against possession and manipulation by powerful, even presidential, adults. If *World War Z* referred to its postwar youth as Generation Z, playing on who will follow Gen X and Gen Y, then perhaps we are experiencing the insurgence of the Dystopia Generation, Generation D—or the D Generation.

The Rise of Young Adult Dystopia

In 1997, *Harry Potter and the Sorcerer's Stone* started teaching a generation of young readers to hope, on their 11th birthday, for an owl with their invitations to Hogwarts School of Witchcraft and Wizardry. The magic of the books was about much more than flying brooms and spell-casting wands—it was the magic, the possibility, of reading itself. Just 11 years later, in 2008, the appeal of *The Hunger Games* seemed radically different: no readers would fantasize about being entered into the Hunger Games' tribute lottery at age 12.

Or would they? *The Hunger Games'* UK website offers online simulations, asking readers-turned-gamers to "test your abilities and see if you will be able to survive the real thing. Remember, there is only one path to survival."[5] Fantasy, for Sigmund Freud and as I have discussed, operates on the contrasting yet simultaneous levels of wishes and fears. *Harry Potter* embodies a range of wish fulfillment—first, magical thinking, another term coined by Freud, where our thoughts alone affect the world, the space between what we imagine and what is vanishing. But the magic of *Harry Potter* is also the childhood wish fulfilment of true friendship, as Harry meets his two best friends almost immediately. The wishes continue on, like magic: a procession of protective surrogate parents—Dumbledore, McGonagall, Lupin, Arthur Weasley, Sirius Black, even Snape—stand in for Harry's lost mother and father and replace the pernicious Dursleys. The childhood ordeal of school—middle school and high school, for many students the worst years—is inverted to be the most wonderful place in the world. Even the food is magically delicious. Of course, the series dramatizes fears as well: in book after book, powerful dark forces try to kill Harry. The *Harry Potter* books transmute childhood fears—of being an orphan, of school, of magic and monsters—into wishes of control. Like many fairy-tale orphans before him, Harry has no parental rules. His school gives him power—enough to take on all of the monsters in his life, even the Dursleys.

The Hunger Games, then, reverses *Harry Potter*. The New Dystopia first revolves around terror: threats of starvation and death; loss of self, mind, and identity; and the loss of freedom and the end of the current social order. Despite the dark premise, though, *The Hunger Games* is also filled with wishes: escape from a stultifying social order; to be chosen and recognized as special; given clothes, food, and servants; allowed—encouraged!—to remove one's rivals; and the fantasy of saving one's self, family, and society just by being true to one's authentic identity. All that, and two handsome love interests. Perhaps most of all, we see teen Katniss Everdeen given adult status and adult responsibilities, a powerful simultaneous wish and fear for prospective YA readers. While the series follows many conventions of literary genres that long predate 9/11, at the same time it recasts its wishes through the culturally specific fears of the post-9/11 generation: of a suffocating life in a society suffused with both rules and spectacle, feelings of generational apathy, a supposed profusion of selfie-styled narcissism, and a barrage of constant media-stoked threats.

Harry Potter's setting and style belong to a genre, I think, of "secret worlds," with predecessors in L. Frank Baum's *Wizard of Oz* (1900), J. M. Barrie's *Peter Pan* (1911), and C. S. Lewis's *Chronicles of Narnia* (1950–1956), and successors in Neil Gaiman's *The Graveyard Book* (2008)—a take-off on Rudyard Kipling's *The Jungle Book* if the boy were left in a haunted cemetery to be raised by ghosts instead of animals—and Lev Grossman's *Magicians* trilogy (2009–2014), which places college-age students in a more realistic school for wizards. In these stories, readers see the people of our world as we know it—Muggles, or Kansans—deadened by lack of magic real and metaphorical. But then the young protagonists —Harry Potter, Wendy Darling, Dorothy Gale, the Pevensie siblings— who are seemingly ordinary, discover, or are invited into, a closet kingdom, by means of some mundane threshold: a hidden train, a magic car, fireplace, or even a boot—or a simple window, or an actual closet in *The Lion, The Witch, and the Wardrobe*. There, they discover that the world is full of previously invisible possibilities and that they are special and integral to saving it. The book's pages function as that magic wardrobe, opening and taking the young reader into its realm. While danger obviously must ensue, the books begin and remain inherently hopeful that the world will be saved and that it is worth saving. Particularly in *Harry Potter* and *Narnia*, a peaceful status quo existed before evil infiltrated the magical world. Their tone is essentially optimistic—the characters and narrative seek to restore order from chaos, even if part of that restoration means sending the satisfied protagonist back home, to apply the valuable lessons of the adventure to what he or she comes to understand as real life. By the end of the series, Harry Potter has reinstated what we understand to be the proper pillars of love, family, and community, the Voldemort Years and corruption of the

Ministry of Magic as awful aberrations rather than the way the world is supposed to be.

Conventional wisdom dictates that the *Harry Potter* books began as lighter reading before the series grew up, becoming more and more adult as its readers aged with it. With *Harry Potter and the Goblet of Fire* (2000), the series darkens: Voldemort becomes embodied once again; a Hogwarts student, Cedric Diggory, dies; and the wizard community begins to turn against Harry. *The Hunger Games* seems to pick up where *Harry Potter* grows up, even down to the teen tournament that turns fatal. A *New York Times* article about the possible audience for *The Hunger Games* film adaptation (2012) suggested that the books and films may be trying to "follow the 'Harry Potter' model, which succeeded as perhaps the first middle-grade novel to bring in adults to both the reading experience and the movie theater. As Harry and his Hogwarts friends made their way into the upper grades, the stories themselves became darker and more sophisticated—decidedly young adult."[6]

In Suzanne Collins's *Hunger Games* series, as well as other books such as *The Bar Code Tattoo* (2004), *Uglies* (2005), *Unwind* (2007), *The Knife of Never Letting Go* (2008), *Gone* (2008), *The Maze Runner* (2009), *Ashes, Ashes* (2011), *Divergent* (2011), *Feed* (2012), and more, including several movie adaptations, the new YA genre is not secret worlds but, like the film, the world's end.[7] Narnia, *Harry Potter*, Neverland, and Oz were always utopian, if also utopias in peril. Some of that threat included an apocalyptic sensibility, especially the Christian-inflected *Last Battle* in Narnia, but also late-series *Harry Potter*, with its sense of an impending showdown between the forces of good and evil. But the postmillennial books are different. They are dystopian, not just apocalyptic but postapocalyptic. The world never does come to an end for Harry Potter, Narnia, or even Lev Grossman's Filory, despite his mature revisions to the secret worlds idea. Panem, the totalitarian state in *The Hunger Games*, comes to exist after some unknown natural disaster has eradicated the United States as we know it, and, presumably, the forces of democracy have already lost. Sixteen-year-old Katniss Everdeen has never known anything other than the perpetual famine and strategic deployments of fear by Panem's seat of power, the Capitol. The battle, it seemed, was over before she was even born.

The New Dystopia owes more to George Orwell, Aldous Huxley, and Ray Bradbury than to J. K. Rowling, but it also seems indebted to the Cold War melancholy of 1960s through the 1980s that led to literary science fiction by Kurt Vonnegut, J. G. Ballard, Margaret Atwood, and adult end-of-the-world films like *Planet of the Apes* and *Mad Max*, both of which have been brought back out for the 2010s. Who in 2000 would have guessed that the most influential YA novel published in the 1990s would not be *Harry Potter*, but rather Lois Lowry's *The Giver* (1993),[8] about a dystopian society controlled by The Elders, bent on eradicating difference, and that must be rescued by a 12-year-old? Even in 1993, book reviewer Natalie Babbitt wrote, "The story has been told before in a variety of forms—Ray Bradbury's *Fahrenheit 451* comes to mind—but not, to my knowledge, for children."[9] The previous generation's dystopian narratives were not aiming for YA readers—or the malls, the suburbs, and multiplexes. But this one clearly is.

Perhaps in addition to being influenced by 1950s dystopias like *Fahrenheit 451* (1953), the New Dystopia also develops thematically from *The Lord of the Flies* (1954). That book is, or was, a staple of high school reading, in part because its initial childhood wish fulfillment—complete freedom from adult supervision and even adult society—quickly turns to adult cautionary tale. Reading it, high school students are compelled to understand just what would happen if they stopped listening to grown-ups. It may seem exciting to live in a world without adults, but the kids' adult-free tropical desert island utopia turns dystopically deadly even more quickly than it did on *Lost*.

The nature of adults in the New Dystopia is very different as well. In *Gone*, as the title suggests, all of the adults simply disappear, so that unlike the unfathomable "sudden departure" in the adult novel *The Leftovers*, or the entirely fathomable rapture in *Left Behind*, *Gone* becomes a domestic, science-fictionalized *Lord of the Flies*, with the wish fulfillment of a world without grownups but not the guilt of internecine violence.[10] In *Gone*, *Uglies*, *Unwind*, and *The Hunger Games*, the reader comes to grasp how fragile, how flimsy, and how arbitrary the veneer of adult society really is. In these stories—taking place at or after the end of our world, rather than, like *Harry Potter*, *Narnia* and the others, parallel to the world that we know—the absence of protection is adult society's fault, not an accident, like in *Lord of the Flies*, or the act of a single, evil individual, like Voldemort. The true fear of the books goes beyond food or even death. As *The Giver* makes explicit, the nightmare is that these dystopias came about deliberately, because of trusted adults' calculations, and that most of the adults do not consider their world dystopian at all. Instead, they represent some adult version of utopia, the good place. The revelation of the world's end is not a shock or twist, like Charlton Heston classics *Planet of the Apes* or *Soylent Green*, or the ending of Shirley Jackson's story "The Lottery" (1949), another precursor to *The Hunger Games* where children are selected for sacrifice. It is a given, simply the way the world is—and, for the adults in power, the way it should be.

The shift from wardrobes and broomsticks to teenage death matches should not come as a surprise. With their dark subject matter and end-of-the-world anxieties, the genre's popularity suits its time. As writer and teacher Melissa Ames puts it,

> [T]he post-9/11 climate . . . has instilled and perpetuated a climate of fear, which they [young adults] have become a part of (e.g. the rhetoric of the Bush administration; media pundits with their endless prophetic predictions of future disasters). Teens are now entrenched in the culture of the 24-hour news networks and connected to social media, which constantly expose them to depictions of terror, extremism, and violence. Arguably, the cultural "mood" created by the abovementioned factors influences their literary choices. Although teens may not be conscious of fears related to 9/11, they are a part of the social and political climate—a climate that provides a ripe context for these dystopian texts.[11]

Or as Julie Bertagna, author of the YA *Exodus* trilogy, writes, "Have teenagers, fed on an everyday diet of terror—war, recession, floods, hurricanes, earthquakes, swine flu—become disaster junkies?"[12] Consider that 12-year-old middle-schoolers reading *Mockingjay*, the third book in the *Hunger Games* series, when it was published in 2010 would have had no memory of a time before 9/11 and the twenty-first century. They have only, and always, known social media and cyber-bullying, TSA checkpoints, NSA surveillance, the Patriot Act, U.S. military presence in the Middle East, economic crises, increased media attention to police violence against civilians, and the greatest income divide between the rich and the poor since the age of robber barons. Dystopian novels exaggerate and make literal the metaphorical power struggles and hungers that teens—and, based on their readership, many adults—immediately recognize and that the era of terror has thrown into sharp relief. But one series in particular deserves specific attention.

The Hunger Games

From the title onward, *The Hunger Games* separates itself from the whimsically British sounding *Harry Potter and . . .* series as well as the single-word titles of its dystopian contemporaries (*Gone, Uglies, Unwind*). Like so many YA titles, *Harry Potter* is eponymous, while many of the New Dystopian series, whose characters are in search of their identities, are named after events. The juxtaposition of "hunger"—somber—and "games"—playful—is striking but not unique. German author Franz Kafka had already written his short story "A Hunger Artist," a candid and depressing mediation about a man who starves himself for the entertainment of others. Although the story was published in 1922, it is already nostalgic, looking back on the golden era of starvation artists, a real-life phenomenon where men would live in cages, their wasting made public for gawking spectacle. As the story opens, "During these last decades the interest in professional fasting has markedly diminished. It used to pay very well to stage such great performances under one's own management, but today that is quite impossible."[13]

The story, like all of Kafka's work, is difficult to interpret. Is it autobiographical and symbolic, with emphasis on the word "artist": starving artists as hunger artists, sacrificing themselves for their art? Is the hunger artist a Christian martyr or Christ symbol himself, sacrificing his body for the seeming benefit of others, even if those others do not know it? Is the story sincere or ironic: does Kafka really think that slow starvation is a "great performance"? Is the hunger artist a victim of a vicious society, or the perpetuator of a con, making a living literally doing nothing? Is he misunderstood, as he believes, or does he misunderstand himself? The tone of the story is spiritual and existential, but in the twenty-first-century cultural context of eating disorders, reality television, and viral video micro-celebrities of dubious talent, he now seems anorexic and narcissistic, equally food and attention starved, and psychiatrically disordered rather than acetic, otherworldly, or even especially alienated.

The Hunger Games seems a contemporary heir to Kafka's hunger for answers. Like "A Hunger Artist," *The Hunger Games* is also nostalgic, not because the days of starvation are behind it, but because they are ahead. In this futuristic, totalitarian dystopia, America is now Panem, a strange amalgam of technological advancement amidst a semifeudal society of gaping inequality. In order to circumvent rebellion, Panem's Capitol uses a lottery to select two teenaged contestants—"tributes," one boy and one girl—from each of the 12 districts, elevates them to celebrity status, has them model haute couture and eat haute cuisine, makes them smile and wave on state-run television, and then broadcasts their gory fight to the death, with a single winner rewarded with permanent income and safety (or so we are led to believe). The name Panem comes from the Roman expression "panem et circenses," or "bread and circuses": that is, if the poor are given enough to subsist on and a healthy distraction from their own penury, they will not rise against the system—or if the poor are kept struggling, they will not have the strength to rebel even if they wanted to.

The Hunger Games themselves are obviously central to the plot, but for adult readers they may not make literal or political sense, especially since Panem seems to have neglected to provide its namesake bread (a recurring image throughout the series), and its circus consists of boys and girls, not professional gladiators, killing one another. While *The Hunger Games* frequently alludes to Ancient Rome,[14] despots throughout the twentieth century have successfully fomented fear and quashed insurrection through straightforward, low-concept mass murder: concentration camps, pogroms, public executions, killing fields, and disappearances. The Hunger Games, instead, serve as state-sanctioned terrorism directed at its own people, "intended to intimidate or coerce a civilian population," part of the FBI's legal definition of terrorism.[15]

The Hunger Games may be best understood as a narrative device and metaphor rather than a realistic political tool, yet one that young adults coming of age in the era of terror may relate to all too well. The tournament allows author Suzanne Collins to establish and build conflict—the bread and butter of story—in a methodical and incremental manner. The built-in narrative arc of the elimination competition explains its frequency, from reality TV shows of the 2000s (*Survivor*, *The Biggest Loser*, *The Weakest Link*, *The Bachelor*) to novels (Stephen King's *Running Man* and *The Long Walk*, Koushun Takami's *Battle Royale*) to gladiator films (*Spartacus*, *Gladiator*, *Pompeii*). As a metaphor, however, the idea of the Hunger Games is even more powerful. At their most basic and in their capriciousness, the Hunger Games embody fear: fear of being chosen, or not being chosen and therefore fear of a loved one being chosen instead; the fear of killing, and the fear of being killed, repeated year after year. Those fears, as we have seen in the 9/11 novels, *Twilight*, *Lost*, and *The Road*, vary widely in range, from the narrowest—about only the self—to the family, city, country, and the world. Rather than minimize or domesticate personal fears, *The Hunger Games* collapses the space between them and public fears. Fear for one's friends and family, or for one's self, becomes indistinguishable from fears for the whole society. The series dramatizes the mantra of 1960s counterculture, that the personal is political.

Early in *Catching Fire*, for example, when Katniss kisses Gale during her politically expedient public engagement to Peeta, she first thinks of the illicit romance in the way any teenager working through her emotions might: "I tried to decide how I felt about the kiss, if I had liked it or resented it, but all I really remembered was the pressure of Gale's lips and the scent of the oranges that still lingered on his skin. It was pointless comparing it with the many kisses I'd exchanged with Peeta. I still hadn't figured out if any of those counted."[16] This seeming domestic love triangle immediately has life or death consequences, however, as Katniss fears that now the despotic ruler of Panem, President Snow, might harm Gale, Peeta, or her family because of the kiss. Relationships in the novels of 9/11 seemed symbolic of rifts in the culture, but in the post-9/11 New Dystopia, they *are* the rifts. The title of *Catching Fire* refers to the political uprisings that spread after Katniss defies the Capitol with her feigned love for Peeta in *The Hunger Games*, but it could just as easily refer to her relationships with Gale and Peeta themselves, while the icy President Snow works to extinguish them both, and Katniss's life as well.

Terror is central to the would-be participants in the Hunger Games just as it is central, if in less heightened form, to its readers. The series combines ancient cultural fears that have arguably been magnified since 9/11. Collins herself suggested that the book's genesis came from a juxtaposition of the ancient and modern. On the one hand, Collins explains, the series is

> very much based on the myth of Theseus and the Minotaur, which I read when I was eight years old. . . . As punishment for displeasing Crete, Athens periodically had to send seven youths and seven maidens to Crete, where they were thrown into the labyrinth and devoured by the Minotaur, which is a monster that's half man and half bull. Even when I was a little kid, the story took my breath away, because it was so cruel, and Crete was so ruthless.[17]

In the same interview, Collins continues that she was inspired to write when "[o]ne night, I was lying in bed, and I was channel surfing between reality TV programs and actual war coverage. On one channel, there's a group of young people competing for I don't even know; and on the next, there's a group of young people fighting in an actual war. I was really tired, and the lines between these stories started to blur in a very unsettling way. That's the moment when Katniss's story came to me."[18] Even young adults who have not participated in reality television or the military, however, understand the scrutiny of today's heightened surveillance; the image of life as a competition, emblemized best by reality TV but including the Likes, Shares, Friends, and Followers that young adults both loathe and covet; conformity versus independence; and inequality, whether of money, appearance, or status. Readers don't need to go to war, appear on TV, or wait for the catastrophes of *The Hunger Games* to recognize their everyday incarnations. Being crowned prom queen or king and selective college admissions are zero-sum games. Unlike Hogwarts, real-life high school already feels like a dystopia, so Collins wrote a dystopia that feels like high school. As *Uglies* author Scott Westerfeld puts it, "Dystopian literature is just like high school: an oscillation between extremes of restraint."[19] In *Uglies*, all teens receive full-body plastic surgery at age 16 to eliminate every flaw, but in doing so, their authentic identities—as well as the critical thinking sectors of their brains—are wiped out as well. *Uglies* represents the tension between wanting to be yourself and wanting to fit in, that contradiction of aspiring to be a part of an accepted group while also yearning to be noticed as an individual, the paradox of adolescent attention. *The Hunger Games* embodies Westerfeld's "oscillation between extremes of restraint" even better than his own series. When the Capitol isn't forcing Katniss into extravagant clothing and depilation so she can be on her best behavior in front of strangers, it is forcing her to kill her friends.

The Hunger Games becomes an era-of-terror hyperbolic high school, where each kid competes for limited resources, hoping yet fearing that she will be catapulted into the spotlight, going back and forth between fashion show and death match, pushed by a hypercompetitive culture of achievement and selectivity to view her friends as rivals. The most powerful adults, like President Snow—a white-bearded patriarch so unlike benevolent Dumbledore—lurk behind the scenes of the operations, adversarial upholders of their self-sustaining, crooked status quo. Even if, as political policy, the Hunger Games fall short, or, unlike the novels of 9/11, the *Hunger Games* books do not attempt to incorporate real-life events, "only someone insensitive to the emotional tenor of the story could regard social criticism as the real point of Collins's novel," critic Laura Miller writes. "*The Hunger Games* is not an argument," Miller continues. "Dystopian fiction may be the only genre written for children that's routinely *less* didactic than its adult counterpart. It's not about persuading the reader to stop something terrible from happening—it's about what's happening, right this minute, in the stormy psyche of the adolescent reader."[20] No wonder YA and adult readers find the genre so enticing, then: YA literature provides an emotional and narrative urgency—crucial to contemporary culture—that other forms of writing choose not to.

In another shift from the *Harry Potter* series, *The Hunger Games* books indeed prop the reader directly into the "stormy psyche" of Katniss Everdeen, who is not only the main character, but also the first-person narrator. Even more than its magic, *Harry Potter*'s third-person narration, with Rowling's ability to seamlessly change perspectives between her own arch commentary and a character's way of perceiving the world, lent the books much of their appeal. Literary critic Harold Bloom condemned Rowling's writing a few years after the first book was released, stating, "Her prose style, heavy on cliché, makes no demands upon her readers. In an arbitrarily chosen single page—page 4—of the first 'Harry Potter' book, I count seven clichés, all of the 'stretch his legs' variety."[21] But Bloom, who also recommends reading the book "very quickly," was not reading closely enough. The "legs" of the offending "stretch his legs" passage belong to Mr. Dursley, as does the passage's third-person limited perspective. Dursley has yet to learn that his magical infant nephew Harry will soon be living with him. At this point, he is merely suspicious about an assembly of owls in daylight, eerie people in cloaks, and a strangely sentient cat who is loitering outside his insistently ordinary home. However, Dursley then proceeds to have "a perfectly normal, owl-free morning. He yelled at five different people. He made several important telephone calls and shouted a bit more. He was in a very good mood until lunchtime, when he thought he'd stretch his legs and walk across the road to buy himself a bun from the bakery."[22] The clichés are not Rowling's but Dursley's, the unselfconscious musings of a portly, cruel, and utterly conventional man. The language represents the way in which he sees the world, through the ironic distance of the narrator, who knowingly understands that walking across the street, especially for a sweet, does not count as exercise. When Rowling employs clichés, she does so purposefully, in this case to allow the reader to understand—and dislike—the character under examination.

In an otherwise favorable *New York Times* review, YA author John Green writes, "The concept of [*The Hunger Games*] isn't particularly original. . . . Nor is there anything spectacular about the writing—the words describe the action and little else."[23] At first, the writing does seem prosaic. If Harold Bloom felt as though the prose style of *Harry Potter* makes no demands upon the reader, he would have chaffed even more at the writing in *The Hunger Games*. Rowling's often long, complicated sentences and uses of rhetorical figures of speech give way to Collins's stripped-down syntax and concision, a style consistent across YA dystopia. In keeping with Bloom, here is an arbitrarily chosen single paragraph from early in the first *Hunger Games* book:

> In the fall, a few brave souls sneak into the woods to harvest apples. But always in sight of the Meadow. Always close enough to run back to the safety of District 12 if trouble arises. "District Twelve. Where you can starve to death in safety," I mutter. Then I glance quickly over my shoulder. Even here, even in the middle of nowhere, you worry that someone might overhear you.[24]

If Bloom were still counting clichés, he might cite "brave souls," "trouble arises," "glance ... over my shoulder," and "middle of nowhere," four clichés in as many lines. Yet again, the number of clichés is less important than how the passage positions them. The writing style, then, is misleadingly unsophisticated. Instead, the prose works in several ways. Again, as in *Harry Potter*, the narrator is calling attention to contrasts—"brave souls" is sarcastic, just as the notion of state-provided "safety" is ironic, since the state is the sole source of danger; it supposedly keeps its citizens secure from outside threats even as they waste away within the electrified fences, which we learn about on the same page. The seeming cliché of "middle of nowhere" also becomes ironic, since no place is free from surveillance; there is no middle of nowhere. Most importantly, the language and perspective belong to Katniss, and they help us to understand her—terse, stressed, constantly fighting for survival with no spare energy for frivolous thought or poetic language. Her verbal austerity represents the way in which she sees and treats the world, reminiscent of Cormac McCarthy's implication in *The Road* that a lack of material possessions makes its way into a character's very thought process. Words and punctuation marks, like food, energy, or, for Katniss, arrows, are scarce and valuable resources, even within Katniss's internal monologue. Katniss speaks even fewer words aloud than she thinks, knowing that the Capitol may use any word she utters against her—or worse, against those she cares for.

Green concedes that the style—again, that "the words describe the action and little else"—suits the story: "by not calling attention to itself, the text disappears in the way a good font does: nothing stands between Katniss and the reader, between Panem and America." But I think the writing does even more. In passage after passage, Katniss herself tries to disappear, so that the seeming disappearance of the text becomes another lens into her thoughts, as opposed to simply a recitation of her thoughts themselves. Katniss, ironically for a first-person narrator but emblematically of adolescence, is trying not to be seen or heard even as she thrusts herself in the public eye.

While critics like Bloom would see little in common between Suzanne Collins and Irish novelist James Joyce, often considered the greatest fiction writer of the twentieth century, in *The Portrait of the Artist as a Young Man* (1916), his coming-of-age novel, Stephen Daedalus famously proclaims, "I will tell you what I will do and what I will not do. I will not serve that in which I no longer believe, whether it call itself my home, my fatherland, or my church: and I will try to express myself in some mode of life or art as freely as I can and as wholly as I can, using for my defence the only arms I allow myself to use—silence, exile and cunning."[25] Stephen's eloquence meets its flipside in Katniss's sometime simplicity, yet their weapons—"silence, exile and cunning"—are the same, the armaments of underdogs, youth, and terrorists alike. Unlike Stephen, though, Katniss's fight is more than spiritual, so she must also use arrows.

Yet Katniss is not an artist or a young man. *The Hunger Games* succeeds as a narrative despite that the odds are not in its favor: through Katniss, Collins provides a believable lens into a story line that at once feels familiar yet improbable. She creates suspense even when the reader knows that Katniss must survive and makes a story of child-on-child murder acceptable for children. Unlike the bloodthirsty denizens of the Capitol or cowed population of the Districts, readers witness the brutality but neither cheer nor cower.[26] We hear the story through Katniss and feel her pain. But more than creating a compelling story, the series advances ideas about gender that complicate Susan Faludi's assertion that "in the post-9/11 reenactment of the fifties Western, women figured largely as vulnerable maidens."[27]

It could seem, after films like *Aliens* (1986) and *Terminator 2* (1991), that female heroes were at last the norm. But in their time, Ripley and Sarah Connor were still regarded under the subset of female heroes, not just heroes. Unlike them, Katniss is simply, unselfconsciously herself, not a representative of gender awareness. Katniss is tough and cunning, but not book-smart; often as self-preserving as she is altruistic, even if, like Kafka's hunger artist, she seems to sacrifice herself for her sister, Prim, and others whom she loves. She is skilled at traditionally masculine tasks like hunting, and she is often lucky, but cursed with the kind of luck that comes after the self-evident disasters of living in Panem and fighting in the Hunger Games. In other words, she is far more like Harry Potter than Hermione Granger, more Peter Pevensie than Susan. When Susan Pevensie receives a bow and arrow from Father Christmas in *The Lion, The Witch, and The Wardrobe*, unlike the boys and their swords, she is admonished to use it " 'only in great need ... I do not mean for you to fight in the battle,' " for " 'battles are ugly when women fight.' "[28] Fictional girls are the smart ones, the boy's sister, the main character's girlfriend, the protected or rescued: supporting characters, in every sense of the word. In *Harry Potter*, Ginny Weasely manages to be every one of these; in *The Hunger Games*, Katniss is not any of them. She is the narrator, protagonist, and hero. But she is not nearly invincible—readers rightly fear for her safety, just as we feared for Harry's, and her soul, her integrity. Yet at the same time, the book, by being narrated through Katniss's perspective, never says, or needs to say, anything overt about gender at all.

On the surface, Katniss's two love interests seem to set up another *Twilight*-like romantic triangle, but the dynamic and resolution run contrary to conventional representations of gender in popular culture. Like Edward Cullen and Jacob Black, Gale Hawthorne and Peeta Mellark have opposite characteristics; their only trait in common seems to be their love for Katniss Everdeen. Gale is tall and physically powerful, and like Katniss he has "straight black hair, olive skin, [and] gray eyes" (8); Peeta is "medium height, stocky build, [with] ashy blond hair that falls in waves over his forehead" (25). Unlike the names in *Twilight*, however, the names of the romantic leads are all androgynous, as is each character. Gale, whose name means a strong wind current, shares his name with Dorothy's surname in *The Wizard of Oz*, and hawthorn is a genus of tree or shrub.

As his name and behavior suggest, Gale is an outdoorsman and a man of nature. The novel introduces him as he and Katniss enjoy the morning before the reaping, the lottery in which the names of the tributes will be selected: "From this place, we are invisible but have a clear view of the valley, which is teeming with summer life, greens to gather, roots to dig, fish iridescent in the sunlight. The day is glorious, with a blue sky and soft breeze" (9). In context, the description seems more foreboding than comforting. Once again, Katniss's own narration functions like a clear window, allowing the reader to see through her, to observe what she observes. Yet Collins, unlike Katniss, is more self-aware, ironically foreshadowing the way in which Katniss will soon lose her invisibility, and that this Eden just outside the electrified barbed wire cannot be sustained. True to their botanical names, Katniss and Hawthorne are subject to reaping.

Like hawthorn, katniss is also a plant, but unlike it, Katniss's name is one of the few that is explicated in the novel:

> In late summer, I was washing up in the pond when I noticed the plants growing around me. Tall with leaves like arrowheads. Blossoms with three white petals. I knelt down in the water, my fingers digging into the soft mud, and I pulled up handfuls of the roots. Small, bluish tubers that don't look like much but boiled or baked are as good as any potato. "Katniss," I said aloud. It's the plant I was named for. And I heard my father's voice joking, "As long as you can find yourself, you'll never starve." (52)

While John Green is right that usually Katniss's "words describe the action and little else," this passage describes the action but also much more. The appearance of the plant resembles an arrowhead, appropriate for an archer. Katniss, like her namesake, also "does not look like much," the casting of Jennifer Lawrence in the film adaptations to the contrary. Katniss describes herself (and Gale) as looking like "most of the families who work in the mines" (8). But beneath the surface, literally for the kat-niss root, Katniss is life giving and life sustaining. And her father's advice, "As long as you can find yourself, you'll never starve," sounds far less lit-eral, about food and the body, than spiritual and philosophical. Again and again, Katniss indeed needs to find herself, her integrity, even as she strives for silence and invisibility.

Unlike many female YA or fairy-tale heroes, and more like Oskar Schell in *Extremely Loud and Incredibly Close*, Katniss seems to have learned far more from her father, who died in a mine explosion before the books began, than from her mother, about whom she is often ambiva-lent. Katniss thinks of her father and hears his voice in her head fre-quently. She inherits her bow from him (5), tells us that her father "was particularly fond of mockingjays," (43) the bird that comes to symbolize hope and the rebellion against the Capitol, and she learned to shoot rab-bits "with my father's guidance" (51). At the end of the Hunger Games, in symmetry with the voice that reminds her of her namesake's nourish-ment, Katniss thinks, "I lean down to scoop up a few [berries], rolling them between my fingers. My father's voice comes back to me. 'Not these, Katniss. Never these. They're nightlock. You'll be dead before they reach your stomach' " (318). Her father's voice saves her (and Peeta's) life, and her training and quick thinking allow her to improvise the ploy that frees them both from the games. Ultimately, the combination of opposite foods that Katniss learned about from her father—the sustaining katniss and the deadly nightlock—sets in motion the series of events that will end Panem's famines and the Hunger Games themselves.

If Katniss is a hunter, Peeta, the baker's son whose name is a phonetic spelling of a kind of bread, is a gatherer. While Katniss goes on the offen-sive, Peeta protects himself in the Hunger Games passively, by hiding and painting himself, a skill he learned by decorating "fancy cakes with flowers and pretty things painted in frosting. . . . Somehow the whole thing—his skill, those inaccessible cakes, the praise of the camouflage expert—annoys me"; " 'It's lovely,' " Katniss tells him. " 'If only you could frost someone to death' " (96). Peeta behaves more like *Twilight*'s Bella—sensitive, romantic, pining for Katniss—while Katniss and Gale are both more like Edward—aloof, noncommittal, prone to disappear-ance. This dynamic alone would be an interesting gender reversal for the novel, since the outdoors, hunting, and activity are traditionally associ-ated with masculinity, while decorating, baking, and passivity have been associated with femininity. But the story does more: during the Hunger

Games, after Peeta's leg is severely injured, and an improvised rule change forces Katniss and Peeta to team up, Peeta's injuries make him more of a liability than an asset for Katniss. Yet not only does she need to protect Peeta, she also needs to protect his male ego, so that as she's protecting him, she has to make him believe that he is, in fact, comforting her:

> Twenty-one tributes are dead, but I still have to kill Cato. And really, wasn't he always the one to kill? Now it seems the other tributes were just minor obstacles, distractions, keeping us form the real battle of the Games. Cato and me.
>
> But no, there's the boy waiting beside me. I feel his arms wrap around me.
>
> "Two against one. Should be a piece of cake," he [Peeta] says.
>
> "Next time we eat, it will be in the Capitol," I answer.
>
> "You bet it will," he says. (327)

Edward may continuously rescue and protect Bella without any self-consciousness or subterfuge, yet Katniss must win the Games, support Peeta, and convince Peeta that the fight is really "two against one." Even as Peeta's fighting skills are minimal and his noisy walking gives away their position, she lets him believe it "should be a piece of cake." (Even Peeta's clichés are domestic and derived from baking.) Once the games are over and she has recovered, Katniss discovers that Peeta's leg has been amputated. In his name, vocation, position as rescued rather than rescuer, the one who longs for love rather than the one who dispenses it, and now in his symbolic castration, Peeta is rendered less conventionally male and masculine than the typical hero or romantic love interest—certainly less so than Edward Cullen, Gale, or even Katniss.

But unlike Bella, who was always going to choose Edward, her cold, white, bad boy vampire, over Jacob Black, the warmhearted, loyal boy in puppy love, in the end, Katniss chooses Peeta, not Gale. Her last name, Everdeen, like evergreen and her plant-like first name, symbolically could have paired her with nature boy Gale Hawthorne. But Katniss is not naive—not ever green—and she rejects the somber worldview of Gale's other namesake, Nathaniel Hawthorne, the author of *The Scarlet Letter* and other moralistic tales. Unlike Bella Swan, Katniss and Peeta subvert their gender roles, but, like the narration, do so invisibly. And unlike her Victorian counterparts in fairy tales or the novels of Jane Austen or the Bronte sisters, Katniss marries the nice guy who has always loved and sustained her when she was hungry. In a flashback, we learn that Katniss's first meeting with Peeta came when he deliberately burned loaves of bread—incurring his parents' corporal punishment—so that Katniss could have it when she was starving (30–31). And with that bread, and the glance she shared with him, Katniss saw "the first dandelion of the year. A bell went off in my head. I thought of the hours spent in the woods with my father and I knew how we were going to survive" (32). Peeta provided the bread that Panem, despite its name, never did.

Near the end of *Mockingjay*, Katniss eavesdrops on Gale and Peeta's conversation as they talk "almost like friends. Which they're not."[29] Gale says,

> "I think it's unlikely all three of us will be alive at the end of the war. And if we are, I guess it's Katniss's problem. Who to choose." ...
>
> "I wonder how she'll make up her mind."
>
> "Oh, that I do know." I can just catch Gale's last words through the layer of fur. "Katniss will pick whoever she thinks she can't survive without." (329)

Katniss is angered by the remark: "It's a horrible thing for Gale to say, for Peeta not to refute. Especially when every emotion I have has been taken and exploited by the Capitol or the rebels. At the moment The choice would be simple. I can survive just fine without either of them" (330). But after the final traumatic events of the series, survival is not trivial, and like the end of *World War Z*, no one survives "just fine." Survival alone may be the most that former citizens of Panem's districts can hope for. Like Chuck Palahniuk's survivor Tender Branson, in the end what Katniss needs most now is to write her own story: "I got the idea from our family's plant book. The place where we recorded those things you cannot trust to memory" (386). And like Oskar Schell and the traumatized families in the novels of 9/11, she needs to love the people around her:

> We learn to keep busy again. Peeta bakes. I hunt. . . . We're not alone. A few hundred return because, what has happened, this is our home. . . . Peeta and I grow back together. . . . I wake screaming from nightmares of mutts and lost children. But his arms are there to comfort me. . . . What I need to survive is not Gale's fire, kindled with rage and hatred. I have plenty of fire myself. What I need is a dandelion in the spring. The bright yellow that means rebirth instead of destruction. The promise that life can go on, no matter how bad our losses. That it can be good again. And only Peeta can give me that. (387–388)

The image of the dandelion—another plant, a weed, and a hearty survivor itself—returns, and so does the image of Peeta putting his arms around Katniss, a gesture during the first Hunger Games that she did not find reassuring and may have seen as a sign of weakness. Now, she finds consolation. While again, the ending of domestication, marriage, and heteronormativity puts the series in line with the endings of the other novels—from *Fight Club* to *Extremely Loud and Incredibly Close* to *The Road*—and films—from *World Trade Center* to *World War Z*—*The Hunger Games*' overall treatment of gender, particularly for a YA series, deserves attention, in part because it does not call for it. In the novels of secret worlds, the girl is a Hermione Granger or a Susan Pevensie—laudable, but never the title character: the Harry Potter, or even Aslan, who is male, as opposed to the villainous White Witch. Yet in *The Hunger Games*, the female protagonist is not demoted from the title, like Wendy Darling, who once shared the novel's name with Peter Pan,[30] or set aside, as Lucy and Susan Pevensie are from their own Peter, who gets to slay the wolf and is crowned Peter the Magnificent, High King of Narnia, with authority over his siblings. *The Hunger Games* has no Peter—only Peeta.[31] And Katniss chooses him, not the other way around.

The World's End in the Real World

In the wake of the New Dystopia's popularity, popular culture for adults is trying to catch up with YA. Journalist Alan Weisman published *The World Without Us* (2007), and the History Chanel ran *Life After People* (2008–2010), examples of what might be called apocalyptic speculative nonfiction. Margaret Atwood, who laid the groundwork for the New Dystopia, continued developing her dystopic vision in the Madd-Addam trilogy. Novels like Edan Lepucki's *California* (2014) borrow from the same influences as the New Dystopia. And movie reboots or prequels like *Dawn of the Planet of the Apes* (2014) and *Godzilla* (2014) update the originals' Cold War subtexts for post-9/11 apocalypticism.

Yet for all their current popularity, and all of our familiarity with them, dystopian worlds can still feel like political Rorschach tests, where readers see the meanings that reflect their own minds, or simply what they want to see. Like *The Road*, *The Hunger Games* feels allegorical. But an allegory for what? The books and films may be YA entertainment, but popular culture lends itself to analysis, discussion, and even action. Still, Laura Miller cautions critics from reading the books as social criticism. Unlike previous literary dystopias like *1984* and *Brave New World*, which "detail the consequences of political authoritarianism and feckless hedonism [, describing] what will happen if we don't turn back now," readers of *The Hunger Games* are not looking for political implications: "Children," Miller continues, "don't run the world, and teen-agers, especially, feel the sting of this."[32]

But Miller's restraint has not stopped adult readers from responding, and rightly so. Writing from the perspective of the left in the *Huffington Post*, Russell C. Smith and Michael Foster say that *The Hunger Games* seems like a critique of free-market capitalism. Like Miller, they cite Orwell, but for the opposite reason:

> In the same way Orwell wrote about 1948 and titled his novel *1984*, one can ask whether *The Hunger Games* is a reflection of our current world or a warning of horrific things to come. Is the tip-off also in the title? Aren't we all hungry for a world where innocence doesn't have to be needlessly killed off, much less where blood sport as entertainment sinks down to appeal to younger and younger audiences, becoming more real as it continues in a downward spiral? In the meantime, *The Hunger Games* poses the question: Is all of this the inevitable result of Winner-Take-All Capitalism?[33]

Yet because the teen heroes are not struggling against usurpers, but rather against the legitimate machinations of an overreaching government, conservatives have a very different reading.

Writing from the right in *Forbes*, John Tammy says, "The novel is a boisterous comment about the certain horrors of big government," concluding that "Back in the real world, something similar is at work. Though agreement is not uniform, and our government not nearly as oppressive as the one in 'The Hunger Games', many Americans simply want to be left alone, to get their lives back. 'The Hunger Games' seems to channel this natural, and very American, urge to be free."[34] And Andrew O'Hehir splits the difference, noting that "the politics of Katniss Everdeen's struggle against the effete and decadent elite of the Capital in the 'Hunger Games' series are impossibly vague, as if designed to allow both left-wing anarchists and right-wing black-helicopter paranoids to sign on." O'Hehir then provides a more interesting and sophisticated reading: "When we convince ourselves that 'Divergent' or 'The Hunger Games' contains any sort of lesson about resisting authority or speaking truth to power, we have already accepted their central premise that personal liberty, as defined by contemporary capitalism, is a precious virtue and that it might someday be under threat from somebody, somewhere."[35]

Writing in March 2014, however, O'Hehir may have been too provincial and hasty. Just months later, in November 2014, protestors on the other side of the world would appropriate an image from *The Hunger Games* in genuine real-life dissent:

> A Thai theater chain has withdrawn the latest "Hunger Games movie after several student protesters were detained for using a gesture taken from the films, a three-finger salute of resistance to authoritarian government. The salute, which in the movies is a daring act of silent rebellion, began to appear here in the weeks after the May 22 coup [by military dictator General Prayuth Chan-ocha]. The authorities warned that anyone raising it in public could be subject to arrest.[36]

Perhaps *The Hunger Games* has a lesson about resisting authority after all. As a direct result of the novel-turned-movie, Thailand suppressed protest and a film about an authoritarian government's suppression of filmed protest.

The story from Thailand made it to the *New York Times*. But another connection to *Mockingjay*, despite being closer to home, did not. A different news story was dominating American headlines and screens. Just days earlier, a grand jury decided not to indict white police officer Darren Wilson for shooting Michael Brown, an unarmed 18-year-old African American, in Ferguson, Missouri. In anticipation of the verdict, and even more so in the aftermath of the decision, protests developed across St. Louis and Ferguson (part of St. Louis County), which would spread to other American cities and cities around the world over the following weeks. Yet missing from most of the reports—about the grand jury, the rallies, and what turned into violence and property damage—was that, while awaiting the grand jury's decision, protestors graffitied the line "If we burn, you burn with us," from *Mockingjay* (100), onto the base of St. Louis's national monument, the Gateway Arch.[37] Katniss's metaphorical fire had spread beyond the pages of the novel, beyond the screen, and into what at least some protestors felt to be their own dystopia, a world where police forces could take citizens' lives without consequence.

Michael Brown's death, the grand jury's decision, and the subsequent protests separated American opinion starkly, often across political and racial lines. The same white readership who saw Katniss and the rebellion against the Capitol as fighting against the oppressive force of state-sanctioned violence did not extend the parallel to the real-life demonstrators. Some members of the audience who cheered for protests in imaginary

Districts or the attacks against the state in *Mockingjay*, in District 5 and District 8, condemned real-life protestors as criminals, although to citizens of the Capitol, that is what Katniss's rebels are as well. Peaceful protesters were lumped together with looters and rioters, yet their voices were sometimes silenced, and their efforts ignored. Readers will sympathize with Katniss, in *Catching Fire*, when the use of emetics during parties in the Capitol—" 'Everyone does it, or else how would you have any fun at a feast?' " (79)—makes her "think of ... the emaciated bodies of the children on our kitchen table as my mother prescribes what the parents can't give" (80). But they may be slower to accept the staggering rates of income inequality in America—that, for example, "St. Louis' 20 percentage point gap between the unemployment rate of African Americans and white Americans is the largest of any city in America, according to the Census," conditions that potentially lead to feelings of anger and powerlessness.[38] When *Forbes* writer John Tammy says, "The Hunger Games' seems to channel this natural, and very American, urge to be free," he means free from federal taxation, the only specific example provided, not police overreach; overall, more conservatives and whites disagree that the police and justice system discriminate, while many liberals and blacks agree.[39] The protestors of the Darren Wilson decision did not see exaggerated allegories of high school or capitalism, for better or worse, in *The Hunger Games*. They saw themselves—not in the future, but right now. The protests for Michael Brown—and, subsequently Eric Garner and Tamir Rice, also killed by police after Brown—created an American dialogue about police power and brutality, and the language of *The Hunger Games* gave protestors the image that they needed. Dystopia was not in the future, not hyperbole or allegory, but the world as it is, right now. And if some readers did not recognize that protestors might feel that their America was dangerously close to Panem, a familiar if fictionalized version of a violent police state, then perhaps they now have a sense of what it must have been like to live in the Capitol during *Mockingjay*'s revolution.

Yet when young adults read the book in the years to come, they will not think about Kafka's Hunger Artist, or the book's unpoetic, survivalist language. They may or may not think of the protests set off by Michael Brown's death in Ferguson, although I believe they will think deeply about power, inequality, and violence. They may not notice that Katniss has ushered in a new literary era of nonchalantly female heroes, or the wave of movies, for young adults and adults alike, that have made the end of the world trendy. Readers will simply take Katniss for herself. And they will read the book as it is: a coming-of-age story that is about terror, then survival.

In the end, aren't they all?

The secret worlds of Neverland, Narnia, and Harry Potter may have aspired toward utopia, but the stories set in literary dystopias have, ironically, made readers feel optimistic: about their fears and their futures; their hope and their voices; millennial representations of power, youth, and gender; and even the possibility of justice. *The Hunger Games* is Katniss's story, even as her narrative transparency allows readers to feel her fear and her persistence. At the very end, she finally claims her story from her manipulators, no longer concerned, as she was at the beginning of *The Hunger Games*, "that even in the middle of nowhere, you worry someone might overhear you" (6). Perhaps dystopia does not mean the end of the world after all. Katniss and Peeta will not party like it's 1999, but neither do they die young. It turns out that the reports of the world's end have been greatly exaggerated.

CHAPTER 7

The Absurd Hero: Escapism, *The Dark Knight* Trilogy, and the Literature of Struggle

From *The Dark Knight Rises* (2012): Bane and Batman, foils in battle and contrasting masks. (Warner Brothers/Photofest)

In this chapter: *Batman Begins* (2005), *The Dark Knight* (2008), and *The Dark Knight Rises* (2012), directed by Christopher Nolan. Additional discussion: *The Amazing Adventures of Kavalier & Clay* (2000), Michael Chabon; *X-Men* (2000), directed by Bryan Singer; *Man of Steel* (2013), directed by Zack Snyder; *The Myth of Sisyphus* (1942), Albert Camus.

After 9/11, stories about the end of the world were rewritten for kids, while stories about saving it turned dark, for adults. And while 2000 provided readers and viewers with a Pulitzer Prize–winning superhero novel and debut X-Men *film that changed the direction of superhero stories, subsequent films all clearly take place in a post-9/11 context. In its imagery, story, and tone, Christopher Nolan's* Dark Knight *trilogy remains the most dynamic yet morally ambiguous, overtly drawing upon the conflicts and symbolism of terror even as it does not present a coherent message about the post-9/11 world—or a conventional superhero story line. Superheroes present a reversal of war-on-terror narratives that reimagine monsters as alluring—here, heroes are outsiders, even if they have audience allegiance and sympathy. And if young adult dystopia is in the end ironically optimistic, are the never-ending sequels and never-ending fights in superhero films signs of hope in the war on terror, or futility?*

In the year 2000, predictions to the contrary, the world did not end. In fact, it proved to be a fateful year for the pop-cultural icon best known for saving the world: the superhero.

Even as Brad Pitt's charismatic killers of the 1990s would give way to the 2000s and its cinematic zombies, sparkly vampires, sympathetic aliens and amnesiacs, and postapocalyptic adolescents, their seeming flipside was the explosion of superhero movies. Until the millennium, superfans had to be content with the once-a-decade anomalies of Richard Donner's *Superman: The Movie* (1978), Tim Burton's *Batman* (1989), and their sometimes uninspired sequels, with Teenage Mutant Ninja Turtles as the only significant new comic-book adaption of the 1990s. While comic-book industries themselves were enjoying record-breaking profits (which, like other economic bubbles of the 1990s, would not last),[1] superhero movies languished. *The Punisher* (1989), which would be rebooted not once but twice in the 2000s; *Captain America* (1990), not to be confused with the eventual 2011 success *Captain America: The First Avenger*; and comic-movie nadir *Fantastic Four*, produced in 1993 and never released: the 1990s proved to be as dark for cinematic superheroes as they were a boon for celluloid split personalities.

That changed after the 9/11 attacks. The word "hero" was everywhere: one political cartoon, representative of many, asked, "Who is your favorite superhero? Superman [] Batman [] Fireman []." DC comics released *9-11: The World's Finest Comic Book Writers & Artists Tell Stories to Remember*, its cover featuring a small Superman looking up at a huge billboard of firemen, policemen, and rescue workers while uttering the word "Wow."[2] During his September 16, 2001, speech, President George W. Bush vowed to "rid the world of the evil-doers," referring to "evil-doers" five times, along with "evil people," "evil folks," "a new kind of evil," and "this kind of evil."[3] In time, the public would stop directly conflating 9/11 and superheroes. But as critic Shaun Treat writes, "It seems hardly coincidental that superheroes flourish during traumatizing wars abroad and an economic crisis inherited from Gilded Age corporate corruption at home, but a post-9/11 superhero zeitgeist? Since 2001, more comics-based superhero movies have been released than in all the prior years combined, doubling their domestic box-office average ($3 billion conservatively) with 'darker' superhero franchises ahead."[4] Treat goes on to treat this "post-9/11 superhero zeitgeist" cynically. Yet, as this chapter will explore, the surfeit of superhero films seem plaintive expressions of post-9/11 anxieties, with their prevailing atmosphere of fear and recurring plots about terrorists attacking New York (or Gotham, or Metropolis). Yet at the same time, they represent primal wishes about how the world could have been different, and, perhaps, despite our era of terror, still may be.

Revising the Golden Age: *The Amazing Adventures of Kavalier & Clay and X-Men*

Superheroes, however, seemed poised to fly before 9/11. The year 2000, not 2001, provided readers with Michael Chabon's superhero novel *The Amazing Adventures of Kavalier & Clay*, which won the Pulitzer Prize in 2001, and the first movie to revitalize the genre, Bryan Singer's *X-Men*.

The Amazing Adventures of Kavalier & Clay begins with the 1939 creation of comic-book hero The Escapist by Sammy Clay, né Clayman, a closeted 17-year-old gay Brooklyn Jew, and his cousin, Josef Kavalier, a 19-year-old Czech émigré, magician, and escape artist. But the novel goes on to encompass World War II, the 1954 Senate hearings about comic books and juvenile delinquency, the Golem of Prague, and more. A work of fictional history and historical fiction, Chabon's 639-page novel appropriates aspects from the lives of Jerry Siegel and Joe Shuster, the real-life creators of Superman, along with comic-book legends Will Eisner,

Stan Lee, and Gil Kane, all of whom spoke with Chabon,[5] while the Author's Note ends with an acknowledgment of "the deep debt I owe in this and everything else I've ever written to the work of the late Jack Kirby, the King of Comics" (639).

More than the context of superheroes, though, the novel brings their subtexts to light. In Chabon's deft prose and narrative structures, themes of lost fathers and homelands, alienation and difference, love and identity, and, of course, heroism—sometimes difficult for nonfans to see beneath comics' Ben-Day dots of masks, muscles, and macho posturing—interconnect and surface. As the novel dramatizes, during the Golden Age of comics (for most readers, the late 1930s to the mid-1950s), writers often drew directly from the American prewar and World War II–era experiences—particularly, those of immigrants and Jews; all of the seminal figures named above are Jewish. These experiences led to a powerful "assimilationist fantasy," as comic great Jules Feiffer put it, that "underneath the schmucky façade live men of steel."[6] Superman, perhaps the first and greatest comic superhero, is a kind of super-immigrant, one who, like the immigrants of his day, assimilates flawlessly, speaks the language, and knows the natives better than they know themselves. As Sammy Clay realizes late in *The Amazing Adventures of Kavalier & Clay*, "They're all Jewish, superheroes. Superman, you don't think he's Jewish? Coming over from the old country, changing his name like that. Clark Kent, only a Jew would pick a name like that for himself" (585).

As the novel makes clear, superhero fantasies long predate their renewed imagery after 9/11 and postwar on terror context.[7] And they have been political from the beginning. Superheroes went to war in the pages of comic books even before America itself had been attacked at Pearl Harbor or became a superpower. The most dramatic illustration of this phenomenon comes from the cover of 1941's *Captain America* #1, a hero co-created by Kirby, who, like Jerry Siegel and Will Eisner, enlisted to fight in World War II. The comic featured the red, white, and blue super-soldier punching out Adolph Hitler himself. As historian Bradford Wright explains, "Like many patriotic superheroes of World War II, Captain America declared war on the Axis months before the rest of the nation did."[8] Chabon writes the scene into his novel—with his hero The Escapist doing the punching, and then, naturally, escaping.

In featuring these conflicts—and much more—Chabon rejects the notion that somehow superheroes may not be the appropriate subject matter for a supposedly serious novel, treating his heroes and characters with affection as well as critical introspection. While other writers, including philosopher and novelist Umberto Eco in his essay "The Myth of Superman" (1972), had begun to analyze superheroes, Eco's approach, typical of semiotics, implied that anything, even comics, could be parsed if the analyst were clever enough. Chabon insisted that the comics themselves—as well as their creators, characters, and story lines—merited consideration, even celebration. Nearly the end of the novel, which features an imaginary hero whose symbol, anticipating Jonathan Safran Foer's novel, is a key, and an aspiring escape artist who breaks free from real manacles as well as Nazi-occupied Europe, Chabon makes the metaphor of escape explicit: "The newspaper articles that Joe had read about the upcoming Senate investigation into comic books always cited 'escapism' among the litany of injurious consequences of their reading, and dwelled on the pernicious effect, on young minds, of satisfying the desire to escape. As if there could be any more noble or necessary service in life" (582). The same charge of mere escapism would be directed against postmillennial superhero films by, among others, film producer Ted Hope, who complained, "There's no reality whatsoever ... Our entire culture is still based on escapism, on not living in the real world."[9]

At the same time, however, much of the appeal of Chabon's novel—as well as its contemporary, *X-Men*, also released to commercial and critical acclaim in 2000—is precisely the way in which it navigates the spaces *between* reality and fantasy. Like Chabon (who, in 1996, himself wrote an *X-Men* film treatment that was solicited and then rejected by 20th Century Fox[10]), director Bryan Singer and screenwriter David Hayter take the emotional yearning and political undertones beneath the spandex seriously. This handling was considered a gamble at the time, even as in retrospect *X-Men* should have seemed a safe bet. *X-Men* was adapted from a best-selling comic, came after a successful 1990s television cartoon, and starred two accomplished British thespians, Patrick Stewart and Ian McKellen, who brought gravitas rather than condescension to their roles as the telepathic Professor X and his friend and enemy, Magneto. The film's harrowing opening scene, depicting a young Erik Lehnsherr—who will become Magneto—torn from his parents in a Nazi concentration camp, is distinctly un-comic book-like, far from "not living in the real world," despite the mysterious magnetic powers young Erik begins to manifest. And the film's deliberate pace, somber story line, and austere color scheme already signaled that the superheroes of the new millennium would look very different from Donner's *Superman* or even Burton's *Batman*, which seemed far less dark in retrospect.

In the aftermath of the Holocaust, comic writers and readers began to see Golden Age simplicities as hollow and naïve; not surprisingly, after World War II, Captain America disappeared for decades. Meanwhile, the appearance of the X-Men in the 1960s, its 1970s revision, its 1980s and 1990s popularity, and 2000s film radically complicate the positive assimilation imagery of its comic forebears. The X-Men's own precarious relationship to humanity, as the 2000 film makes clear, challenges Superman's—and The Escapist's—integrationist ethos. Clark Kent is a nerd and nebbish on the outside but an Aryan ideal inside, yet crucially in the service of truth, justice, and the American way. Superman embodies a perfect prewar fantasy: an American who uses Fascist-style power in the service of freedom; a salt-of-the-earth Midwesterner, like anyone else in all the ways that count, and his small difference—god-like powers—does not affect how he treats humans, or how humans treat him. (As photographer and friend Jimmy Olsen always says, "Thanks, Superman!") Feiffer—and later, a similar monologue in the film *Kill Bill: Vol. 2*—suggest that Superman is the true, not secret, identity; Clark Kent is the disguise. In the aftermath of the Holocaust, and later, in the post–Cold War era of terror, the X-Men are poised to tackle disturbing truths. Unlike Clark Kent, X-Man Cyclops can never remove his glasses for fear of killing anyone around him with his optic blasts. Wolverine's healing factor makes him virtually invincible, but he, unlike Superman, is pierced by, and feels the pain of, each bullet. And mutant Colossus may be a Man of Steel, but he has, in a sense, no secret identity; both flesh and organic metal are his true form.

If Superman represents a wish fulfillment, that immigrant and assimilation experiences make people who they are—different, powerful—rather than what they look like—mild mannered, bland—then the X-Men provide the reverse. Despite how they frequently look different or are treated like freaks, the experience of being a minority adapting to a majority culture makes them the same, not different: they are entitled to equal and fair treatment and tolerance. Yet the series suggests more. The only human in Superman's world who feels threatened by the presence of an omnipotent alien hiding among them is arch-villain Lex Luthor.[11] Stan Lee, writing decades after Siegel and Shuster, knew better. Luthor's reaction isn't that of a psychopath, but the way humans have always responded to those who are different from themselves. And by 2000, after sympathizing with protagonists from the novels of Chuck Palahniuk and films of David Fincher, Quentin Tarantino, and Oliver Stone, mainstream movie-going America had finally caught up with Lee's prescient pop-cultural vision. The black-and-white, good guys saving the world from bad guys Manichaeism of Superman's day would be replaced; the villains, and heroes, would become more complex. Gene Hackman plays Superman's Lex Luthor for bluster and laughs; his evil scheme boils down to a big real estate swindle. Magneto, the X-Men's Luthor, does not see himself as evil as much as enlightened. He believes that the endgame of intolerance is death and that it is better to inflict than receive violence. When Magneto was first introduced in *X-Men* #1 (1963), he was, like Luthor, a standard-issue megalomaniac, with a shiny, domed helmet instead of Luthor's bald pate. But by the time of the first X-Men film, he had evolved into a Jewish Holocaust survivor who is chastened enough to know that, as he tells the test subject of his mutation-inducing machine, "Mankind has always feared what it doesn't understand. Well, don't fear God, Senator, and certainly don't fear me. Not anymore."

Magneto is not interested in power or money, wanting only to make the world safe for his kind. To do so, he commandeers a New York monument for his own symbolic purposes—in this case, the immigrant's icon of the Statue of Liberty—so that he can use his machine to mutate the world leaders convening for a summit on Ellis Island, thus ending fear and discrimination. The X-Men stop him, in part because they disagree ideologically and do not want to force humans to accept—or become—mutants. Indeed, as the world's most powerful telepath, Professor Charles Xavier, leader of the X-Men, could simply use his own powers to change people's minds. But Magneto does not know that the effects of his machine prove fatal, so he must be stopped, the pre-9/11 attack on a New York iconic structure by a foreign-born terrorist foiled—at least on film. And, less symbolically and more cinematically, the film would establish that no superhero movie can conclude without a large-scale battle at the end.

With the success of *X-Men*, viewers soon had more superhero films than they could handle, including subsequent *X-Men* sequels and pre-quels, the *Iron Man*, *Captain America*, *Thor*, and *Avengers* intercon-nected franchise, two different *Spider-Man* series, *Superman* and *Batman* reboots, Pixar's animated *The Incredibles*, and more. Yet unlike the first *X-Men* movie, which, like *The Giver*, continued to draw upon dystopian tropes of the 1970s, the more recent films all clearly take place in the post-9/11 world. Unlike Captain America, who got to sock Hitler in the 1940s, these heroes would not participate in anything that too closely resembled the wars in Iraq or Afghanistan. Instead, they incorpo-rated the signifiers, images, and tropes of the war on terror—particularly the image of a terrorist attack on New York City (or a fictionalized version), while minimizing real-life references to the war on terror or wars abroad. As a result, as critics like Sean Treat (quoted earlier) and fans quickly noticed, unlike World War II–era comics or the celluloid Superman's emulation of the Golden Age, these films eschewed BAM!

POW! ZAP! levity: the new superhero films were inevitably dark. And none was darker, more ambiguous, or more narratively daring than Christopher Nolan's *Dark Knight* Trilogy.[12]

Batman Begins and the Iconography of Terror

Batman Begins (2005) does not begin with Batman. Instead, it opens with a scene of pure, distilled terror: young Bruce Wayne falls into a well and is swarmed by bats. Viewers know that Bruce will eventually appropriate the image as his own, to terrify those who would terrify others. But in the beginning, bats symbolize Bruce's pain and powerlessness, abandonment later on, and fear itself. It will take time for him to redirect his internal fear outwardly. This post-9/11 Batman does not begin with a Depression-era street crime gone wrong, his parents' murder by a mugger, introduced six months into Batman's first comic book run. The murder of Thomas and Martha Wayne is now the second trauma, further rewritten as part of a systemic, terroristic effort to destroy Gotham, not a random crime, the death of the single family representing the death of community, like other post-9/11 domestic dramas. The new Batman begins with a fall—yet another fall, after 9/11's falling towers, falling planes, and falling men.

   Batman Begins manages to maintain the modern mythos that comics, television, and film have developed and cultivated since his comic book debut in 1939. Yet at the same time, it adapts its now-familiar signifiers for the era of terror. What in 1939 looked backward in homage to film noir and *Zorro* becomes another reenactment of the 9/11 attacks and the world that those attacks ushered in—except this time, unlike the amnesia films discussed in Chapter 5, they will not take place only to be forgotten. Unlike the stories of the apocalypse, the city, however beleaguered, will not fall. Batman will stop the terrorist attack on Gotham City—his symbolic New York—set forth by a mysterious cabal from the East, before it is complete, redeeming and avenging not just himself, but America. And by the end of the film, Bruce Wayne, having found his shadow self in Batman, will pick himself, and Gotham City, back up from their mutual fall. For all of its celebrated darkness, Batman, like the key image from Michael Chabon's novel, is a fantasy of escape, but of a different kind: a caped escape, a flight from the traumatizing fall of his childhood, which the film visually entwines with 9/11. By the end of the series, the falling man, like the image that concludes *Extremely Loud and Incredibly Close*, will rise. As Bruce's father, Dr. Thomas Wayne, says after he carries him from the well, "Why do we fall, Bruce? So we can learn to pick ourselves up." [13] Father figures of all kinds abound in the era of terror, as we have seen. Yet the contrast of the film's visual darkness and paternal optimism may not quite resolve, even by the series' conclusion.

Unlike Superman, whose two post-9/11 relaunches were met with mixed reception, but like X-Men, Batman was ripe for a comeback because of the ways in which his story fit seamlessly into the post-9/11 interconnected narratives of trauma, family, and fear. With America's renewed interest in monsters, Batman himself is a vampiric figure. He is not Edward Cullen: in keeping with the heroic archetype, Batman can never settle down or find love.[14] Yet in a reversal consistent with Chapter 3, after 9/11, as our monsters have grown ever more sparkly and lovable, our heroes seem darker and more alone—another fall. Still, Batman is not like the vampires fighting U.S. troops on the *Weekly World News* cover. Instead, he is a version of the troops themselves, an American Dracula waging his one-man war against terror, even as terror is his own key tactic. Crucially, the film, like Chuck Palahniuk's novels, *World War Z*, *Lost*, and the amnesia films, is not narrated linearly. Instead, until the last act's inevitable attack on Gotham and Batman's equally certain rescue, the film works as a series of memories and associations from within Bruce Wayne's traumatized psyche. Fears, rather than chronology, move the story in time and Bruce's interior war on terror, a battle that turns outward and becomes nearly literal by the end.

Bruce also shifts from personal vengeance to public protection. Initially, college-age Bruce wants to kill Joe Chill, his parents' murderer. But Chill, who was about to testify to a larger anti-Gotham conspiracy, is killed first by mob boss Carmine Falcone, whose avian name implies danger to our hero—falcons eat bats. So Bruce ventures into the criminal underworld, literally—Gotham City seems to possess a downward ramp leading directly to what the screenplay refers to as the "basement club," another of the series' subterranean images of fear. There, Falcone lectures Bruce on the true nature of power: "I don't have a second's hesitation blowing your head off in front of them [a judge and several cops, all present in Falcone's club] . . . that's power you can't *buy*" (32). Falcone knows Bruce has plenty of money; what Falcone has, he continues, is "the power of fear. . . . This is a world you'll never understand. And you'll always fear what you don't understand" (33). An inadvertent father figure, Falcone sets orphaned Bruce on his quest to stop fearing what he does not understand, by understanding what he fears.

In his attempt to find and defeat his fears, Bruce seems like yet another post-9/11 lost child—Oskar Schell,[15] *Lost*'s Jack Shephard, *The Road*'s unnamed son, Katniss Everdeen—searching for the lock that will open the secret of his departed father. Instead, though, he finds an even darker mentor than Falcone in Henri Ducard, servant of the mighty and fearful Ra's Al Ghul, leader of the League of Shadows, a kind of ninja Illuminati. Ra's Al Ghul's name, like Falcone's, plays against the image of the bat; it means "head of the demon" in Arabic. Following Falcone, Ducard asks Bruce, "What do you fear?," administering a hallucinogen created from the blue flower Bruce was told to bring to the mountaintop compound, symbolic opposition to underworld and cave. "Face your fear," Ducard implores—and the film dissolves back in time to Thomas Wayne's death, the Oedipal moment that Bruce feels guilt for but also draws power from. As Ducard explains, "To conquer fear, you must *become* fear . . . you must bask in the fear of other men . . . and men fear most what they cannot see. It is not enough to be a man . . . you have to become an idea . . . a terrible thought . . . a *wraith*" (38, screenplay's ellipses). And so Bruce does. Yet Ducard, Bruce's new father and foil, never quite replaces the memory of his angelic father, a healer, philanthropist sponsor of Gotham's trains, and bringer of comfort, the man who drives away darkness rather than embraces it.

Bruce must become a symbol of "something terrifying," and so the narrative again shifts to the bat from his fall, his childhood fear, and he turns the site of his trauma into his place of refuge, his Bat Cave. Bruce wants to do more than fight his fears—he needs to become a symbol of them, "something elemental. Something terrifying" (43) to find "the means to fight injustice. To turn fear against those who prey on the fearful," as he explains to Ducard (11). "Bats frighten me," Bruce later admits to loyal butler Alfred, "and it's time my enemies shared my dread" (65). The Bat Cave becomes a direct manifestation of Bruce's unconscious, beneath the ego's mansion façade. By remaking the cavern under Wayne Manor into his Bat Cave, Bruce reclaims his own fears in order to sow it in others.

The cave has been a powerful recurring image, appearing in *Lost*, *The Road*, and now *Batman Begins*. For philosopher Plato, the cave provided an allegory of darkness, ignorance, and entrapment. Yet for Carl Jung, the cave represents the paradox of life and death, a symbolic womb and source of plant life, and of death as well, the place where life is buried and decays. For Christians, the cave is the place of Christ's resurrection. For Bruce Wayne, it is each of these, and for Christopher Nolan, it makes a dark, fearsome set. But the cave also represents a more recent war on terror image: the (supposedly) hidden refuge of Osama bin Laden. The U.S. military searched and bombed caves in Afghanistan pursuing the founder of al-Qaeda. (In what was an act of misdirection or bad intelligence, bin Laden turned out to be in Pakistan, and not in a cave after all.) *Batman Begins* co-writer David S. Goyer explicitly stated, "We modelled

[Ra's Al Ghul] after Osama bin Laden. He's not crazy in the way that all the other Batman villains are. He's not bent on revenge; he's actually trying to heal the world. He's just doing it by very draconian means."[16]

Bruce was supposed to lead the effort to eradicate Gotham City, just as the league destroyed "Constantinople or Rome before it" (40). Instead, Bruce fights back, escaping and burning the compound, even as he cannot help but rescue one man: the trapped, unconscious Ducard. Bruce is unable to allow another father figure to die. Still, despite that Ra's Al Ghul is modeled on the twenty-first century's most infamous terrorist, Bruce appropriates what he has learned from him, from the cave's seclusion to the ninja outfit he refashions as a batsuit. Later, of course, Ducard reveals himself to have been the real Ra's Al Ghul all along, so that by saving him, Bruce inadvertently perpetuated the plan to destroy Gotham.

Like Bruce Wayne/Batman, Ducard/Ra's Al Ghul understands the power of deception; in revealing himself, Ra's Al Ghul says, "Surely a man who spends his nights scrambling over the rooftops of Gotham wouldn't begrudge me dual identities?" (119). And he also reveals the League of Shadows' indirect responsibility for the death of Bruce's parents through the weapon of "economics": "You created the depression twenty years ago," Bruce realizes, causing his parents to become, as Ra's Al Ghul replies, "unfortunate causalities in the fight for justice" (123–124). Bruce wanted to kill Chill, then Falcone, but he missed the man who really set up his parents' death, who had been hiding in plain sight through ninja-esque misdirection. In symmetry and retribution, Ra's Al Ghul burns down Wayne Manor and leaves Bruce to die.

With his identity open and metaphorical mask off, Ra's Al Ghul reveals his plan to complete Gotham's destruction. To do so, he uses mobster Falcone and another villain, Dr. Jonathan Crane, the Scarecrow, who, like Bruce/Batman, has a masked identity. Scarecrow terrifies his victims by means of a weaponized version of the fear-inducing flower, and Ra's Al Ghul plans to unleash Scarecrow's toxin. "Then," he tells Bruce, "watch Gotham tear itself apart through fear" (121).

In the aftermath of Ra's Al Ghul's attack on Wayne Manor, Bruce is defeated, lying at the bottom of his elevator shaft, a mirror of his first fall through the well. And Alfred, who observed the first fall and exchange, stands in as the final surrogate father, the one who, like Ra's Al Ghul, had also been hiding in plain sight all along. Alfred reminds Bruce of what his father said, repeating the line, "And why do we fall, sir? So that we can learn to pick ourselves up" (127), rallying him to fight his fears again. Like *The Hunger Games*, the personal is political: Bruce's parents were killed by Ra's Al Ghul, the same man who wants to destroy Gotham now. The individual fall is directly tied to the fall of the city. If Bruce is personally defeated in this moment, all of Gotham falls as well. The fate of everyone rests on the individual, in keeping with popular culture in the era of terror but going back to the Western and frontier literature.[17] Alfred, not Falcone, not Ra's Al Ghul, represents the final return of the father figure, and he reminds Bruce to pick himself up. It is the reversal of the falling man, taken off the page of Jonathan Safran Foer's novel and concretized through Batman's willpower, cables, and grappling guns.

In the film's final act, Batman battles a literal war on terror, fighting fear itself, or at least Gotham City's reaction to the drug that causes it. The fear drug distils the very essence of terrorism—the ability to create and propagate fear so that civilians destroy themselves, with no additional threats or violence necessary. With the help of ally Sergeant James Gordon, Batman averts disaster and indeed rescues Gotham—however dark, it is still a superhero movie—in the process allowing him to let Ra's Al Ghul die instead of saving him again, correcting his earlier mistake. In symmetry, Batman puts an end to the man who killed Bruce's father and tried to be his father substitute by means of his father's greatest legacy to Gotham, the train.

Ultimately, the conclusion of *Batman Begins* is ambivalent about the use of terror. Batman is clearly indebted to terrorist Ra's Al Ghul: the application of fear as a method of asymmetrical warfare, solitude and shadow, deception and a staged identity (Bruce Wayne rescues his cover at the end by pretending to be a drunk who burns his own house down), and of course the nonstop, routine threats and physical violence over all other means. Batman perpetuates against criminals the acts that Ra's Al Ghul would conduct against all of Gotham. Ra's Al Ghul potentially seems an extreme version of Batman, since both believe that they are Gotham's saviors. In their final confrontation, Ra's Al Ghul suggests as much, joking, "You took my advice about theatricality a bit literally, don't you think" (137).

With the threat of the League of Shadows at bay, Batman tells now-Lieutenant Gordon that "Gotham will return to normal," once again in keeping with monomythological hero's journey: the goal of the ending is ultimately to restore the status quo. Yet the film breaks form, or perhaps updates it, as I will discuss, with the immediate arrival of a new adversary, the Joker, thus setting up the conflict of the next film, *The Dark Knight*. Yes, Batman saved Gotham City, but as Gordon warns, "What about escalation? ... You're wearing a *mask* and jumping off rooftops" (149–150). Gordon is concerned—correctly, we will learn—that Batman's presence in

Gotham has thwarted one terrorist only to create another, just as researchers across the political spectrum have argued that real-life post-9/11 counterterrorism measures have had the unintended consequence of increasing terrorism.[18] Terrorist Ra's Al Ghul believes that he and Batman are not so different. But the Joker, if he believes anything at all, thinks that Batman has, in Gordon's words, only escalated, not won, his war on terror, and that, as we will see, it is a war that the superhero narrative will not allow its heroes to win.

Rising and Falling: *The Dark Knight*'s Duality

Batman Begins seems a clear fantasy of the 9/11 attacks averted—the threat of terrorism against a New York–like city from a shadowy cadre, led by a tall bearded man with an Arabic name who spouts jihadist proclamations that Gotham City has reached "the pinnacle of its decadence" (121), foiled by the man who declares a war on terror. Yet *The Dark Knight* (2008), placing Batman in a seemingly unwinnable war against an adversary who, unlike Ra's Al Ghul, has no story, no identity, no principles, and no political motive, has garnered much more analysis as a film about politics and terrorism than *Batman Begins*.

Andrew Klaven, in the *Wall Street Journal*, writes, "There seems to me no question that the Batman film 'The Dark Knight' . . . is at some level a paean of praise to the fortitude and moral courage that has been shown by George W. Bush in this time of terror and war. Like W, Batman is vilified and despised for confronting terrorists in the only terms they understand. Like W, Batman sometimes has to push the boundaries of civil rights to deal with an emergency, certain that he will re-establish those boundaries when the emergency is past."[19] Responding to Klaven in the *Washington Independent*, Spencer Ackerman sees the film as aligning "so perfectly with those of the Office of the Vice President that David Addington, Cheney's chief of staff and former legal counsel, might be an uncredited script doctor," yet he comes to a completely different conclusion: "In the real world, this concept [becoming like the monster so he can vanquish him] is ludicrous and anti-American. . . . It gives Al Qaeda exactly what it wants—open-ended wars of occupation that deplete U.S. military and financial resources, increase Muslim discontent at U.S. policy and, ultimately, makes the world a more dangerous place."[20]

More than any overtly political film—including *Lions for Lambs*, *In the Valley of Elah*, *Redacted*, *Rendition*, or *Extraordinary Rendition*, all released in 2007—this sequel to a reboot of a nearly 70-year-old comic book provided the basis for a national conversation on the ethics of the war on terror. Yet for all the attention to political allegories that *Dark Knight* engendered, its most significant contribution to the superhero genre, and to popular culture in the era of terror, may not be directly political at all, but rather its concomitant possibilities and problems of storytelling and symmetry.

As a villain, Ra's Al Ghul may want to destroy Gotham, but at least he has a clear purpose, and he does not want to die. The Joker of *The Dark Knight* is unlike any conventional action villain. Ra's Al Ghul and Batman are, in many ways, similar. The Joker is less a character than a cypher—as James Gordon learns, "*Nothing*. No matches on prints, DNA, dental . . . No name, no other alias . . . nothing" (259)—and the embodiment of conflict itself, a means to make Batman betray himself and his values. Only actor Heath Ledger's virtuoso performance, licking his lips and channeling Richard Nixon's voice through gleefully psychotic contortions, chortles, and tics, makes us feel as though there must be more to the character than his crimes and lies. As Alfred, the fatherly voice, tells Bruce, "Some men just want to watch the world burn" (229). The Joker has no rational motives, certainly not money, which, like the world, he would see burned, or authority—in the usual villain parlance, to take over the world. If we can trust him for just a moment, the Joker says, "I'm an agent of chaos" (287). And so he injects chaos not just into Gotham or Batman's life, but into the film's very narrative.

While *Batman Begins* eschews linear chronology for the interior logic of Bruce Wayne's fragmented memories so that it becomes the free associations of Bruce Wayne's fears, it nevertheless maintains a conventional three-act structure, as I suggested of *World Trade Center* in Chapter 1. The film presents exposition: establishing Bruce Wayne's character, motivation, and backstory. It provides the rising action: Bruce must learn to face his fears, his internal conflict, and become Batman, just as in parallel external conflict; he must discover and thwart Ra's Al Ghul's plans for Gotham's destruction. And it concludes with its resolution: Bruce conquers his own fears, Ra's Al Ghul, and the fear-producing toxin. Christopher Nolan had already experimented with complicating story structures in *Memento* (discussed in Chapter 5), and he would later go on to confound viewers' perceptions though multiple framing devices and plots in plots in *Inception* (2010). Taking the trilogy as its own single three-act story, *Batman Begins* provides the exposition, while *Dark Knight Rises*, its name to the contrary, provides the resolution.

The Dark Knight, then, the middle child and murkiest of the three and yet the most daring, completely eschews the three-act structure of its own or even, like other era of terror narratives such as Don DeLillo's *Falling*

Man, the basic conventions of plot. Instead, it provides continuous rising and falling action, less like a roller coaster, as film cliché has it, than an exploration into the very nature of rises and falls, of dramaturgical and symbolic pairings. *The Dark Knight* is a sustained study in duality—the dichotomies of "Either you are with us, or you are with the terrorists," to reach back to Chapter 1, and of "civilians" and "evildoers." The narrative, and every scene and image throughout the film, is presented as a series of interconnected binaries: doubles, foils, and twos, appropriate for the second movie of the series. Yet despite its painstaking methodology, the result is not an orderly film at all, but rather a deconstruction of structure and symmetry. The Joker's seeming chaos turns out to be highly orchestrated. Batman's order isn't very orderly. And Christopher Nolan's perfectly Manichean film comes across as finely wrought disarray.

The film opens with a bank heist, perpetuated in broad daylight by the Joker and his accomplices, all wearing rubber clown masks, each of whom, except Joker, dies. The next scene, at night, features Batman foiling a deal between Scarecrow and a crime boss, but Batman is joined by three fake "Batmen" who purport to help but only get in the way; Batman leaves them tied up with the rest of the criminals. The entwined scenes both feature dispensable doubles, and they double each other. Then the action falls, for expository scenes involving District Attorney Harvey Dent and James Gordon, who are struggling to prosecute organized crime using legitimate, nonvigilante means, and their own foils, a caucus of criminals teleconferencing with Lao, a criminal accountant, crashed by the Joker, who accounts for nothing and threatens to blow them all up. The film shifts to its next set. First, during the day Bruce Wayne use his superpower—money—to gain access to Lao, hiding in Hong Kong; Lucius Fox, yet another father figure and as cunning as his animal namesake, devises and plants a cellphone that uses sonar to image its surroundings. Then the action literally rises: at night, assisted by Lucius's invention, Bruce's alter ego Batman flies through the high-rises in order to capture and extradite Lao, giving Dent and Gordon the means they need to prosecute the entire criminal underworld.

Scenes continue to alternate between day and night, in the air and below ground, action and exposition. The doubles continue to fly by and quickly accumulate, becoming exhaustive and exhausting. Rachel Dawes must choose between the love of Bruce, irresponsible playboy on the outside and dark knight inside, and Harvey Dent, prosecutor and Gotham's white knight, as the Joker calls him. The Joker and his criminals disguise themselves as police officers, the keepers of law and order, so that they can kill the mayor, who is saved when James Gordon jumps in the way of the bullet. Prodded publically by the Joker, Bruce feels compelled to reveal his identity, so Alfred burns evidence that would incriminate anyone aside from Bruce, just as the Joker burns the underworld's mountain of money, but foil Harvey Dent claims to be Batman first, with Aaron Eckhart's chin making a compelling case. After a monumental chase scene in which Batman uses a cable to take down Joker's truck and Joker uses a cable to take down a police helicopter, Batman and Gordon, who was secretly alive in his Joker-esque act of disguise, take the Joker into custody. In the meantime, however, Joker had had the other two angles in the love triangle, both Dawes and Dent, kidnapped, so that Batman must choose whom he will rescue, even as Joker has lied and reversed their locations. Then, Joker escapes custody via an explosive cellphone implanted in a prisoner's stomach, even as a cellphone is the same device Batman used to locate Lao and eventually uses to find the Joker. Rachel Dawes is killed in yet another explosion, but Harvey Dent lives, now horribly burned and disfigured symmetrically down the middle of his face in the film's clearest depiction of dual identity. Dressed as a nurse, the profession most opposite his real vocation, Joker says he will blow up a hospital if a particular man is not killed, threatening further detonations on Gotham's bridges and tunnels, in the film's clearest nod to treating Gotham as Manhattan, an urban island. Anticipating the response, in yet another doubling, Joker rigs two ferries —one with civilians and the other with Dent's arraigned criminals—with still more explosives and gives the detonators to the people on the opposite ferry, saying that he will destroy both if no one destroys the other. After Joker's reversal of Dent's and Dawes's locations, viewers would be right to suspect another switch. Yet the ferries instead reverse: the criminals lawfully throw the detonator overboard, while the law-abiding citizens seem eager to capitulate to evil and flip the switch, although in the end neither does, and Batman stops the Joker before he can detonate both. To do so, Batman must rescue the doctors whom the Joker's men have kidnapped. But of course, like the expendable clowns and false Batmen, like the psychopaths dressed as cops and the crooked cops whom Joker coerced into crime, like Joker's transparent disguise as a nurse or the ferries of prisoners and regular people who would switch detonators and ethics, Joker has dressed the hostages as criminal clowns and the outlaws as the hostages, so that Batman must fight both the villains and the SWAT team, ostensible rescuers, from killing the captives.

Despite multiple climaxes and false endings, the film, unbelievably, goes on. At the end, Harvey Dent, now Two Face, creates another doubling by placing Gordon in the situation of hearing a loved one die, as Harvey heard Rachel, and the *Sophie's Choice* of which of his two children will live. Previously, after throwing him off a skyscraper (after Lao, the second time Batman has taken this action on an enemy), Batman catches the Joker with his grappling cable, suspending him upside-down, a visual evocation of 9/11's falling man. And for a moment, finally, the action is suspended as well: Batman and Joker have reached a stalemate. By now, the film has established the most significant double of all, between Batman, the force of order, and his foil the Joker, representing chaos. As the hanging Joker gleefully expresses, "*You* won't kill me out of some misplaced sense of self-righteousness . . . and *I* won't kill *you* because you're too much fun. We're going to do this forever." Batman tells Joker, "You'll be in a padded cell, *forever*," but Joker, letting Nolan's hand show, replies, "Maybe we can share it. They'll have to double up" (314).

Throughout, we have come to see Batman and Joker as a dichotomy, two sides—to borrow from Harvey Dent's recurring image—of the same coin, each needed to complete the other. Earlier, Bruce Wayne says criminals have "crossed a line" by turning to the Joker, but Alfred wonders whether Batman had "crossed it first," inviting the Joker to Gotham by pushing criminals "to the point of desperation" (228). Thinking her husband dead, Barbara Gordon shouts to Batman, "You brought this on us! This craziness! *You* did" (237). By the end, Batman must take the Joker's place as the public villain of the story and take the fall for Dent's death and the deaths of the officers. At the same time, in a montage, father figure Alfred burns Rachel's letter as he burned documents before, so Bruce will never know he was not loved, and second father Lucius, dismayed that his invention would be corrupted by Bruce to spy on the entire city, resigns as the machine goes up in smoke.

Alfred's earlier insight into the Joker, "Some men just want to watch the world burn," has been quoted by political pundits many times since the movie's release.[21] But they leave out the follow-up: Alfred was describing a bandit much like the Joker, a nihilist with no reasonable motives. Eventually, Bruce thinks to ask whether Alfred caught the bandit. Alfred, uneasily, explains how they did it: "We burned the forest down" (276). To kill the bandit, they had to destroy everything. By the film's end, like Wayne Manor in *Batman Begins*, everything—the dichotomy of order and chaos, our perceptions of heroes and evil-doers, even the way a story is supposed to be told—has been burned down as well. *Spider-Man 2* screenwriters Alfred Gough and Miles Millar called *The Dark Knight*, in keeping with its many flames, "a 'hot mess' with plot holes and bloated second acts."[22] They are partially right, but not for the reasons they believe.

In describing himself as an "agent of chaos," the Joker tells Harvey Dent, "You had plans. Look where it got you. I just did what I do best—I took your plan, and I turned it in on itself. Look what I've done to this city with a few drums of gas and a couple of bullets. Nobody panics when the *expected* people get killed. Nobody panics when things go according to plan, even if the plan is horrifying" (287). Batman and Gordon repeatedly call Joker a terrorist, and of course, like Tyler Durden in *Fight Club*, a double of a double, he is. But what is the point, politically or otherwise, of his terror? Durden's Project Mayhem had a point. Ra's Al Ghul and Tyler Durden—and terrorists from Osama bin Laden to the Unibomber—used terror as a tactic in service of a cause, however wrong, however misguided. The chaos Joker wreaks is not only upon Batman, Gotham, or its civilians. In the end, the Joker takes the traditional superhero story and also turns it on itself. Gough and Millar are still looking for plans, for first, second, and third acts, but they, like Gotham, are panicking. The Joker is a narrative terrorist. He burns the plans and the plot—or better yet, makes Batman do it. And he manages to steal the story from Batman, as well—not despite his lack of motivation and backstory, but because of it. Order, it turns out, is not just disorderly. It's not nearly as interesting as terror.

The Many Masks of *The Dark Knight Rises*

The Dark Knight Rises once again lays waste to Gotham City, again resembling New York, continuing the imagery of 9/11 from *Batman Begins*. But comparisons now feel less allegorical. Metaphors accumulate, drawing on post-9/11 realities even as, in their accretion, the film grows more and more surreal and phantasmagorical. The film opens with CIA agents abusing hooded prisoners, on a plane hijacked so it can be crashed. Police officers are trapped beneath rubble, evoking the same 9/11 as *World Trade Center*. The film depicts extradition and detention centers and unnamed countries resembling the Middle East, with a pit recalling Iraq's Abu Ghraib prison, site of torture and humiliation by smiling American soldiers, its most famous image the Batman-esque pose of prisoner Satar Jabar, with his own mask and cape as an international emblem of systemic American abuse. The film seems to reference the war on terror. It criticizes stockbrokers for fleecing the American worker yet also seems anti–Occupy Wall Street by putting its rhetoric in arch-villain Bane's masked mouth. It makes homegrown class warfare literal even as the war is manipulated by a New World Order conspiracy. We witness symbolic pits with real walls to be scaled, references to the French Revolution, Kafka-esque—or perhaps Lewis Carroll-esque—kangaroo courts, a *Fight Club*-like Project Mayhem intent on taking down financial centers and no longer interested in finding out if they are vacant, and a final quotation from Charles Dickens's *A Tale of Two Cities*. What is the meaning behind these masks?

In this final film, the imagery of the mask, prevalent throughout Batman's symbolism since his beginnings, grows more striking, even as it challenges how the mask should be interpreted after 9/11. Before he appears or we hear his name, Bane, Batman's new film adversary, is referred to as "the masked man," to a CIA man who cannot see that Bane stands right in front of him, since his mask is masked by a hood (352). As Bane soon tells, him, "No one cared who I was until I put on the mask" (354). And Bane's face remains covered, unlike Batman, who appears unmasked as Bruce Wayne through the first third of the film. Even then, the Batman mask neither conceals nor creates his identity: a semiconscious James Gordon still recognizes Batman even when he substitutes his usual cowl with a simple ski mask. Officer Blake, an orphan like Bruce, similarly recognizes the mask—but he means Bruce's public face: "You have to hide the anger. Practice smiling in the mirror. Like putting on a mask ... When I saw you I *knew* who you really were. I'd seen that look on your face. Same one I taught myself" (381).

Critics, however, were not kind to Bane. Anthony Lane writes in the *New Yorker* that "Bane wears a crablike mask over the lower part of his face—a disastrous burden for Tom Hardy, whose mouth, sensual and amused for such a tough customer, is his defining feature."[23] Dana Stevens similarly feels as though "the mask is a mistake because we never get a good look at Bane's face. With nothing to work with but a pair of darting eyes, Hardy can't endow Bane with motivation enough to make him more than a generic bogeyman."[24] We eventually see the reason for Bane's mask, revealing his humanity and full face, if just for a moment, in flashback. The mask is certainly not meant to hamper Hardy's performance, since the film could have used a mask more like the comic's, that of a *lucha libre*-style wrestler.

Instead, Bane's movie mask makes a perfect symbolic foil to Batman's cowl, and scowl. This chapter's opening still, one of the most frequently featured promotional images for *The Dark Knight Rises*, shows a close-up Batman's and Bane's heads as they brawl, and in doing so it emphasizes the visual and metaphorical contrast between them. Bane's face is a kind of negative, a reverse mirror image, of Batman's. What is exposed on Batman—the mouth, the jaw, the chin—is concealed on Bane. Batman's head and eyes are disguised, whereas Bane's are exposed. Batman's guttural voice is an affectation, a frightening front; Bane's is the result—in a major revision of the comic-book character—of the mask he cannot remove without his feeling severe pain. When we first meet Bane at the beginning of the movie, he is hooded, but removing one mask only reveals another. Covering the mouth, even more than the eyes as the source of his humanity, forces Hardy to act entirely kinesthetically. Together with Batman's costume and mask covering him almost completely, Bane's and Batman's choreographed fight scenes become a version of Japanese Noh drama, where the masks themselves represent the characters' roles and personalities, freeing the actors to use their bodies, rather than their faces, as their sole vehicles of stylized, even ritualized, expression.

When Bane finally breaks Batman, his final humiliation is removing Batman's mask. In doing so, he does not reveal Batman's true identity, which he already knew—he takes it from him. Then he throws him into a pit, in a visual reference to the first well that Bruce fell down as a boy. Once again, Bruce has fallen so that he may pick himself back up, yet Batman's real adversary turns out to be Miranda Tate, whom we first see masked at a charity ball, now unmasked as Talia al Ghul, Ra's Al Ghul's daughter. Batman stops the threat of a rogue weapon of mass destruction, and the series concludes with the adult Bruce Wayne rising, just as it began with young Bruce's fall, and disappearing, as he did at the opening of *Batman Begins*, casting off the mask of Batman—and his real mask, that of billionaire playboy Bruce Wayne.

All of the faces of the *Dark Knight* series have been masks. Harvey Dent—Two Face—is crucial to the new film even in his absence. Gotham is presented only with his good side—he is Gotham's white knight, the foil and reversal of Batman's dark knight. Dent's ugliness stays hidden, an omission that now-Commissioner Gordon and Batman consider a necessary fiction but one that inevitably, in mask-like fashion, must be revealed. Two Face, like Bane, provides a reversal of Batman's face, not the negative but a vertical rather than horizontal divide, like Batman and Bane. His perfectly symmetrical split visually represents both his fractured psyche and his Manichaeism, his belief in the world as divided as he is, a partition that proved in the last movie unstable within himself, and now unstable for Gotham.

Bane's mask-in-a-mask revelation was the same ploy used to introduce Heath Ledger's Joker in the *Dark Knight*—one clown mask removed to uncover another clown's face beneath it, and the film uses mask-under-mask imagery for Selina Kyle and Bane again, with a motorcycle helmet. But unlike Batman, even unlike Bane, whose history is briefly revealed at the end, the Joker has no secret face. He can don the clown mask, the police hat, or the nursing cap, but his mask is his face and his face is his mask. He is exactly as he appears to be as well as a complete walking fiction, capable of revising the origin of his scars to suit his audience and need. He is his own shadow, his own mask. And what sometimes appears as Cat Woman's cat ear mask is really her goggles flipped up onto her head, the only whimsical mask in the film. Cat suit and cat burglar aside, Selina Kyle of *Dark Knight Rises* is not the comic's Cat Woman at all, and she is never referred to as such. She wears a domino mask under her goggles seemingly to hide her identity, but we discover that her one true desire is to be free of her identity, not to protect or hide it. Masks expose more than they shield or even conceal.

Even after three films, Bruce Wayne/Batman, an "and/or" identity, remains an enigma, more than ever in the era of terror. He is a hero, again rescuing Gotham from terrorism, but an antihero, willing to use brutal, sometimes terroristic means to achieve his goal. Despite his self-imposed rule that he does not kill, he leaves a high body count in his wake, often through technicalities: letting Ra's Al Ghul die, being unable to stop Harvey Dent's death, or letting Selina Kyle kill Bane for him. He is a cautionary tale of unchecked ego, thinking himself better than and above law and democracy—or, perhaps, a superhero of superego, the orphan who cannot shut out the authoritarian voice of the imaginary parent. Yet he is also a case of noblesse oblige, the wealthy man who feels obligated to help the underprivileged, even putting himself in mortal danger to protect them. In the language of the Occupy Wall Street movement, which the film evokes, Bruce Wayne is the poster boy for the 1 percent, having inherited his privilege and his billions of dollars. Yet he is also a quintessential self-made man, leaving his wealth behind at the end of *Dark Knight Rises*, as he did *Batman Begins*, having trained exhaustively to build his mind, body, and skills to create his own identity. He is a libertarian and rugged individualist. In his tough-on-crime attitude, he is a conservative. In his staunch opposition to guns and the death penalty, he is a liberal. In his use of force and surveillance he is right-wing to the point of borderline fascism, even as conservative talk radio host Rush Limbaugh accused *The Dark Knight Rises* of being anti-Republican for calling its villain Bane as 2012 Republican Presidential candidate Mitt Romney was being criticized for his role with the venture capitalist firm of the same name, if different spelling.[25] In Gotham's recalling of the crime wave and financial crisis of New York City in the 1970s and Cold War sensibility that pervaded the original *Dark Knight* comic by Frank Miller, Batman seems dystopian. In his ultimate belief in the viability of the criminal justice system and that people are inherently good, Batman is utopian.

It's a spectacular show, of course—Batman wears the bat mask at least in part for its theatricality. But what lies beneath Christopher Nolan's mask? What is his political ambition? When asked about the politics of *Dark Knight Rises* in a *Rolling Stone* interview, Nolan put on his own best Noh mask: "We throw a lot of things against the wall to see if it sticks. We put a lot of interesting questions in the air, but that's simply a backdrop for the story. . . . It's just telling a story. . . . The films genuinely arent intended to be political. You don't want to alienate people, you want to create a universal story."[26] His artistic aspirations for the films seem clear. On the surface, universality, action, and big sound and bigger spectacle. Beneath his mask, however, he seems much more interested in manipulating the conventions of time and storytelling, an auteur more than a Hollywood hack hired to parade spandex-clad superheroes. But is provocation enough? Is story?

Even more than the masks, *Dark Knight Rises* provides the metaphor for understanding the series' politics. Lucius Fox, or maybe Christopher Nolan, grants Batman "The Bat," a great chiropteran hovercraft, a visual emblem of putting "a lot of interesting questions in the air," and the most appropriate means of grasping the *Dark Knight* trilogy's political import. Just as the Bat is capable of floating and accommodating whatever airborne circumstance Batman finds himself in, so the films are their own series of what structuralist Claude Lévi-Strauss called "floating signifiers," and what semiotician Roland Barthes amended to a "floating chain of signifieds." Batman's meaning continuously floats, moves, and shifts, representing whatever viewers are able to see in it, whether an entire narrative and political spectrum, or nothing: it is a movie—entertainment, and nothing more. Yet in the aftermath of a mass shooting in Aurora, Colorado, on July 20, 2012, at a premier of *The Dark Knight Rises*, the cinematic gunfire, mayhem, bloodshed, and masks—shooter James Holmes wore a gas mask during the massacre and had a Batman mask in his house when police searched it—inevitably seem like another link in the chain of signifiers.[27] The films appropriated images of terror; a terrorist appropriated images of the films.

William Butler Yeats's poem "The Mask" begins, "Put off that mask of burning gold / With emerald eyes" so that "I would but find what's there to find, / Love or deceit," before concluding, "O no, my dear, let all that be; / What matter, so there is but fire / In you, in me?" Like the *Dark Knight* series, the poem is an exercise in sustained ambiguity, although not nearly as long, in the challenge of determining desire or deceit, who is a lover or enemy, and what is behind the mask. It can be interpreted in many ways, or, for people who don't read poetry, as a bore, or nothing. Yet one implicit meaning may be the notion that readers—and viewers, and lovers—can stop being concerned about what is behind each of our masks. The face we put forward is our real face, even if it's a mask. Similarly, Christopher Nolan crowds his film with contradictory expressions but then asks to be taken at face value. He provides a sustained mood of terror, and multiple allegories for our postwar on terror world, but tells us not to be afraid. He has created a meticulous three-act structure and also dismantled it. He has provided the most Manichean movie imaginable, pivoting on every double, foil, and duality imaginable, that as a result feels anarchic. And he has deepened and developed one of the oldest symbolic superheroic conceits, the mask that conceals the hero's face, and used it to reveal Batman's identity. It is a film version of shock and awe. Perhaps its big sound and bigger spectacle are all there is. Nolan insists, "It's just telling a story." Batman escapes, and so do the viewers. Sometimes, escape is fantastic, as if, Michael Chabon said, there could be any more noble or necessary service in life. On the other hand, a figure like Batman, still ripe for revisionism, politicization, and mythopoeia for a septuagenarian, has consistently defied dichotomies or clear categories. He predates the war on terror. But can he outlast it?

Sequels, Reboots, and Camus's *Myth of Sisyphus*; or, Why Can't the World Stay Saved?

The *Dark Knight* series was far from the only superhero storyline to incorporate imagery from the war on terror. *The Avengers* (2012) thwart another terroristic attack on New York City, which sets up Captain America, in *The Winter Soldier* (2014), to contend with government surveillance—and attendant infiltration and retribution—gone too far, a version of Batman's city-wide sonar rendered globally, itself a pre–Edward Snowden fear of NSA overreach. *Iron Man* (2008) and the rebooted *Robocop* (2014) present a plaintive form of technological wish fulfilment: armor to make soldiers invulnerable, after revelations that "a secret Pentagon study has found that as many as 80 percent of the marines who have been killed in Iraq from wounds to the upper body could have survived if they had had extra body armor."[28] But even more than protection, Iron Man and Robocop have internal viewscreens that accurately detect the difference between harmless civilians and hostiles so that they can effortlessly shoot down the threats without any collateral damage, something that, unlike armor, still remains in the realm of fantasy.

In the comics, Marvel's *Civil War*—soon to be incorporated into the films—shows the U.S. government treating heroes as potential weapons of mass destruction, after an inexperienced superhero accidently destroys most of Stamford, Connecticut, with its accompanying image strongly resembling the pieces of skeletal frame left after the Twin Towers' collapse. The storyline begins with 9/11 imagery but quickly becomes a post-9/11 allegory of America's reaction, pitting Captain America as the force of liberty against Iron Man as the force of law, an embodiment of American's conflict between individual and society, freedom and safety, that goes back to the very beginning of the republic. DC has a nearly identical storyline in *Injustice*: after the Joker detonates a bomb in Metropolis—with nearly the same image of crossbeams to stand in for the city's destruction—Superman decides to end all war and crime in the world, at any cost. Here, the Man of Steel plays the Iron Man role, with Batman, another hero who, like Captain America, has no super powers, defending individual liberty.[29]

The search for the missing or unobtainable father continues to dominate post-9/11 popular culture; a country searching for father figures found that superheroes, in their obsessions with origins and orphans, provided readymade storylines. *The Amazing Spiderman II*, a reboot of the series, rewrites *Extremely Loud and Incredibly Close*—Peter Parker is now the son with special, particular abilities trying to solve a mystery left behind by his dead father, the clues being little pieces of New York bric-a-brac, culminating in the old subway token substituting for the found key. The film ends with the metaphorical father/son reunion that Peter craved: during yet another villain's attempt to destroy Manhattan, a young boy whom Spiderman protected from bullies earlier dons the red and blue suit to stand up to a foreign menace, in this case, the Rhino. Spiderman, now the father figure himself, returns to protect him. Thor's film centers on the Asgardian family drama of brothers warring for a sometimes-absent father's love. Even arrogant *Iron Man*'s Tony Stark suffers from unresolved Oedipal conflicts with deceased genius Howard Stark.

Images of 9/11 and a rescued New York; war-on-terror-like story lines; missing fathers and orphaned sons; sequels, prequels, reboots every decade: even as the wars in Iraq and Afghanistan wound down in 2014, our superheroes' wars rage on. Marvel and DC have already planned their releases for the next decade. Yet after three Batman films and co-producing/co-story-writing *Man of Steel*, Christopher Nolan will not return for *Batman vs. Superman*, scheduled for release in 2016. Film critic Matt Zoller Seitz suggests that "the problem" he has with superhero movies "is the visual and rhythmic sameness of the films' execution": "The buzz for the next one begins within days of the latest film's opening"[30] "It's become convoluted corporate destinies," as screenwriter Miles Millar puts it.[31]

Superman's 2013 reboot, *Man of Steel*, emblemizes Seitz's point, as well as the problem of post-9/11 darkness permeating a once–Golden Age character. Visually and narratively, the film borrows heavily from *Avatar*, *Star Wars*, *Aliens*, television's *Smallville*, and the *Dark Knight*, in the process jettisoning the bright tone and narrative devices of previous Superman stories. Clark Kent's nerdy persona, generator of decades-long dramatic irony, is absent, as is the name "Superman," never uttered. Instead, Clark Kent must learn to hide his true self from a world that fears his power, appropriating what had been X-Men's reversal of the classic Superman story. In *Man of Steel*'s revision, Superman is not only an alien but alienated. Clark Kent, sans glasses but clad in flannel, is dark and brooding, not just orphaned but orphaned twice, on Krypton by Jor El and Earth by Jonathan Kent. The predictable final battle appropriates *War of the Worlds*, down to the giant menacing tripods, along with *Cloverfield* and other 9/11-influenced films, with its de rigueur shaky camera shots and civilian masses fleeing the dust, paper, and debris of falling buildings. A *Transformers*-like CGI battle ensues, but Superman, unlike Batman, has no compunction against killing super-villain General Zod. Triumphant, Clark kisses Lois Lane, even as the resulting wreckage in Metropolis looks like a dozen 9/11s. No matter. In the final scene, Clark Kent shows up in a miraculously restored Metropolis, even as One World Trade Center alone took over a decade to construct, and we're ready for the next adventure.

Whereas before 2000, superhero movies were once in a decade, now, like their flipside, dystopian films, viewers can expect them as a summer rite of passage. But is their postwar on terror popularity a danger—not just to villains, but to their own stories? *X-Men* began as a single, risky film in 2000. By 2015, it had generated *X2: X-Men United* (2003), *X-Men: The Last Stand* (2006), *X-Men Origins: Wolverine* (2009), *X-Men: First Class* (2011), *The Wolverine* (2013), and *X-Men: Days of Future Past* (2014), with *Deadpool* (2016), *X-Men: Apocalypse* (2016), *Gambit* (2016), and another Wolverine film all in production or preproduction. And its film run pales in comparison to comics' multiple titles, manifold timelines, and separate realities and continuities.

The decades to come will bring more reboots and newer television and movie incarnations. The multiple versions, variable timelines, and alternate universes that proliferated throughout comics have made their way into mainstream movies. Together, they demonstrate the ways in which these, too, are part of the fear, yet also fantasy, inherent to the superhero story. For better or worse, terror never ends. Political critics feared that the war on terror was by definition a never-ending war. Superheroes, ever

American, have an existential problem—and not in the sense of a threat to their existence. If YA utopia is, in the end, ultimately hopeful, what if superhero films are ultimately pessimistic—the fight can never be won? A never-ending war on terror would be spiritually desiccating, certainly in life but perhaps even in our stories.

These never-ending conflicts recall literary critic M. H. Abrams's textbook definition of literature of the absurd, which is, in part,

> to view a human being as an isolated existent who is cast into an alien universe, to conceive the universe as possessing no inherent truth, value, or meaning, and to represent human life—in its fruitless search for purpose and meaning, as it moves from the nothingness whence it came toward the nothingness where it must end—as an experience which is both anguished and absurd.[32]

Abrams's multipart definition lets us see how superheroes stand as agents of existentialism. "Isolated existent": Aside lending itself to X-Men puns, each member of the X-Men, or Batman, or Spider-Man, or the new Superman, demonstrates a lonely, isolated, and dangerous existence. To be a superhero is to be alone, even when surrounded by mentors, like Batman, or teammates, like the X-Men or Avengers. Each hero must learn to accept and control his or her particular powers and body, and the responsibility—sometimes even danger—that it inevitably brings.

"Alien universe": Abrams didn't mean the worlds of the Krypton, Asgard, or the Days of Future Past, although these alien worlds and alternate timelines and dimensions underscore the main point: how can we respond to the vast strangeness and unknowability that surrounds us? And I'll skip to the end of Abrams's description for a moment: "anguished and absurd." While these words typically have negative connotations, they accurately describe the plight of many superheroes: orphaning, obsessions, secrecy, violence, one terrorist or maniacal killer after another. The portrayal seems apt. As the Joker says, "What doesn't kill you . . . simply makes you *stranger*" (173). The description applies to heroes and villains alike.

The middle section of Abrams's definition, however, seems debatable: "the universe as possessing no inherent truth, value, or meaning" and the "fruitless search for purpose and meaning" that "moves from the nothingness whence it came toward the nothingness where it must end." That's dark, even for the Dark Knight or the X-Men, and sounds suspiciously relativist for upholders of truth, justice, and the American way. Or consider the opening of author and philosopher Albert Camus's

Myth of Sisyphus, one basis for Abrams's formulation: "There is but one truly serious philosophical problem, and that is suicide."[33] Not the self-sacrifice of James Gordon or Nick Fury in *The Winter Soldier*, since neither is really dead anyway, or Superman's father, Jor El, who dies so his son can live and yet manages to appear in hologram form throughout *Man of Steel*. In the end, because of the never-ending battles in never-ending timelines in never-ending universes, and now, their never-ending sequels to never-ending reboots, do superheroes, and by extension, do we, struggle for nothing? Does popular culture's capitulation to unending struggle ironically represent a form of surrender in the war on terror? Indeed, if one chronicles the plight of any superhero, particularly in the comics but now in the films as well—X-Men's Jean Grey or Wolverine, Captain America, Batman—it is a series of one severe trauma after another: torture, amnesia, displacement, disappearance, the death of loved ones, even, sometimes, one's own seeming, or at least temporary, death.[34] Yet they come back, and move on, often, seemingly, unscathed, as if their psyches had some version of Iron Man's armor or Wolverine's mutant healing powers. Despite the stories' heightened realism, they can cope. But can we?

Alive and recovered, our heroes move on to yet another storyline rewriting human history through the lens of superhero science fiction, where New York—and the world—can be saved yet again. Or, if not saved, time can be traversed, or reality reformed, the wish fulfilled in *Superman: The Movie* and revived in *X-Men: Days of Future Past*. Yet even when the world is saved, the next existential threat immediately segues from the last, without painful self-reflection or commentary. As hero Mr. Incredible said, finally and reasonably, in the movie *The Incredibles*: "No matter how many times you save the world, it always manages to get back in jeopardy again. Sometimes I just want it to *stay saved*, you know?"

Mr. Incredible's predicament, shared and magnified by Batman, the X-Men, and the rest, is Sisyphus's problem as well. Condemned by the gods to Hades for punishment, Sisyphus must roll a boulder up a hill, only to have it tumble back down to the bottom before he can complete his task, forever. Yet the problem of suicide, and the question of whether existence is pointless, belies Camus's optimism near the end:

> You have already grasped that Sisyphus is the absurd hero. He *is*, as much through his passions as through his torture. His scorn of the gods, his hatred of death, and his passion for life won him that unspeakable penalty in which the whole being is exerted toward

accomplishing nothing. This is the price that must be paid for the passions of this earth. Nothing is told us about Sisyphus in the underworld. Myths are made for the imagination to breathe life into them.[35]

Superheroes, like Sisyphus, whom Camus calls an absurd hero, do not suffer for nothing. Before their post-9/11 resurgence, pop culture critics generally read superheroes as a kind of modern mythology, not involuntary emblems conscripted in the war on terror.[36] Through their pursuits and struggles, their deaths and rebirths, their anguish and absurdity, we, as a readership and viewership, get to exercise our collective imagination, and that deeply human superpower, our empathy. In light of the comics' Jewish origins, as evinced by Michael Chabon's novel, and the aftershock of 9/11, the notion of never-ending narratives and alternate universes seems especially compelling rather than especially hopeless. Who, in the aftermath of national trauma, doesn't wish that somewhere, somehow, the world could be different, and saved? That a sequel, time jump, or a reboot—a kind of existential do-over, as I suggested of *Lost*—could somehow make things right again? While the seemingly futile struggle, the notion that the world cannot ever stay saved, seems like Sisyphus rolling the rock up the hill only to watch it come crashing down, Camus understood that Sisyphus's plight is not torment, but the most basic incarnation of narrative itself. The rock, up, then down the other side, is precisely how the dramatic arc works, as evidenced by the plotted parabolas of every high school English class. The rock starts at the bottom, then rises, as the action rises, conflicts ensue, and characters develop, before it rolls back to bottom in resolution—or, for superheroes, serial narratives, and Sisyphus, resetting the counter for the next adventure.

Fittingly, then, Camus ends *The Myth of Sisyphus* this way:

> I leave Sisyphus at the foot of the mountain! One always finds one's burden again. But Sisyphus teaches the higher fidelity that negates the gods and raises rocks. He too concludes that all is well. This universe henceforth without a master seems to him neither sterile nor futile. Each atom of that stone, each mineral flake of that night-filled mountain, in itself forms a world. The struggle itself toward the heights is enough to fill a man's heart. One must imagine Sisyphus happy.[37]

Life is complicated. As the *Dark Knight* trilogy implies, a war on terror may very well escalate terror's response. The United States may have ushered in its own era of sequels and serial narratives, its own never-ending war to save a world that refuses to stay saved. So let's imagine, then, like Sisyphus, superheroes—even Batman—are happy in their struggle. Perhaps there is narrative satisfaction—for the reader or viewer, since of course superheroes are ink on paper or images on a screen—in the never-ending story, not in its completion. Superheroes represent the fantasy of living and fighting forever, even as, we understand, real people cannot. Like Sisyphus, and in a world transfixed with terror, we are happy to begin each adventure anew, even if we already know how it must, inevitably, end.

CONCLUSION

Undo: Is the Sky Falling?

"Trying to Remember the Color of the Sky on That September Morning," with its inscription from Virgil, Memorial Hall at the National 9/11 Memorial Museum at Ground Zero. (Cpenler/Dreamstime.com)

In literary theory, sometime between the end of World War II and the 1960s marked the beginning of postmodernism. Many discussions of postmodernism begin by debating what the term can possibly mean, since it creates an etymological problem: "modern" comes from the Latin for "just now." So what can possibly come "post"—after—"just now"? Yet over the decades, certain characteristics have emerged: postmodern work tends to blend different literary and formal elements, often from different genres, sometimes as parody but often as what theorist Frederic Jameson described as pastiche or bricolage—bits and pieces of everything formed into a sometimes fragmentary whole. Postmodern work often unsettles distinctions between what might have been considered high (elite, intellectual) and low (folk, vernacular, or mass-market) culture. Postmodern work blends the fictional with the real in order to challenge what we think of both, often revolving around themes of technology, paranoia, and their intersections, while employing experimental, nonlinear, ironic, or playful approaches to perspective, theme, and story structure. Postmodernism is often conflated with cultural relativism, an idea from anthropology that all ethical systems are equal, or, for detractors, a rejection of absolutes and fundamental, universal truth. Novelists like Don DeLillo, novels and films like *Fight Club*, TV shows like *Lost*, and filmmakers like Christopher Nolan, with their disconcerting narrative approaches and ambivalent political messages, can easily fall under the mantle. So can writing a book like this one, imposing a real-world context on to fictions, or even analyzing the significance and meaning of popular culture in the first place.

Along with postmodernism, the prefix *post-* became an operative way of understanding popular culture, and the world: post-war, post-structuralism, post-colonialism, post-industrialism; later, post-human, post-Baby Boomer, and post-punk; more recently, post-millennial, post-apocalyptic, and post-9/11; and for at least a little while in 2008, with the promise of President Barack Obama's new kind of politics, post-partisan and post-racial. *Post-* became more than a prefix—it became a worldview, an epistemological category.

But what, students in my class on postmodern literature have reasonably asked, can possibly come after postmodernism, or *post-* anything? The redundancy of *post-postmodernism*, possibly a viable historical category or genre, but a clunky, redundant term that people are rightly reluctant to embrace. *Post-* is the prefix that devours itself, since it is always after, belated, still waiting, or deferred. Nothing can come after *post-*.

Nothing except, perhaps, a new kind of nothing: *Un-*, the prefix that devours everything it precedes.[1]

Un-, like *post-*, is not a word. Unlike other prefixes, however, like *pre-* or *post-*, or *re-* or *un-*'s near relative, *under-*, *un-* does not describe, affix in time, suggest repetition, or, like *mis-* or *mal-*, even suggest that something is wrong. Unlike *with-*, *dis-*, *de-*, *counter-*, *anti-*, or even the powerful *non-*, *un-* does not suggest opposition, working against. *Un-* suggests more than reversal or opposite: it is negation, disappearance, taking out of existence. And if *post-* described the world after about 1945, *un-* describes the world from 2000, or maybe 2001, to the present. We are living in the era of terror, and the age of *un-*: of *undo*, *undead*, *unfollow*, *uninstall*, *unfriend*, *unlike*. I don't mean *unlike* the way I used it earlier in this paragraph, as a preposition meaning "dissimilar from." On Facebook, *unlike* is a verb: if we Like something and then decide not to Like it anymore, we can Unlike to erase the Like. Since Facebook, unlike YouTube, does not have a Dislike button, Unlike is as close people can get to disapproval. But Unlike is different from Dislike. Both suggest opposition, but *dis-* implies an active opposition, expending energy to repel. *Un-* feels passive, a kind of vanishing—or worse, the suggestion that the Like never existed in the first place. When we Unfriend or Unfollow online, we do something we cannot do in real life or face to face, which is presumably why the word had to be invented. We don't Unfriend corporeal people. We just—what, exactly? Stop being friends? Spend less time together? Drift apart? Or something stronger—not a drift but a rift. A fight, a falling out, not on speaking terms anymore. But not Unfriend. We can't Unfollow in person. Unfriend and Unfollow seem like electronic versions of Untouchable, with the implications of prohibition, exclusion, disappearance: that which is Unclean.

Like many people who spend a lot of time at their keyboard, I have become reliant on Delete, on Backspace, on Undo. When I knock down a real glass and wish it would unshatter and float back to its place in a *Memento*-esque cinematic backwind, or I misplace my book and want it to reappear, or say something that I want to take back, I can picture Ctrl Z clearly in my mind's eye. But it does not Undo. Glasses do not unbreak; books are not unlost but rather must actively be found (without Ctrl F, either). Words that are unspoken were never spoken, not spoken and stricken. We can say *I take it back*. But the words cannot be unsaid. Judges instruct juries to ignore testimony, but lawyers know that jurors cannot unhear. Judges cannot unstruct. Traumatized viewers cannot unsee.

And so *Un-* fails at complete erasure. Like a palimpsest—and like Tyler Durden, like the skyline of the Twin Towers, like zombies, like the memories of characters on *Lost* and in amnesia movies, like traces of the world before the apocalypse, like the fear of falling in Bruce Wayne's psyche—*Un-* leaves traces of its former self behind. The close reader can see what once was, the residue of virtual Friendship, the electronically unsettled path left behind after one has Followed, or been Followed. And perhaps this failure is for the best. The only thing more powerful than *Un-*'s fever dream of retroactive disappearance is that the wish cannot come true. If anything, the electronic world that birthed the fantasy of Undo is the same one that never lets us scrub our online prints away.

Blue Skies and Green Grass

In some ways, the era of terror is also the *Un*-age. The novels of Chuck Palahniuk self-destruct, undoing themselves. The narratives of 9/11, particularly Jonathan Safran Foer's image of his falling man reversed and rising, attempt to unmake the fall. Vampires and zombies are undead: reanimated but not alive, bearing the resemblance of the humans they were, yet completely unmade. The amnesia films do not just rewrite but *unwrite* the story we thought we were seeing. The New Dystopian YA novels that end the world wind up optimistic, while the never-ending time travel, sequels, and reboots of superhero films erase, negate, and undo their previous films—but never completely.

In other ways, though, perhaps popular culture's terror obsession has been misguided all along. What if popular culture has gotten it all wrong and terror is not the most apt image for our post–Cold War period? For many Americans, in many ways, the new century has been a great time and place to be alive. "If you watch the nightly news, it feels like the world is falling apart," President Barack Obama said in an August 2015 speech. "I promise you things are much less dangerous now than they were 20 years ago, 25 years ago, or 30 years ago. This is not something that is comparable to the challenges we faced during the Cold War."[2]

In their own similar attempt to undo popular perception, to Ctrl Z the mainstream narrative, psychologist Stephen Pinker—author of *The Better Angels of Our Nature: Why Violence Has Declined*—and One Earth Future Foundation fellow Andrew Mack take great pains to lay out this un-argument in their essay "The World Is Not Falling Apart," echoing Obama's phrase and providing the statistics to prove it. Crime rates in America dropped sharply in the 1990s and have continued to fall, and "kids are undoubtedly safer than they were in the past."[3] But not only is America a safer place; the world is as well, with homicide rates, prevalence of mass killings, violence against women and children, and rates of battle deaths all falling: "By any standard, the world is nowhere near as genocidal as it was during its peak in the 1940s, when Nazi, Soviet, and Japanese mass murders, together with the targeting of civilians by all sides in World War II, resulted in a civilian death rate in the vicinity of 350 per 100,000 per year." Pinker and Mack wonder, "Why is the world always 'more dangerous than it has ever been'—even as a greater and greater majority of humanity lives in peace and dies of old age?" They conclude by suggesting that, rather than looking to quantitative data sets, "[t]oo much of our impression of the world comes from a misleading formula of journalistic narration."[4] As if to prove their point, after Obama's speech, Republican senator Lindsey Graham said, "The president tried to tell us we're safer today than we've ever been. Do you believe that? I don't . . . we are not safer than we were before 9/11."[5] For Graham, like most Americans, belief trumps fact. For Pinker and Mack, numbers, not narratives, tell the true story.

But even their Ctrl Z is subject to its own undo, or redo: its Ctrl Y. Why, indeed? Pinker elsewhere suggested a psychological theory that "people are biased to overestimate the likelihood of the sorts of events that stand out in our memory, as violence and mayhem do, and as peace and quiet do not."[6] But what about literary and cultural theory? Why, when statistics suggest that we've never been safer, do Americans crave stories about terror, mortal peril, and the end of the world? If audiences are scaring themselves into believing the world more dangerous than it is, then why do stories about traumas and collapses feel so good? It's a question that far predates American pop culture or America itself, going back to Aristotle's notion of catharsis: the theory that dramatizing others' fear might allow the viewer to purge his or her own bad feelings. Some of humanity's oldest stories are the mythological (and Biblical) tales of ever-impending apocalypses. Stories thrive on conflict. Peace and prosperity in life may be what we all wish for. But in stories, safety is boring. Viewers long to see characters fall, often so that they can pick themselves up again. But a fall alone will suffice.

In life, fear—of terrorism; of state-sanctioned torture, violence, or incarceration; or of global climate change, none of which Pinker and Mack address—can be very powerful. As postmodern and era-of-terror stories show us, our perspectives and perceptions are even more powerful. Is gun violence really less of a problem today than in the past? Yes—but in another sense, no. As a headline in *The Economist* puts it, "[m]ass shootings are up; gun murders down."[7] The FBI's *Study of Active Shooter Incidents in the United States Between 2000 and 2013* found "an increasing frequency of incidents annually. . . . This trend reinforces the need to remain vigilant regarding prevention efforts and for law enforcement to aggressively train to better respond to—and help communities recover from—active shooter incidents."[8] And even as overall death rates have fallen, "most Americans are unaware that gun crime is lower today than it was two decades ago. According to a new Pew Research Center survey, today 56% of Americans believe gun crime is higher than 20 years ago and only 12% think it is lower."[9] Gun homicides *are* down—but that's also because of better emergency room care, a fact that is only somewhat comforting.[10] Yet the public doesn't *feel* safer—perhaps because mass shootings are increasing even if overall homicides are down, or perhaps because of the nature of the stories we continue to tell ourselves. Beginning with the Columbine school shooting—raised in Chapter 1, to come full circle—mass shootings, unlike even other homicides, have attracted massive media attention and provoked concomitantly massive fear, by design. Yes, statistically, violence in America is down. But terror is up. Is the sky falling? Maybe it depends on where you look.

Or maybe it depends on where you're standing. Sometimes, terror really is up. Not only do stories scare us—symbols do as well. Just as the blue sky became an American representation of the calm and beauty before the sudden shock of the 9/11 attacks, the meaning of the blue sky has changed for victims of American drone attacks in the ensuing war on terror, in frightening symmetry: "Zubair ur Rehman is afraid of blue skies. After all, it was a bright, clear day when his grandmother, Mamana Bibi[,] was killed by a drone strike in a field outside of his home in Pakistan's Waziristan region. ... 'When the sky brightens and becomes blue, the drones return and so does the fear,' the thirteen-year-old told members of Congress."[11] For Obama, violence is down. American drone strikes are up. Is the sky falling?

The mosaic at the September 11 Memorial & Museum, "Trying to Remember the Color of the Sky on That September Morning," features an inscription from Virgil's epic poem, the *Aeneid*: "No day shall erase you from the memory of time."[12] Narrative grants us the ability to determine what comes next, after, or *post*—to redo, remake, and revisit the sites of our dramas and our traumas. Language allows us the luxury to undo—or, as the inscription suggests, to guard against its erasure. But in life, terror cannot be undone. Despite the signs, the era of terror continues. "I am the grass/Let me work," Carl Sandburg's poem, which opened the Introduction, concludes. Under the blue sky, the grass, Sandburg's image for the natural passage of time, will grow. Yet as an audience, we refuse to let it work. It will never completely cover the graves, or prevent new ones, anyway.

Notes

Introduction

1. George W. Bush, "President: The World Will Always Remember September 11," December 11, 2001, accessed March 30, 2015, http://george wbush-whitehouse.archives.gov/news/releases/2001/12/text/20011211-1.html

2. "Area Man Not Exactly Sure When To Take Down American Flags," *Onion*, Issue 38, January 16, 2002, accessed March 30, 2015, http://www.the onion.com/articles/area-man-not-exactly-sure-when-to-take-down-americ,229/

3. Charles P. Webel, *Terror, Terrorism and the Human Condition* (New York: Palgrave, 2004), 10. The original sentence appears entirely in italics.

4. Susan Faludi, *The Terror Dream: Myth and Misogyny in an Insecure America* (New York: Picador, 2007), 2–3.

5. Richard Gray, *After the Fall: American Literature Since 9/11* (West Sussex: Wiley-Blackwell, 2011), 30.

6. Jonathan Rauch, "Barack Obama is right—we've never been safer," *Dallas Morning News*, March 13, 2015, accessed March 26, 2015, http://www .dallasnews.com/opinion/sunday-commentary/20150313-jonathan-rauch-barack -obama-is-right—weve-never-been-safer.ece

Chapter 1

1. Richard Lacayo, "Tower Terror," *Time*, March 8, 1993, accessed March 20, 2015, http://content.time.com/time/magazine/article/0,9171,977933,00 .html

2. Bruce Hoffman, *Inside Terrorism* (New York: Columbia UP, 2006), 194–195.

3. Joseph B. Treaster, "Terror in Oklahoma City: The Bomb; The Tools of a Terrorist: Everywhere for Anyone," *New York Times*, April 20, 1995, accessed January 11, http://www.nytimes.com/1995/04/20/us/terror-in-oklahoma-city -the-bomb-the-tools-of-a-terrorist-everywhere-for-anyone.html

4. Federal Bureau of Investigation, *Terrorism in the United States*, 1999, 36, accessed January 11, http://www.fbi.gov/stats-services/publications/terror_99.pdf

5. Jeffrey Gettleman, "Suspect in '96 Olympic Bombing And 3 Other Attacks Is Caught," *New York Times*, June 1, 2003, accessed March 26 2015, http://www.nytimes.com/2003/06/01/us/suspect-in-96-olympic-bombing-and-3-other-attacks-is-caught.html

6. Greg Toppo, "10 Years Later, The Real Story Behind Columbine," *USA Today*, April 14, 2009, accessed March 26, 2015, http://usatoday30.usatoday.com/news/nation/2009-04-13-columbine-myths_N.htm

7. Don DeLillo, *Libra* (New York: Viking, 1988), 221.

8. Philip Roth, "Writing American Fiction," *Reading Myself and Others* (New York: Farrar, Straus and Giroux, 1975 [first published 1961]), 120.

9. Robert Chalmers, "Chuck Palahniuk: Stranger Than Fiction," *Independent*, August 1, 2004, accessed October 4, 2014, http://enjoyment.independent.co.uk/books/interviews/article49383.ece

10. Alex Tuss, "Masculine Identity and Success: A Critical Analysis of Patricia Highsmith's *The Talented Mr. Ripley* and Chuck Palahniuk's *Fight Club*," *The Journal of Men's Studies* 12, no. 2 (Winter 2004), 94.

11. Chuck Palahniuk, *Fight Club* (New York: Henry Holt, 1996), 49. Hereafter cited parenthetically.

12. Michiko Kakutani, "Designer Nihilism," *New York Times*, March 24, 1996, section 6, 30.

13. As I write, Palahniuk is preparing a sequel to *Fight Club*. Tyler may be back by the time you read this.

14. See Chapter 5 for a discussion of America's attempt to temporarily purge popular culture of anything that seemed too close to the events of 9/11.

15. See Palahniuk's website, *The Cult*, for updates on this on-again, off-again project, http://chuckpalahniuk.net/movies/survivor/. Not surprisingly, the film for the less-topical *Choke* beat *Survivor* to the screen as Palahniuk's second adaptation.

16. Peter Murphy, Interview with Chuck Palahniuk, *New Review*, 2005, accessed October 4, 2007, http://www.laurahird.com/newreview/chuckpalahniuk.html

17. Chuck Palahniuk, *Survivor* (New York: Anchor, 1999), 160. Hereafter cited parenthetically.

18. Andrew O'Hehir, "Fight Club," *Salon*, October 15, 1999, accessed October 4, 2007, http://dir.salon.com/ent/movies/review/1999/10/15/fight_club/index.html?sid=350202

19. Henry A. Giroux, *Public Spaces, Private Lives: Beyond the Culture of Cynicism* (Lanham: Rowman and Littlefield, 2001), 67.

20. Kakutani, "Designer Nihilism."

21. The narrator is not nameless, of course. The novel refers to his name without ever revealing it. And he has many names: "Joe," in the frequent personification of body parts (revised to "Jack" in the film); "Cornelius" and 12-step

pseudonyms; and of course the name everyone in Project Mayhem associates with him: Tyler Durden.

22. I use "begins" here because it is early in the story, even as Palahniuk's readers know that the novels begin with the ending. The distinction in Russian Formalism, a form of literary criticism, between "story" ("*fabula*"), or the chronological sequence of events, and "plot" ("*syuzhet*"), or the events in the order in which they are presented to the reader, seems crucial to understanding his work. The *fabula/syuzhet* incongruity is so pronounced in *Survivor* that Palahniuk uses reverse pagination.

23. National Commission on Terrorist Attacks upon the United States, *The 9/11 Commission Report*, Final Report, 2004, 231.

24. Alex Tuss, "Masculine Identity," 97.

25. National Commission on Terrorist Attacks upon the United States, *The 9/11 Commission Report*, 241.

26. Thomas Friedman, *Longitudes and Attitudes: The World in the Age of Terrorism* (New York: Anchor, 2002), 33–34.

27. "Chuck Explains the Ending of *Survivor*."

28. Alexander Kevin Boon, "Men and Nostalgia for Violence: Culture and Culpability in Chuck Palahniuk's *Fight Club*," *The Journal of Men's Studies* 11, no. 3 (Spring 2003), 267.

29. Jodi Wilgoren, "After the Attacks: The Highjackers; A Terrorist Profile Emerges That Confounds the Experts," *New York Times*, September 15, 2001, A, 2.

30. Of course, the charges fail in the novel while succeeding in the film, for me the key revision of the adaptation. Palahniuk opts for a surprisingly conventional ending: the building stands, the narrator is institutionalized, and Tyler Durden and Project Mayhem lie dormant—for now. The big-budget film surprisingly proves more subversive in allowing the buildings to fall and the narrator to go unapprehended. While the audience understands that the buildings are evacuated, this ending is far more morally ambivalent than Palahniuk's own.

31. Don DeLillo, "In the Ruins of the Future," *Guardian*, December 22, 2001, accessed October 2014, http://books.guardian.co.uk/departments/generalfiction/story/0,,623732,00.html

32. Ibid.

33. Philip Roth, "American Fiction," 135.

34. Chuck Palahniuk, *Stranger Than Fiction: True Stories* (New York: Doubleday, 2004), xv.

35. Palahniuk, "Introduction," *Fight Club*, xviii.

Chapter 2

1. George W. Bush, "Address to the Nation on the Terrorist Attacks," September 11, 2001, *The American Presidency Project*, accessed March 12, 2015, http://www.presidency.ucsb.edu/ws/?pid=58057

2. George W. Bush, "National Day of Prayer and Remembrance Service," September 14, 2001, *Selected Speeches of President George W. Bush 2001–2008*, 59, accessed March 12, 2015, http://georgewbush-whitehouse.archives .gov/infocus/bushrecord/documents/Selected_Speeches_George_W_Bush.pdf

3. "Portraits Redrawn," *9/11: The Reckoning*, *New York Times*, accessed March 12, 2015, http://www.nytimes.com/interactive/us/sept-11-reckoning/ portraits-of-grief.html

4. Susan Faludi, *The Terror Dream: Myth and Misogyny in an Insecure America* (New York: Picador, 2007), 3.

5. One could, of course, make a case that the Space Shuttle Challenger disaster in 1986 was the first televised disaster, although it was not an attack on American soil.

6. Stephen Prince, *Firestorm: American Film in the Age of Terrorism* (New York: Columbia UP, 2009), 74.

7. Tom Pollard, *Hollywood 9/11* (Boulder, CO: Paradigm, 2011), 18.

8. Ibid., 18.

9. Prince, *Firestorm*, 109.

10. Frank Rich, "Too Soon? It's Too Late for 'United 93,' " *New York Times*, May 7, 2006, accessed January 11, 2014, http://www.nytimes.com/2006/05/07/ opinion/07rich.html?pagewanted=all&_r=0. Rich's point, however, is larger than whether or not *United 93* is exploitative. He is far more concerned that Americans are conflating the attacks on 9/11 with the war in Iraq: "When Americans think about war now, they don't think about the war prompted by what happened on 9/11 so much as the war in Iraq, and when they think about Iraq, they don't say, 'Let's roll!', they say, 'Let's leave!' "

11. Faludi, *Terror Dream*, 3.

12. Mohsin Hamid, *The Reluctant Fundamentalist* (New York: Harcourt, 2007), 72–73.

13. Jonathan Safran Foer, *Extremely Loud and Incredibly Close* (New York: Mariner, 2005), 299. Hereafter cited parenthetically.

14. Richard Gray, "Open Doors, Closed Minds: American Prose Writing at a Time of Crisis," *American Literary History* 21, no. 1 (Spring 2009), 34. I mention this quotation in the introduction as well.

15. Michael Rothberg, "A Failure of the Imagination: Diagnosing the Post-9/11 Novel: A Response to Richard Gray," *American Literary History* 21, no. 1 (2009), 153.

16. Gray, "Open Doors," 34.

17. Rich, "Too Soon?"

18. Anis Shivani, "The 15 Most Overrated Contemporary American Writers," *Huffington Post*, August 7, 2010, accessed March 12, 2015, http://www. huffingtonpost.com/anis-shivani/the-15-most-overrated-con_b_672974.html

19. Harry Seigel, "Extremely Cloying & Incredibly False," *New York Press*, April 20, 2005, accessed March 15, 2015, http://nypress.com/extremely-cloying -incredibly-false/#sthash.EVwMkQA.dpuf

20. "Book Club: Jonathan Safran Foer's *Extremely Loud and Incredibly Close*," *Yankee Pot Roast*, June 3, 2005, accessed March 12, 2015, http://www.yankeepotroast.org/archives/2005/06/jonathan_safran.html

21. Seigel, "Extremely Cloying."

22. The word "close" appears on pages 9, 13, 16, 30, 70, 80, 96, 97, 145, 163, 165, 179, 196, 207, 228, 217, 273, 278, 279, 299, and 304. "Closer" appears on 10, 52, 135, 207, 245, 259, and 292.

23. The book does not burden the reader with any real-life diagnoses, which would impinge upon its fairytale qualities.

24. A. O. Scott, "In Search of the Best," *New York Times*, May 21, 2006, accessed January 11, 2014, http://www.nytimes.com/2006/05/21/books/review/scott-essay.html?pagewanted=2&_r=0

25. Don DeLillo, *Falling Man* (New York: Scribner, 2007), 3. Hereafter cited parenthetically.

26. In 2008, performance artist Luke Jerram simulated the Falling Man using parabolic flight, just as DeLillo suggested of the performance artist in his novel; see http://www.lukejerram.com/projects/falling_man, accessed March 12, 2015.

27. Don DeLillo, *Mao II* (New York: Scribner, 1991), 87.

28. Ibid., 87.

29. Don DeLillo, *Underworld* (New York: Scribner, 1997), 184, 372.

30. James Wood, "Tell Me How Does It Feel?" *Guardian*, October 6, 2001.

Chapter 3

1. "White House: 'War on terrorism' is over," *Washington Times*, August 6, 2009, accessed March 18, 2015, http://www.washingtontimes.com/news/2009/aug/06/white-house-war-terrorism-over/?feat=home_headlines

2. Heather Havrilesky, "Steve Jobs: Vampire. Bill Gates: Zombie," *New York Times Magazine*, October 28, 2011, accessed March 16, 2015, http://www.nytimes.com/2011/10/30/magazine/steve-jobs-vampire-bill-gates-zombie.html?pagewanted=all

3. "Zombify Yourself," *Zombieland*, Sony Pictures, accessed December 13, 2011, http://www.sonypictures.net/movies/zombieland/zombify/; the link was removed after the 2014 cyberattack.

4. Max Brooks, *World War Z: An Oral History of the Zombie War* (New York: Crown, 2006), 1. Hereafter cited parenthetically.

5. Bruce Hoffman, *Inside Terrorism* (New York: Columbia UP, 2006), 131, 132.

6. Max Brooks, "Transcript: Zombie Wars," *Washington Post*, October 6, 2006, accessed March 18, 2015, http://www.washingtonpost.com/wp-dyn/content/discussion/2006/10/03/DI2006100300686.html

7. Matthew Inman, "What the World War Z movie has in common with the book," *Oatmeal*, accessed March 16, 2015, http://theoatmeal.com/comics/wwz

8. Nafeez Ahmed, "Iraq invasion was about oil," *Guardian*, March 20, 2014, accessed March 18, 2015, http://www.theguardian.com/environment/earth-insight/2014/mar/20/iraq-war-oil-resources-energy-peak-scarcity-economy

9. Ben Hoyle, "War on Terror backdrop to James Cameron's Avatar," *Australian*, December 11, 2009, accessed March 2015, http://www.theaustralian.com.au/arts/film/war-on-terror-backdrop-to-james-camerons-avatar/story-e6frg8pf-1225809286903?nk=031636a3a195bdeb789d81321a5d79ab

10. Dave Gilson, "Hobbit Fans Unleash Geek Fury on Rick Santorum," *Mother Jones*, October 18, 2006, accessed January 13, 2015, http://www.motherjones.com/mojo/2006/10/hobbit-fans-unleash-geek-fury-rick-santorum. Gilson goes on to point out numerous flaws in Santorum's analogy between the war in Iraq and *Lord of the Rings*.

11. Bram Stoker, *Dracula*, 1897, eds. Nina Auerbach and David Skal (New York: Norton Critical, 1997), 23–24. Hereafter cited parenthetically.

12. Stephen Arata, "The Occidental Tourist: Dracula and the Anxiety of Reverse Colonization," reprinted in Aurbach and Skal, *Dracula*, 462.

13. Franco Moretti, "A Capital Dracula," reprinted in Aurbach and Skal, *Dracula*, 433–434.

14. Mary Shelly, *Frankenstein*, 1818, ed. J. Paul Hunter (New York: Norton, Critical, 1996), 30, 32. Hereafter cited parenthetically. The Norton Critical Edition is based on the 1818 text. As Anne K. Mellor discusses in an essay included with the novel, the 1818 edition should be preferred ("Choosing a Text of *Frankenstein* to Teach," 160). It is worth noting that the 1818 version supports the readings of this essay more than the 1931 edition does.

15. The novel is, of course, ambiguous on this point.

16. Steve Coll, *Ghost Wars: The Secret History of the CIA, Afghanistan, and Bin Laden, from the Soviet Invasion to September 10, 2001* (New York: Penguin, 2004), 17.

17. Richard Devetak, "The Gothic scene of international relations: ghosts, monsters, terror and the sublime after September 11," *Review of International Studies* 31 (2005), 640.

18. Milly Williamson, "Let Them All In: The Evolution of the 'Sympathetic' Vampire," in *Screening the Undead: Vampires and Zombies in Film and Television*, eds. Leon Hunt, Sharon Lockyer, and Milly Williamson (London: I.B. Tauris, 2014), 78.

19. Brooks, "Transcript: Zombie Wars."

20. Stephenie Meyer, *Twilight* (New York: Hachette, 2005), 93. Hereafter cited parenthetically.

21. Laura Miller, "Touched by a vampire," *Salon*, July 30, 2008, accessed February 13, 2015, http://www.salon.com/2008/07/30/twilight_3/

22. Susan Elgin, "Q&A: 'Twilight' Author Stephenie Meyer," *Newsweek*, July 25, 2008, accessed February 13, 2015, http://www.newsweek.com/qa-twilight-author-stephenie-meyer-93139

23. Stephenie Meyer, *New Moon* (New York: Hachette), 85–92. Hereafter cited parenthetically.

24. Don DeLillo, *Cosmopolis* (New York: Scribner, 2003), 203. Hereafter cited parenthetically.

25. Cornel Bonca, "Contact With The Real: On 'Cosmopolis,' " *Los Angeles Review of Books*, September 12, 2012, accessed March 18, 2015, https://lareviewofbooks.org/essay/contact-with-the-real-on-cosmopolis

26. Don DeLillo, "The Border of Fallen Bodies," *Esquire* (April 2003), 124.

Chapter 4

1. Wayne Friedman and David Goetzl, "Few 'Survivors' as Reality Bites," *Advertising Age* 72, no. 43 (October 22, 2001), 61.

2. J. Wood, *Living Lost: Why We're All Stuck on the Island* (New Orleans, LA: Garret County Press, 2007), ix.

3. Mikal Gilmore, "Get Lost," *Rolling Stone* (May 31, 2007), 44.

4. Seth Stevenson, "More Literary References," *Slate*, March 17, 2010, accessed June 6, 2010, http://www.slate.com/id/2242745/entry/2248149/

5. Chadwick Matlin, "Sweet Mother of God," *Slate*, March 17, 2010, accessed June 6, 2010, http://www.slate.com/articles/arts/tv_club/features/2010/lost_season_6/season_6_more_literary_references.html

6. Andy Serwer, "The '00s: Goodbye (at Last) to the Decade from Hell," *Time*, November 24, 2009, accessed June 23, 2010, http://www.time.com/time/nation/article/0,8599,1942834,00.html

7. Fareed Zakaria, "The Politics of Rage: Why Do They Hate Us?" *Newsweek*, October 15, 2001, accessed June 4, 2010, http://www.newsweek.com/2001/10/14/the-politics-of-rage-why-do-they-hate-us.html

8. This reversal or negation of what the audience thought it understood is also one of the major features of Chuck Palahniuk's novels, as Chapter 1 discussed.

9. Glenn Beck, "Mission Statement," *The 9.12 Project*, 2009.

10. Mayo Clinic Staff, "Symptoms," *Mayo Clinic*, April 10, 2009, accessed June 6, 2010, http://www.mayoclinic.com/health/post-traumatic-stress-disorder/DS00246/DSECTION=symptoms

11. David Hastings Dunn, "LOST: (Adventures in the American Psyche after the 9/11 Fall)," *Defence Studies* 6, no. 3 (September 2006), 318.

12. Frank Kermode, *The Sense of an Ending*, 1966 (New York: Oxford UP, 2000), 5. Hereafter cited parenthetically.

13. Wood, *Living Lost*, 110.

Chapter 5

1. Slavoj Zizek, *Welcome to the Desert of the Real* (London: Verso, 2002), 12. "*Jouissance*," a term used by French cultural theorists like Roland Barthes and Jacques Lacan, suggests pleasure so extreme (and, in French, implicitly sexual) that it violates accepted boundaries.

2. Julie Salamon, "The Relevance of 'Sex' in a City That's Changed," *New York Times*, July 21 2002.

3. James Barron, "Lost Towers, Reflected in a Coffee Can," *New York Times*, June 19, 2004.

4. Max Page, *The City's End: Two Centuries of Fantasies, Fear, and Premonitions of New York's Destruction* (New Haven: Yale UP, 2008), 204.

5. Ibid., 206–207.

6. Ibid., 204.

7. Gayatri Chakravorty Spivak, introduction to *Of Grammatology* by Jacques Derrida (Baltimore: Johns Hopkins UP, 1967), xiv.

8. Artist Damien Hirst and composer Karlheinz Stockhausen were both excoriated for viewing the destruction of the Twin Towers as a work of art. It does seem clear, though, that the attacks were a form of criticism, although not in the analytical sense of the word, yet to put it that way feels as though it diminishes the lives lost. In *In the Shadow of No Towers* (New York: Pantheon, 2004), Art Spiegelman sardonically writes that "if not for all the tragedy and death, I could think of the attack as some sort of radical architectural criticism" (unpaged).

9. Wheeler Winston Dixon, "Introduction: Something Lost—Film after 9/11," in *Film and Television after 9/11*, ed. Winston Wheeler Dixon (Carbondale: U of Southern Illinois P, 2004), 3.

10. Art Spiegelman, *In the Shadow of No Towers* (New York: Pantheon, 2004), unpaged.

11. Dan Amira, "Rudy Giuliani Keeping Score on Terror Attacks, Poorly," *New York Times*, January 8, 2010.

12. Ibid.

13. Carlin Flora, "Amnesia's Allure," *Psychology Today*, September 1, 2005, 24.

14. Terrence Rafferty, "The Last Word in Alienation: I Just Don't Remember," *New York Times*, November 2, 2003.

15. Jonathan Lethem, *The Vintage Book of Amnesia: An Anthology of Writing on the Subject of Memory Loss* (New York: Vintage, 2000), xiii.

16. The fact that many of the amnesia films are remakes or adaptations whose sources long predate September 11 does not discount them; I see them as suggesting a sudden interest, immediacy, and relevance to the material.

17. John Leland, "On Film as in Life, You Are What You Forget," *New York Times*, December 23, 2001.

18. Harald Merckelbach et al., "A Skeptical Look at a Remarkable Case Report of 'Overnight' Amnesia," *Skeptical Inquirer* 35, no. 3 (May/June 2011), 37.

19. James Gorman, "Only in the Movies: Living a Life Unencumbered by Memory," *New York Times*, April 20, 2004.

20. Zizek, *Welcome*, 16.

21. Jess Walter's novel *The Zero* (New York: Harper, 2007) provides an interesting intersection between the explicitly 9/11 novel and amnesia.

22. Lethem, *The Vintage Book of Amnesia*, xvi.

23. The distinction in Russian Formalism between "story" ("*fabula*"), or the chronological sequence of events, and "plot" ("*syuzhet*"), or the events in the

order in which they are presented to the reader, seems crucial to understanding how these films work, just as they were in the novels of Chuck Palahniuk. In *Memento*, the *fabula* essentially runs in reverse of the *syuzhet*, making the film's opening shot an important visual, narrative, and symbolic cue to the viewer, even as he or she cannot appreciate its significance during the initial viewing.

24. Jean Baudrillard, "Requiem for the Twin Towers," *The Spirit of Terrorism and Other Essays*, trans. Chris Turner (London: Verso, 2002), 48.

25. Jean Baudrillard, "The Gulf War Did Not Take Place," 1995, *Selected Writings*, 2nd ed. Ed. Mark Poster, trans. Paul Patton (Stanford: Stanford UP, 2001), 253.

26. Gore Vidal, "The State of the Union," *Nation* (September 13, 2004).

27. Alice Park, "Erasing Bad Memories May Soon Be Possible," *Time*, August 27, 2014, accessed March 15, 2015, http://time.com/3194849/how-memories-are-made-and-manipulated/

28. Richard Gray, *After the Fall: American Literature Since 9/11* (West Sussex: Wiley-Blackwell, 2011), 39–40.

29. Cormac McCarthy, *The Road* (New York: Vintage, 2006), 12. Hereafter cited parenthetically.

30. Another post-9/11 post-apocalyptic movie, *The Book of Eli* (2010), serves as a foil to the film adaptation of *The Road* (2009): both revolve around a male survivor's journey through dangerous, burned-out landscape. Yet *The Book of Eli* is a straightforward adventure with attendant Hollywood violence; despite that the quest turns out to be the delivery of the last Bible. In *The Road*, the violence is far more harrowing, in part because the characters' survival does not seem self-evident, and because the film, thanks to its source material, dramatizes the love between the man and his son.

31. The range of allegorical interpretations is wide, from John Vanderheide's "allegorical daemonism" (111) to Carl James Grindley's reading of *The Road* as an unambiguous "document of the so-called Tribulation of Judeo-Christian mythology" (11). See John Vanderheide, "Sighting Leviathan: Ritualism, Daemonism and the Book of Job in McCarthy's Latest Works," *The Cormac McCarthy Journal* 6 (Autumn 2008), 107–120; and Carl James Grindley, "The Setting of McCarthy's The Road," *Explicator* 50.1 (September 2008), 11–13.

32. David Kushner, "Cormac McCarthy's Apocalypse," *Rolling Stone*, December, 27, 2007.

33. Gray, *After the Fall*, 39.

34. Stephanie Zacharek, Review of *Cloverfield*, dir. Matt Reeves, *Salon*, January 18, 2008.

35. John Cant, "The Road," *Cormac McCarthy*, ed. Harold Bloom (New York: Chelsea, 2009), 184.

36. Ibid., 191.

37. The shopping cart is another recurring post-9/11 image, appearing in *The Road, War of the Worlds, Zombieland*, and *28 Days Later*. It serves as a powerful metaphor for the late-twentieth-century life and related consumerism that

after disaster must be left behind. Or maybe it's just the easiest way to transport items.

38. Scott Laming, "Bleak Books - the Top 10 Most Depressing Books," *AbeBooks.com*, accessed March 15, 2015, http://www.abebooks.com/books/bleak-miserable-horrible-sad-novels/depressing-stories.shtml

39. Amy Hungerford, *Postmodern Belief: American Literature and Religion since 1960* (Princeton, NJ: Princeton UP, 2010), 135.

40. Gray, *After the Fall*, 47.

Chapter 6

1. In its first usage, Thomas Moore's *Utopia*, the word suggested a fantasy—"no place." But it has since taken on positive connotations.

2. Don DeLillo, *Cosmopolis* (New York: Scribner, 2003), 3.

3. Joe Fassler, "Cormac McCarthy's *The Road* May Have the Scariest Passage in All of Literature: Benjamin Percy, author of Red Moon, makes the case," *Atlantic*, May 14, 2013, accessed February 13, 2015, http://www.theatlantic.com/entertainment/archive/2013/05/cormac-mccarthys-i-the-road-i-may-have-the-scariest-passage-in-all-of-literature/275834/

4. George W. Bush, Speech at the Citadel, December 11, 2001, accessed March 13, 2015, http://www.nytimes.com/2001/12/11/international/12BUSH-TEXT.html

5. See "The Hunger Games Online Game," accessed March 13, 2015, http://www.thehungergames.co.uk/games/

6. Pamela Paul, "Peer Pressure? How About, Like, Fighting to Death?" *New York Times*, March 9, 2012, accessed February 13, 2015, http://www.nytimes.com/2012/03/11/movies/the-hunger-games-books-become-a-movie-franchise.html?scp=23&sq=hunger%20games&st=Search

7. Even the Cartoon Network show *Adventure Time* turned out to be another example of a postapocalyptic world's end series, despite its secret worlds–style swords and sorcery trappings.

8. *The Giver* was also adapted into a movie in the wake of *The Hunger Games*' success in 2014.

9. Natalie Babbitt, "The Hidden Cost of Contentment," *Washington Post*, May 9, 1993, X15.

10. That the teens in *Gone* also develop superpowers later in the series solidifies the idea of wish fulfillment even further.

11. Melissa Ames, "Engaging 'Apolitical' Adolescents: Analyzing the Popularity and Educational Potential of Dystopian Literature Post-9/11," *The High School Journal* (Fall 2013), 8.

12. Julie Bertagna, "Why are teenagers such avid readers of books about dystopias?" *The Scotsman*, June 5, 2011, accessed February 11, 2015, http://www.scotsman.com/news/books-why-are-teenagers-such-avid-readers-of-booksabout-dystopias-1-1667196

13. Franz Kafka, "A Hunger Artist," *Selected Short Stories*, trans. Willa and Edwin Muir (New York: Modern Library, 1952), 188.

14. For further complication of *The Hunger Games*' appropriation of Rome, see Adam Barkman, " 'All of this is wrong' ": Why One of Rome's Greatest Thinkers Would Despise the Capitol," *Hunger Games and Philosophy*, eds. George A. Dunn and Nicolas Michaud (Hoboken: Wiley, 2012), 265–276.

15. "Definitions of Terrorism in the U.S. Code," Federal Bureau of Investigations, accessed March 16, 2015, http://www.fbi.gov/about-us/investigate/terrorism/terrorism-definition

16. Suzanne Collins, *Catching Fire* (New York: Scholastic, 2009), 27. Hereafter cited parenthetically.

17. Rick Margolis, "A Killer Story: An Interview with Suzanne Collins, Author of 'The Hunger Games,' " September 1, 2008, *School Library Journal*, http://www.slj.com/2008/09/authors-illustrators/a-killer-story-an-interview-with-suzanne-collins-author-of-the-hunger-games/#_

18. Ibid.

19. Scott Westerfeld, "Teens and Dystopias," *Scott Westerfeld* (blog), September 13, 2012, accessed March 16, 2015, http://scottwesterfeld.com/blog/2012/09/teens-and-dystopias/

20. Laura Miller, "Fresh Hell: What's Behind the Boom in Dystopian Fiction for Young Readers?" *New Yorker*, June 14, 2010.

21. Harold Bloom, "Can 35 Million Book Buyers Be Wrong? Yes," *Wall Street Journal*, July 11, 2000.

22. J. K. Rowling, *Harry Potter and the Sorcerer's Stone* (New York: Scholastic, 1999), 4.

23. John Green, "Scary New World," *New York Times*, November 7, 2008, accessed February 13, 2015, http://www.nytimes.com/2008/11/09/books/review/Green-t.html?pagewanted=all

24. Suzanne Collins, *The Hunger Games* (New York: Scholastic, 2010), 6. Hereafter cited parenthetically.

25. James Joyce, *Portrait of the Artist as a Young Man* (New York: Penguin, 1916), 247.

26. The films complicate the distance that the novel provides, however. In their big-budget enactments, they cannot help but glorify violence even as they also hope to criticize it.

27. Susan Faludi, *The Terror Dream* (New York: Picador, 2007), 6.

28. C. S. Lewis, *The Lion, The Witch, and the Wardrobe* (New York: HarperTrophy, 1950), 118, 119.

29. Suzanne Collins, *Mockingjay* (New York: Scholastic, 2010), 328. Hereafter cited parenthetically.

30. J. M. Barrie's novel was published in abridged form under the name *Peter Pan and Wendy* in 1915.

31. Other writers see a direct connection between Peeta and yet another Peter: Saint Peter, the apostle and closet friend to the savior. For more about

Hunger Games' use of names, see Miriam Krule, "The Hunger Names," *Slate*, November 19, 2014, accessed February 11, 2015, http://www.slate.com/blogs/browbeat/2014/11/19/hunger_games_names_meanings_explanations_for_katniss_everdeen_peeta_mellark.html

32. Laura Miller, "Fresh Hell."

33. Russell C. Smith and Michael Foster, "The Hunger Games and the Death of Winner-Take-All Capitalism," *Huffington Post*, April 3, 2012, accessed February 13, 2015, http://www.huffingtonpost.com/russell-c-smith/hunger-games-capitalism_b_1395338.html

34. John Tammy, "Suzanne Collins' 'The Hunger Games' Illustrates the Horrors of Big Government," *Forbes*, March 20, 2012, accessed February 13, 2015, http://www.forbes.com/sites/johntamny/2012/03/20/suzanne-collins-the-hunger-games-is-a-story-about-the-horrors-of-big-government/

35. Andrew O'Hehir, "'Divergent' and 'Hunger Games' as capitalist agit-prop," *Salon*, March 22, 2014, accessed February 13, 2015, http://www.salon.com/2014/03/22/divergent_and_hunger_games_as_capitalist_agitprop/

36. Seth Mydansnov, "Thai Protesters Are Detained After Using 'Hunger Games' Salute," *New York Times*, November 21, 2014, accessed February 13, 20015, http://www.nytimes.com/2014/11/21/world/asia/thailand-protesters-hunger-games-salute.html?_r=1

37. Daniel Bates, "Ferguson protesters scrawl Hunger Games slogan on landmark as tense town waits for grand jury decision on indicting officer Darren Wilson over killing of Michael Brown," *UK Daily Mail.com*, November 24, 2014, accessed March 16, 2015, http://www.dailymail.co.uk/news/article-2847503/Ferguson-protesters-scrawl-Hunger-Games-slogan-landmark-tense-town-waits-grand-jury-decision-indicting-Darren-Willson-killing-Michael-Brown.html#ixzz3SJTBDcQU

38. Stephen Gandel, "The economic imbalance fueling Ferguson's unrest," *Fortune*, August 15, 2014, accessed February 13, 2015, http://fortune.com/2014/08/15/ferguson-income-inequality/

39. Scott Clement, "How race and police became a red-vs.-blue issue," *Washington Post*, December 30, 2014, accessed February 13, 2015, http://www.washingtonpost.com/blogs/the-fix/wp/2014/12/30/how-race-and-police-became-a-red-vs-blue-issue/

Chapter 7

1. Bradford W. Wright, *Comic Book Nation: The Transformation of Youth Culture in America* (Baltimore: Johns Hopkins, 2001), 254.

2. *9-11: The World's Finest Comic Book Writers & Artists Tell Stories to Remember*, vol. 2, DC Comics, 2002, cover.

3. George W. Bush, Remarks by the President Upon Arrival: The South Lawn, September 16, 2001, accessed March 15, 2015, http://georgewbush-whitehouse.archives.gov/news/releases/2001/09/20010916-2.html

4. Shaun Treat, "How America Learned to Stop Worrying and Cynically ENJOY! The Post-9/11 Superhero Zeitgeist," *Communication and Critical/Cultural Studies* 6, no. 1 (March 2009), 103–109, 105.

5. Michael Chabon, The *Amazing Adventures of Kavalier & Clay* (New York: Random House, 2000), 637. Hereafter cited parenthetically.

6. Jules Feiffer, "The Minsk Theory of Krypton," 1996. Reprinted in *ZAP! POW! BAM! The Superhero*, 29.

7. For a more comprehensive overview of the way in which the word "hero" reentered the cultural lexicon after 9/11, see Susan Faludi, "The Return of Superman," in *The Terror Dream* (New York: Picador, 2007), 59–82.

8. Bradford Wright, *Comic Book Nation,* 33.

9. Interview with Ted Hope, "The Problem With Superhero Films: 'Our Entire Culture Is Based On Escapism'," *Huffington Post Live*, September 17, 2014, accessed March 15, 2015, http://live.huffingtonpost.com/r/archive/segment/5419d41afe34446a3c000154

10. Michael Chabon, "Revenge of Wolverine," *Harper's Magazine*, October 2000, 33–38.

11. Even twenty-first-century revisions of Superman are increasingly X-Men-like in the way in which humans fear and distrust the Kryptonian, including TV's "Smallville," DC's 2013 *New 52* comic relaunch, written by Scott Snyder, and *Man of Steel* (2013), discussed later in the chapter.

12. For fans of the comics, however, darkness in superhero stories was nothing new, going back at least to Frank Miller's *Dark Knight* and Alan Moore's *Watchmen* in 1985. But like the YA dystopia *The Giver* in the previous chapter, these print stories would need to wait decades before the mainstream would be ready for adaptations (or, in the case of *Dark Knight*, something closer in spirit). By that time, these now-post-9/11 superheroes would need to update their Cold War political subtexts—as well as the wishes and fears—to accommodate the era of terror.

13. All quotations from *Batman Begins*, *Dark Knight*, and *Dark Knight Rises* are from Christopher Nolan, Jonathan Nolan, and David S. Goyer, *The Dark Knight Trilogy: The Complete Screenplays* (New York: Opus, 2012), 9. Hereafter cited parenthetically.

14. For a full exploration of Carl Jung's monomyth as applied to American tropes, see John Lawrence and Robert Jewett, *The Myth of the America Superhero* (Grand Rapids: Wm. B. Eerdmans, 2002).

15. Coincidently, both Bruce's and Oskar's lost fathers are named Thomas.

16. Tom Ryan "In defence of big, expensive films," *The Age*, July 14, 2005, accessed March 15, 2015, http://www.theage.com.au/news/film/defending-the-blockbuster/2005/07/14/1120934352863.html

17. Again, see Susan Faludi, *The Terror Dream*, for further discussion.

18. See, for example, Karen DeYoung, "Spy Agencies Say Iraq War Hurting U.S. Terror Fight," *Washington Post*, September 24, 2006, accessed March 15, 2015, http://www.washingtonpost.com/wp-dyn/content/article/2006/09/23/

AR2006092301130.html; Russell Feingold, "Bush's Iraq War is Weakening America," *Counterpunch*, September 29, 2005, accessed March 15, 2015, http://www.counterpunch.org/2005/09/29/bush-s-iraq-war-is-weakening-america/; and Glenn Greenwald, "They hate us for our occupations," *Salon*, October 12, 2010, accessed March 15, 2015, http://www.salon.com/2010/10/12/terrorism_28/

19. Andrew Klaven, "What Bush and Batman Have in Common," *Wall Street Journal*, July 25, 2008, http://www.wsj.com/articles/SB121694247343482821

20. Spencer Ackerman, "Batman's 'Dark Knight' Reflects Cheney Policy," *Washington Independent*, July 21, 2008, accessed March 15, 2015, http://washingtonindependent.com/509/batmans-dark-knight-reflects-cheney-policy

21. See, for example, Thomas L. Friedman, "ISIS, Boko Haram and Batman," *New York Times*, October 5, 2014, accessed March 15, 2015, http://www.nytimes.com/2014/10/05/opinion/sunday/thomas-l-friedman-isis-boko-haram-and-batman.html?_r=0

22. Quoted in Sujay Kumar, "How Superhero Movies Lost Their Humanity," *Daily Beast*, February 24, 2015, accessed March 15, 2014, http://www.thedailybeast.com/articles/2015/02/24/eleven-years-after-spider-man-2-what-went-wrong-with-the-superhero-movie.html

23. Anthony Lane, "Batman's Bane" [review of *Dark Knight Rises*], *New Yorker*, July 30, 2012, accessed March 15, 2015, http://www.newyorker.com/magazine/2012/07/30/batmans-bane#ixzz2284fQzTP

24. Dana Stevens, Review of *Dark Knight Rises*, *Slate*, July 18, 2012, accessed March 2015, http://www.slate.com/articles/arts/movies/2012/07/the_dark_knight_rises_reviewed.html

25. *The Rush Limbaugh Show*. "The Batman Campaign?" July 17, 2012, accessed March 15, 2015, http://www.rushlimbaugh.com/daily/2012/07/17/the_batman_campaign

26. Brian Hiatt, "Christopher Nolan: 'Dark Knight Rises' Isn't Political," *Rolling Stone*, July 20, 2012, accessed March 15, 2015, http://www.rollingstone.com/movies/news/christopher-nolan-dark-knight-rises-isn-t-political-20120720#ixzz3TXqGaOva

27. Associated Press, "Aurora shooting suspect James Holmes had Batman mask, calendar, violent drawing in apartment," *Daily News*, Wednesday, October 23, 2013, accessed March 15, 2015, http://www.nydailynews.com/news/crime/aurora-shooting-suspect-batman-mask-police-article-1.1494797

28. Michael Moss, "Pentagon Study Links Fatalities to Body Armor," *New York Times*, January 7, 2006, accessed March 15, 2015, http://www.nytimes.com/2006/01/07/politics/07armor.html?pagewanted=all&_r=0

29. Perhaps complicating the *Injustice* story arc further is that the comics are a tie-in for the video game, not an official part of the DC canon, although the gamification of an ambiguous, allegorical war on terror lends itself to further analysis. From the makers of the game: "What if our greatest heroes became our greatest threat? From the indomitable DC Comics and the makers of the

definitive fighting game franchise Mortal Kombat comes Injustice: Gods among Us, a bold fighting game featuring a large cast of favorite DC Comics icons. Set in a world where the lines between good and evil are blurred, players will experience heroes and villains engaging in epic battles on a massive scale."

30. Matt Zoller Seitz, "Things Crashing into Other Things: Or, My Superhero Movie Problem," *Roger Ebert.com MZS blog*, May 6, 2014, accessed March 1, 2015, http://www.rogerebert.com/mzs/things-crashing-into-other-things-or-my-superhero-movie-problem

31. Quoted in Sujay Kumar, "How Superhero Movies Lost Their Humanity."

32. M. H. Abrams, *Glossary of Literary Terms*, 7th ed. (Fort Worth: Harcourt, 1999), 1.

33. Albert Camus, *The Myth of Sisyphus,* trans. Justin O'Brien (New York: Vintage, 1942), 3.

34. Superman, Wonder Woman, Batman, Aquaman, Cyclops, Jean Grey, Wolverine, Thor, and Captain America, among others, have all died at some point in their comics run.

35. Camus, *Myth*, 89.

36. See, for example, Richard Reynolds, *Super Heroes: A Modern Mythology* (UP of Mississippi, 1994); and *Supergods: What Masked Vigilantes, Miraculous Mutants, and a Sun God from Smallville Can Teach Us about Being Human* Grant Morrison (New York: Spiegel & Grau, 2012).

37. Camus, *Myth*, 91.

Conclusion

1. Of course, as I discussed in Chapter 5, postmodern theory also analyzes erasure. Perhaps there is nothing after *post*.

2. Jonathan Rauch, "Barack Obama is right—we've never been safer," *Dallas Morning News*, March 13, 2015, accessed March 26, 2015, http://www.dallasnews.com/opinion/sunday-commentary/20150313-jonathan-rauch-barack-obama-is-right—weve-never-been-safer.ece

3. Steven Pinker and Andrew Mack, "The World Is Not Falling Apart," *Slate*, December 22, 2014, accessed March 19, 2015, http://www.slate.com/articles/news_and_politics/foreigners/2014/12/the_world_is_not_falling_apart_the_trend_lines_reveal_an_increasingly_peaceful.html

4. Ibid.

5. Ali Watkins, "S.C.'s Graham disputes Obama claim U.S. is safer now than before 9/11," McClatchy Washington Bureau, September 11, 2014, accessed March 26, 2015, http://www.mcclatchydc.com/2014/09/11/239575/scs-graham-says-obama-claim-us.html#storylink=cpy

6. Rauch, "Barack Obama is right."

7. "Mass shootings are up; gun murders down," *The Economist*, September 21, 2013, accessed March 19, 2015, http://www.economist.com/news/united-states/21586585-mass-shootings-are-up-gun-murders-down

8. According to the FBI, "[a]ctive shooter is a term used by law enforcement to describe a situation in which a shooting is in progress and an aspect of the crime may affect the protocols used in responding to and reacting at the scene of the incident. Unlike a defined crime, such as a murder or mass killing, the active aspect inherently implies that both law enforcement personnel and citizens have the potential to affect the outcome of the event based upon their responses." That is, law enforcement still has the capability to respond to a crime still in progress, as opposed to investigating after it is over. See Federal Bureau of Investigation, "A Study of Active Shooter Incidents in the United States Between 2000 and 2013," September 16, 2013, accessed March 20, 2015, http://www.fbi.gov/news/stories/2014/september/fbi-releases-study-on-active-shooter-incidents/pdfs/a-study-of-active-shooter-incidents-in-the-u.s.-between-2000-and-2013

9. D'Vera Cohn et al., "Gun homicide rate down 49% since 1993 peak; public unaware," *Pew Research Center*, May 7, 2013, accessed March 20, 2015, http://www.pewsocialtrends.org/2013/05/07/gun-homicide-rate-down-49-since-1993-peak-public-unaware/

10. "Mass shootings are up."

11. Beenish Ahmed, "Drone victims testify before Congress," *Boston Review*, October 30, 2013, accessed March 20, 2015, http://bostonreview.net/world/beenish-ahmed-drone-rehman-akbar-grayson. This testimony was also featured on John Oliver's *This Week Tonight*, September 28, 2014, which is where I first heard it.

12. The use of this quotation is not without controversy and, according to Caroline Alexander, badly out of context: "To apply [Virgil's intended] sentiment to civilians killed indiscriminately in an act of terrorism ... is grotesque." See Caroline Alexander, "Out of Context," *New York Times*, April 6, 2011, accessed March 19, 2015, www.nytimes.com/2011/04/07/opinion/07alexander.html?_r=0

Selected Bibliography

This list provides some of the major works cited and possibilities for further reading. For a comprehensive list of citations, please see each chapter's endnotes.

Baudrillard, Jean. "The Gulf War Did Not Take Place," 1995, *Selected Writings*, 2nd ed. Ed. Mark Poster, trans. Paul Patton. Stanford: Stanford University Press, 2001.

Baudrillard, Jean. "Requiem for the Twin Towers," *The Spirit of Terrorism and Other Essays*. Trans. Chris Turner. London: Verso, 2002.

Brooks, Max. *World War Z: An Oral History of the Zombie War*. New York: Crown, 2006.

Camus, Albert. *The Myth of Sisyphus*. Trans. Justin O'Brien. New York: Vintage, 1942.

Chabon, Michael. *The Amazing Adventures of Kavalier & Clay*. New York: Random House, 2000.

Coll, Steve. *Ghost Wars: The Secret History of the CIA, Afghanistan, and Bin Laden, from the Soviet Invasion to September 10, 2001*. New York: Penguin, 2004.

Collins, Suzanne. *Catching Fire*. New York: Scholastic, 2009.

Collins, Suzanne. *The Hunger Games*. New York: Scholastic, 2010.

Collins, Suzanne. *Mockingjay*. New York: Scholastic, 2010.

DeLillo, Don. *Cosmopolis*. New York: Scribner, 2003.

DeLillo, Don. *Falling Man*. New York: Scribner, 2007.

DeLillo, Don. "In the Ruins of the Future." *Guardian*, December 22, 2001, http://books.guardian.co.uk/departments/generalfiction/story/0,,623732,00.html

DeLillo, Don. *Libra*. New York: Viking, 1988.

DeLillo, Don. *Mao II*. New York: Scribner, 1991.

DeLillo, Don. *Underworld*. New York: Scribner, 1997.

Dixon, Winston Wheeler. *Film and Television after 9/11*. Carbondale: Southern Illinois University Press, 2004.

Faludi, Susan. *The Terror Dream: Myth and Misogyny in an Insecure America*. New York: Picador, 2007.

Foer, Jonathan Safran. *Extremely Loud and Incredibly Close*. New York: Mariner, 2005.

Friedman, Thomas. *Longitudes and Attitudes: The World in the Age of Terrorism*. New York: Anchor, 2002.

Giroux, Henry A. *Public Spaces, Private Lives: Beyond the Culture of Cynicism*. Lanham: Rowman and Littlefield, 2001.

Gray, Richard. *After the Fall: American Literature Since 9/11*. West Sussex: Wiley-Blackwell, 2011.

Hamid, Mohsin. *The Reluctant Fundamentalist*. New York: Harcourt, 2007.

Havrilesky, Heather. "Steve Jobs: Vampire. Bill Gates: Zombie." *The New York Times Magazine*, October 28, 2011, http://www.nytimes.com/2011/10/30/magazine/steve-jobs-vampire-bill-gates-zombie.html?pagewanted=all

Hoffman, Bruce. *Inside Terrorism*. New York: Columbia University Press, 2006.

Hungerford, Amy. *Postmodern Belief: American Literature and Religion since 1960*. Princeton, New Jersey: Princeton University Press, 2010.

Kafka, Franz. "A Hunger Artist," *Selected Short Stories*. Trans. Willa and Edwin Muir. New York: Modern Library, 1952.

Kalfus, Ken. *A Disorder Peculiar to the Country*. New York: Harper, 2006.

Kermode, Frank. *The Sense of an Ending*. New York: Oxford University Press, 1966.

Klaven, Andrew. "What Bush and Batman Have in Common." *Wall Street Journal*, July 25, 2008, http://www.wsj.com/articles/SB121694247343482821

Lawrence, John and Robert Jewett. *The Myth of the America Superhero*. Grand Rapids: Wm. B. Eerdmans, 2002.

Lethem, Jonathan. *The Vintage Book of Amnesia: An Anthology of Writing on the Subject of Memory Loss*. New York: Vintage, 2000.

McCarthy, Cormac. *The Road*. New York: Vintage, 2006.

Meyer, Stephenie. *Twilight*. New York: Hachette, 2005.

National Commission on Terrorist Attacks upon the United States, *The 9/11 Commission Report*. Final Report, 2004.

Nolan, Christopher, Jonathan Nolan, and David S. Goyer. *The Dark Knight Trilogy: The Complete Screenplays*. New York: Opus, 2012.

O'Neill, Joseph. *Netherland*. New York: Vintage, 2008.

Page, Max. *The City's End: Two Centuries of Fantasies, Fear, and Premonitions of New York's Destruction*. New Haven: Yale University Press, 2008.

Palahniuk, Chuck. *Fight Club*. New York: Henry Holt, 1996.

Palahniuk, Chuck. *Stranger than Fiction: True Stories*. New York: Doubleday, 2004.

Palahniuk, Chuck. *Survivor*. New York: Anchor, 1999.

Pinker, Steven. *The Better Angels of Our Nature: Why Violence Has Declined*. New York: Viking, 2011.

Pollard, Tom. *Hollywood 9/11*. Boulder: Paradigm, 2011.

"Portraits in Grief," *9/11: The Reckoning, The New York Times*, 2001, http://www.nytimes.com/interactive/us/sept-11-reckoning/portraits-of-grief.html

Prince, Stephen. *Firestorm: American Film in the Age of Terrorism.* New York: Columbia University Press, 2009.

Roth, Philip. "Writing American Fiction," 1961, *Reading Myself and Others.* Reprint, New York: Farrar, Straus and Giroux, 1975.

Rowling, J.K. *Harry Potter and the Sorcerer's Stone.* New York: Scholastic, 1999.

Schwartz, Lynne Sharon. *The Writing on the Wall.* New York: Counterpoint, 2005.

Shelly, Mary. *Frankenstein*, 1818. Ed. J. Paul Hunter. Reprint, New York: Norton Critical, 1996.

Spiegelman, Art. *In the Shadow of No Towers.* New York: Pantheon, 2004.

Stoker, Bram. *Dracula*, 1897. Eds. Nina Auerbach and David Skal. Reprint, New York: Norton Critical, 1997.

Walter, Jess. *The Zero.* New York: Harper, 2007.

Webel, Charles P. *Terror, Terrorism and the Human Condition.* New York: Palgrave, 2004.

Wood, J. *Living Lost: Why We're All Stuck on the Island.* New Orleans: Garret County Press, 2007.

Wright, Bradford W. *Comic Book Nation: The Transformation of Youth Culture in America.* Baltimore: Johns Hopkins, 2001.

Zizek, Slovoj. *Welcome to the Desert of the Real.* London: Verso, 2002.

Films

Avatar. Directed by James Cameron. 20th Century Fox, 2009.

Batman Begins. Directed by Christopher Nolan. Warner Bros., 2005.

Catching Fire. Directed by Francis Lawrence. Lionsgate, 2013.

Cloverfield. Directed by Matt Reeves. Paramount, 2008.

Cosmopolis. Directed by David Cronenberg. Alfama Films, 2012.

The Dark Knight. Directed by Christopher Nolan. Warner Bros., 2008.

The Dark Knight Rises. Directed by Christopher Nolan. Warner Bros., 2012.

Dracula. Directed by Tod Browning. Universal, 1931.

Eternal Sunshine of the Spotless Mind. Directed by Michel Gondry. Focus Features, 2004.

Fight Club. Directed by David Fincher. Fox, 1999.

Frankenstein. Directed by James Whale. Universal, 1931.

The Hunger Games. Directed by Gary Ross. Lionsgate, 2012.

Lost (TV series). Created by Jeffrey Lieber, J. J. Abrams, and Damon Lindelof. Bad Robot/ABC, 2004–2010.

Man of Steel. Directed by Zack Snyder. Warner Bros., 2013.

Memento. Directed by Christopher Nolan. Newmarket Capital, 2000.

Mockingjay-Part 1. Directed by Francis Lawrence. Lionsgate, 2014.

Mulholland Drive. Directed by David Lynch. Les Films Alain Sarde, 2001.

New Moon. Directed by Chris Weitz. Temple Hill, 2009.
The Road. Directed by John Hillcoat. Dimension Films, 2009.
Twilight. Directed by Catherine Hardwicke. Summit, 2008.
United 93. Directed by Paul Greengrass. Universal, 2006.
War of the Worlds. Directed by Steven Spielberg. Paramount, 2005.
World Trade Center. Directed by Oliver Stone. Paramount, 2006.
World War Z. Directed by Mark Foster. Paramount, 2013.
The World's End. Directed by Edgar Wright. Universal, 2013.
X-Men. Directed by Bryan Singer. 20th Century Fox, 2000.

Index

About the Author

JESSE KAVADLO, PhD, is a professor of English and Director of the Center for Teaching and Learning at Maryville University of St. Louis. He is the author of *Don DeLillo: Balance at the Edge of Belief*, coeditor of *Michael Chabon's America: Magical Words, Secret Worlds, and Sacred Spaces*, and president of the Don DeLillo Society.